Case Studies in Educational Foundations

Case Studies in Educational Foundations

Canadian Perspectives

Shelley Hasinoff
David Mandzuk

OXFORD
UNIVERSITY PRESS

OXFORD
UNIVERSITY PRESS

Oxford University Press is a department of the University of Oxford.
It furthers the University's objective of excellence in research, scholarship,
and education by publishing worldwide. Oxford is a registered trade mark of
Oxford University Press in the UK and in certain other countries.

Published in Canada by
Oxford University Press
8 Sampson Mews, Suite 204,
Don Mills, Ontario M3C 0H5 Canada

www.oupcanada.com

Library and Archives Canada Cataloguing in Publication

Hasinoff, Shelley, 1949-, author
Case studies in educational foundations : Canadian perspectives
/ Shelley Hasinoff, David Mandzuk.

Includes bibliographical references and index.
ISBN 978-0-19-544854-2 (pbk.)

1. Teaching—Canada—Case studies. 2. Education—Canada—
Case studies. I. Mandzuk, David, 1957–, author II. Title.
III. Title: Educational foundations.

LB1025.3.H43 2015 371.1020971 C2014-907616-9

Cover image: Jamie Farrant/iStockphoto

Oxford University Press is committed to our environment.
This book is printed on Forest Stewardship Council® certified paper
and comes from responsible sources.

MIX
Paper from
responsible sources
FSC
www.fsc.org
FSC® C103567

Printed and bound in Canada

1 2 3 4 — 18 17 16 15

Contents

KEYWORDS	MYTHS									
	This Suit's for Wearing, p. 32	When I Grow Up I Want to Be . . ., p. 35	Who Cares?, p. 38	Flipping Burgers, p. 40	Missing in Action, p. 44	Just in Time, p. 47	Who Pays?, p. 50	Whose Culture?, Who's Teaching?, p. 53	Unmasking Hallowe'en, p. 56	No Space for God Here, p. 60
Ability	X			X			X			
Aboriginal teachers								X		
Accountability, testing	X			X						
Bullying	X									
Cell phones										
Character education										
Commercialization										
Constructivism, inquiry			X		X					
Digital divide						X				
Ethnicity and race	X		X					X		
Full inclusion/ mainstreaming	X									
Gangs										
Gender expectations		X	X							
Identity theft, privacy										
Learned helplessness				X			X			
Multiculturalism	X		X					X	X	
Normalcy	X		X	X						
Parent involvement									X	

KEYWORDS	BANDWAGONS									
	Alone in a Crowd, p. 78	Be the Change, p. 81	Let Them Eat Cake!, p. 85	The Future Is Now, p. 88	Blurred Reflections, p. 91	DEAR Me! , p. 94	A Test of Wills, p. 98	Teaching for Dummies, p. 101	Corporate Takeover, p. 104	Over the Rainbow, p. 108
Ability	X						X	X		
Aboriginal teachers										
Accountability, testing							X	X		
Bullying				X						
Cell phones										
Character education										
Commercialization									X	
Constructivism, inquiry										
Digital divide										
Ethnicity and race										
Full inclusion/ mainstreaming	X						X			
Gangs										
Gender expectations		X								
Identity theft, privacy										
Learned helplessness										
Multiculturalism							X			
Normalcy							X			
Parent involvement									X	X

KEYWORDS	MORAL PANICS									
	A Place to Belong?, p. 128	A Stitch in Time, p. 131	Brave New World?, p. 134	On-line or Off-base?, p. 137	Bang! Bang! You're Dead, p. 141	A Lapse of Judgment, p. 144	A Cougar in the Schoolhouse, p. 147	No Beeping Song!, p. 150	Gangster Fashion, p. 153	Character Counts, p. 156
Ability	X	X								
Aboriginal teachers										
Accountability, testing										
Bullying		X								
Cell phones				X						
Character education										X
Commercialization										
Constructivism, inquiry										
Digital divide				X	X					
Ethnicity and race	X								X	
Full inclusion/ mainstreaming										
Gangs									X	X
Gender expectations							X			
Identity theft, privacy			X							
Learned helplessness										
Multiculturalism	X								X	
Normalcy						X		X	X	
Parent involvement		X								X

	MYTHS										BANDWAGONS										MORAL PANICS									
KEYWORDS	This Suit's for Wearing, p. 32	When I Grow Up I Want to Be . . ., p. 35	Who Cares?, p. 38	Flipping Burgers, p. 40	Missing in Action, p. 44	Just in Time, p. 47	Who Pays?, p. 50	Whose Culture, Who's Teaching?, p. 53	Unmasking Hallowe'en, p. 56	No Space for God Here, p. 60	Alone in a Crowd, p. 78	Be the Change, p. 81	Let Them Eat Cake!, p. 85	The Future is Now, p. 88	Blurred Reflections, p. 91	DEAR Me! , p. 94	A Test of Wills, p. 98	Teaching for Dummies, p. 101	Corporate Takeover, p. 104	Over the Rainbow, p. 108	A Place to Belong?, p. 128	A Stitch in Time, p. 131	Brave New World?, p. 134	On-line or Off-base?, p. 137	Bang! Bang! You're Dead, p. 141	A Lapse of Judgment, p. 144	A Cougar in the Schoolhouse, p. 147	No Beeping Song!, p. 150	Gangster Fashion, p. 153	Character Counts, p. 156
Pedagogy	X				X	X	X	X					X		X	X	X	X				X	X	X	X				X	X
Professional identity			X	X											X			X	X				X			X	X		X	
Reflections, journals															X															
Religion		X						X	X	X										X										
Rewards							X																							
School administration			X	X	X	X	X	X	X	X	X	X	X	X					X	X	X			X		X	X	X	X	X
School libraries													X																	
Secularism								X	X	X																				X
Segregated schools												X									X									
Sexuality, sexual orientation			X																	X						X	X		X	
Social media																							X							
Socio-economic status				X			X																							
Special needs	X			X			X				X						X					X						X	X	
Standards, standardization	X			X													X	X												
Sustained silent reading																X														
Technology				X		X							X	X									X	X	X					
Video games																									X					
Youth culture																			X				X	X	X			X	X	

PREFACE

Learning how to cope with "uncertainties" is a major concern of prospective teachers (Helsing, 2007; Schuck & Buchanan, 2012; van Huizen, van Oers, & Wubbels, 2005) but it is equally important to learn how to challenge the "certainties" of education, especially those that are not supported by evidence. Unwarranted certainties include "myths"—assumptions we accept uncritically about teaching and learning; "bandwagons"—untested ideas, causes, or theories we follow because they are popular, and "moral panics"—unsupported fears about perceived threats to the safety and well-being of society. In this book, we illustrate some of the myths, bandwagons, and moral panics that pervade education with 30 cases contributed by educators from across Canada.

As you read the cases, some will seem familiar to you because they are loosely based on real events that were widely reported, while other cases will be similar to your own experiences in educational settings. The cases and the commentary related to each case reveal that myths, bandwagons, and moral panics guide our thinking and our behaviour, often preventing us from seriously examining our teaching practices. Each case is followed by five questions to help you think critically about the case and how it applies to your own practice. In order to see the entire book at a glance, please refer to the case matrix on pages viii and ix, which illustrates the 30 cases and their major themes.

Until fairly recently, the foundations disciplines were taught as separate courses which were often mandatory for graduation from most Canadian faculties of education. However, in response to pressures from government, schools, and students to increase the number of methodology courses, the history, philosophy, and sociology of education have been either integrated into a single omnibus course, eliminated entirely, or are no longer compulsory. We argue that, regardless of how the foundations are taught, prospective teachers need to adopt the methods of inquiry embedded in the foundations disciplines so that the strength of their certainty will match the strength of the available evidence.

Although teacher education programs are often accused of not preparing teachers adequately for the realities of teaching (Karsenti & Collin, 2013), it is simply not feasible to prepare them for every experience they might encounter in schools. Nevertheless, faculties of education can broaden the preparation of prospective teachers by using case studies, such as the ones in this book. We believe that these case studies confront the messiness of teaching head on, particularly the unwarranted certainties that take the form of myths, bandwagons, and moral panics. Importantly, the cases in this book illustrate the complexity and diversity that characterize real life in today's schools.

The questions following each case are designed to help educators develop the kind of historical, philosophical, and sociological "habits of mind" they will need to be able to think through the uncertainties of the future and challenge the certainties of the past. Although the case questions may be answered individually, we think that their value may be even greater when discussed through collaborative inquiry with others.

How the book is organized

The Overview touches briefly on the major themes of the book. Chapter 1 contains three essays on the history, philosophy, and sociology of education that make the case for why each of those disciplines matters to prospective and practising teachers. Each essay concludes with some of the essential questions that the discipline raises. We argue that teachers who learn to apply such questions reflexively to the myths, bandwagons, and moral panics they encounter are less likely to be swayed by unwarranted certainties.

One chapter is devoted to each of the three unwarranted certainties we highlight in this book. In each of these three chapters, a general discussion is followed by specific commentaries on the particular myths, bandwagons, or moral panics that are illustrated in the 10 cases presented in the chapter. The five questions that follow each case provide readers with opportunities to revisit the facts of the case and to apply them to their own practice as well as to examine the case from the varied perspectives of the history, philosophy, and sociology of education.

Chapter 2 explores the concept of myths in education and comments specifically on the myths of normalcy, gender, ability, digital divide, constructivism, rewards, multiculturalism, and secularism. Chapter 3, which examines the phenomenon of bandwagons, discusses full inclusion, single-sex education, the future of school libraries, privacy of information, reflections, sustained silent reading, accountability, and community involvement. Chapter 4 describes moral panics and considers issues related to diversity, bullying, social media, cell phones, violent video games, professional identity, youth and youth culture, and moral education.

Finally, Chapter 5 affords an opportunity to revisit the essays and cases in the book and to look ahead to four representative trends that are likely to challenge all of our certainties in the future.

Who this book is for

This book is intended for both pre-service and in-service teachers. Teacher candidates enrolled in foundations courses will value the opportunity to prepare for their own practice through the case-study approach. Practising teachers, in professional learning communities, grade-level teams, and whole-staff discussion groups will appreciate the engaging manner in which the cases deal with common issues that arise in schools. Both groups will benefit from using the essential questions raised by the foundations disciplines to confront the messiness of teaching. In addition, the cases can be used selectively for self-study, especially by individuals who are reading the cases to enhance their own professional growth.

The authors

Shelley Hasinoff and David Mandzuk are veteran educators whose combined experiences span every grade from pre-school to university as teachers, school and university administrators, consultants, and specialists at the school, district, and provincial level, in public and private schools, in Canada and in schools in China, Korea, Thailand, and Brazil. They have also published research articles both independently and together and have been engaging in professional conversations about teaching and learning for almost 25 years. *Case Studies in Educational Foundations: Canadian Perspectives* is the second book they have co-authored together; the first was *Slices of Life: Managing Dilemmas in Middle Grades Teaching: Case Studies for Professional Development* (2010).

***Shelley Hasinoff,* PhD,** has been an educator for over 30 years at all levels and in three Canadian provinces. She has been a resource teacher, a coordinator for gifted and talented students, a faculty associate in the Middle Years program at the University of Manitoba, a principal of a private school, and an assessment and evaluation consultant and coordinator of the Independent Education Unit for Manitoba Education. She is currently an independent education consultant. Dr Hasinoff and her husband, Brian, live in Winnipeg. They have a son, Sam, and a daughter, Amy.

***David Mandzuk,* PhD,** taught in the public school system in Winnipeg for 20 years. In 2000 he joined the Faculty of Education at the University of Manitoba as an assistant professor in Middle Years education, in 2003 he was appointed associate dean (Undergraduate Programs), in 2006 he became an associate professor, and in 2013 he was appointed dean of the faculty. He is also currently the chair-elect of the International Council on Education for Teaching (ICET). Dr Mandzuk lives in Winnipeg with his wife, Lynda, and their two daughters, Jayne and Andrea.

ACKNOWLEDGEMENTS

As in any major writing endeavour, there are many people to thank. First and foremost, we want to thank our families for their unconditional support. We would also like to acknowledge our friends and colleagues whose insightful comments and valuable suggestions have made this book so much richer than it might otherwise have been.

This book grew out of concerns voiced at meetings of the Canadian Association of Foundations of Education (CAFE) about the marginalization of the foundations disciplines in teacher education programs. As the book took shape, colleagues from across Canada were invited to contribute essays about the role and purpose of the foundations or to submit cases that would illustrate the myths, bandwagons, and moral panics that pervade education. We were overwhelmed by the response and the quality of the writing.

We are indebted to Theodore Christou and Helen Raptis for their section on the history of education and to Michelle Forrest, William Hare, and Donald Kerr for their section on the philosophy of education. These contributions offer much needed background for understanding why the foundations matter in teacher education. We would also like to thank Sandra Bruneau, Theodore Christou, Kurt Clausen, Anne-Marie Dooner, Melanie Janzen, Luanne Karn, Alan Sears, Shirley Van Nuland, Andrew Volk, and Diane Wishart for their commitment to this project and for sharing their expertise as educators and their talents as case writers. We are proud to have had the opportunity to work with these dedicated professionals.

We also appreciate the work of the editors at Oxford University Press, including Stephen Kotowych, Tanuja Weerasooriya, and Jodi Lewchuk, and the many other staff at Oxford who have helped to guide us through the writing and publishing process. We especially want to thank our copy editor, Freya Godard, for her invaluable suggestions and the manuscript reviewers for their helpful comments. This has been an exciting and gratifying journey.

CONTRIBUTORS

***Sandra Bruneau*, EdD,** is the Executive Director of ABCDE (Association of BC Deans of Education) and has long experience in teacher education, first as an administrator in UBC's Faculty of Education and then as Associate Dean of Education, University College of the Cariboo (now Thompson Rivers University) in Kamloops, BC. Since the 1970s Dr Bruneau has been active in the Canadian Philosophy of Education Society (CPES). She presents regularly at education conferences on topics such as critical thinking, teacher education, moral education, and teacher courage. She writes poems and short stories about education and is an advocate for using poetry and stories in teaching educational foundations to prospective and experienced teachers. In 2013 CPES presented her with the organization's Award for Distinguished Service.

***Theodore Michael Christou*, PhD,** is an Assistant Professor at Queen's University. He began his academic career at the University of New Brunswick in 2009. His teaching and research pertain to the history and philosophy of education. Before beginning his doctoral studies, he worked as a teacher in the Toronto and Durham District School Boards. He is the author of *The Problem of Progressive Education* (2012), a historical consideration of Ontario's educational history, and of *An Overbearing Eye* (2013), a book of verse and short fiction. Dr Christou is also the co-editor (with Shawn Michael Bullock) of *Foundations in Teacher Education: A Canadian Perspective* (2013).

***Kurt Clausen*, PhD,** has been a member of the Faculty of Education at Nipissing University since 2001, and is past chair of Graduate Studies at that institution. Specializing in foundations of education, he has also taught educational administration and curriculum development at the University of Ottawa, and History/Humanities courses at McGill University and Dawson College. Presently writing a book on Ontario's educational history, he has published widely on foundational areas of education and spoken nationally and internationally on the subject. Dr Clausen has been editor of the *Canadian Journal of Action Research* since 2003 and has promoted increased recognition of teachers as professionals.

***Anne-Marie Dooner*, PhD,** has been an educator in the public school system for 10 years. She has taught both single-grade and three-year multi-age classroom communities in French Immersion Middle Years settings, and has been a vice principal in both Middle and Senior Years schools. The title of her dissertation, *Caring Teacher-Student Relationships and the Influence of Teachers' Identities: A Grounded Theory Approach* reflects her research interests in teachers' authority and teacher-student relationships. She has also worked as a registered nurse specializing in blood cancers, as well as a stained glass artist, designing and creating windows. She lives in Winnipeg with her husband, Peter, and their children, Michael, Thomas, Patrick, and Hannah-Mary.

Michelle Forrest, PhD, is an Associate Professor at Mount Saint Vincent University in Halifax. She began her career as a classically trained singer who performed in eastern Canada, London, England, and in Moscow during the Soviet era. She completed her BEd at Dalhousie University and taught English and Drama for seven years in Nova Scotia public and independent high schools. Dr Forrest brings her experience as a working artist to her writing in philosophy of education, focusing on performance and the role of chance in collaboration. Her other research interests include controversy in education, the place of the arts in teaching students to be critical, and feminist perspectives on the philosophy of education.

William Hare, PhD, is Professor Emeritus at Mount Saint Vincent University in Halifax. His research and teaching have focused on philosophy of education, particularly the ideal of open-mindedness and the nature of good teaching. He has published numerous journal articles and books, including *Open-mindedness and Education* (1979), *In Defence of Open-mindedness* (1985), *Attitudes in Teaching and Education* (1993), and *What Makes a Good Teacher* (1993). His most recent work (co-edited with John Portelli) is *Philosophy of Education: Introductory Readings* (fourth edition, 2013). Dr Hare served as President of the Canadian Philosophy of Education Society (CPES) from 1984 to 1986 and received the CPES Distinguished Service Award in 2004.

Melanie D. Janzen, PhD, is a graduate of the University of British Columbia. Her dissertation received the Outstanding Dissertation Award from the Qualitative Research Special Interest Group of the American Educational Research Association. Currently, she is the Director of the School Experiences Office and an Assistant Professor in the Faculty of Education at the University of Manitoba. Dr Janzen's research, published nationally and internationally, focuses on ideas of teacher becoming, teacher identity, and teacher responsibility, specifically in regard to the ethical responsibilities integral to being a teacher. As a former classroom teacher and learning support teacher, she enjoys working with students, teachers, and school leaders in both university and public school settings.

Luanne Karn, MEd, has worked in the field of education in Ontario and Manitoba for over two decades. After completing her BA in Sociology and Women's Studies at the University of Toronto, she worked as a coordinator and advocate developing community-based adult education programs in downtown Toronto. She completed her Bachelor of Education at the University of Toronto (OISE) and her Master's of Education at the University of Manitoba. She has worked as a classroom teacher in vocational and special education settings and is currently working as a resource teacher at the secondary school level in Manitoba. She and her partner, Heather, live in Winnipeg with their daughter, Anna Elizabeth.

Donald Kerr, PhD, is an Associate Professor and Chair of the Department of Professional Development in Education in the Faculty of Education at Lakehead University in Thunder Bay. He has taught in faculties of education at the University of British Columbia, the University of Calgary, and the University of Victoria. He is a former secondary mathematics teacher, with experience teaching in both alternative-educational programs and traditional high schools; more recently, he has served as a trustee of the Lakehead District School Board. Dr Kerr has published nationally and internationally on topics in philosophy of education and on teaching philosophy of education.

Helen Raptis, PhD, began teaching in 1985 after earning a BA (in French Language and Literature) and a British Columbia Teaching Certificate. She earned an MEd in 1991, and a PhD in 2001. She is currently an Associate Professor at the University of Victoria. An award-winning educator, she has taught at the elementary, secondary, and post-secondary levels in Australia, Canada, France, and the United States. She has held a number of SSHRC grants, most recently for a historical investigation of the integration experiences of Aboriginal children and teachers in northern British Columbia from 1949 to 1969. Dr Raptis has published widely on historical and contemporary questions pertaining to minority and Indigenous education, education policy, and effective schools.

Alan Sears, PhD, is a Professor of Social Studies Education in the Faculty of Education at the University of New Brunswick. His research and writing are in the areas of citizenship education, teacher education, educational history, and policy studies in education. He is currently principal investigator on an SSHRC project designed to map how young people in Alberta and the Maritimes conceptualize democratic participation and is a co-investigator on a similar project looking at how young people and teachers conceptualize diversity in Canada. Dr Sears is Editor of the journal *Citizenship Teaching and Learning* and co-editor of the recent book *Globalization, the Nation-State and the Citizen: Dilemmas and Directions for Civics and Citizenship Education*, published by Routledge.

Shirley Van Nuland, PhD, joined the University of Ontario Institute of Technology (UOIT) in 2005 after many years of experience in various positions as a teacher and principal in Ontario elementary and secondary schools, an education officer with the Ontario Ministry of Education, a sessional instructor at several universities, and an Assistant Professor at Nipissing University. While at Nipissing, she was presented the Chancellor's Award for Excellence in Teaching (2004). She also received the 2012 Publications Award and the 2013 Service Award from the Canadian Association of Foundations of Education. Currently, Dr Van Nuland teaches in the Bachelor of Education program at UOIT. Her research focuses on codes of conduct, Charter issues, and teacher and teacher candidate development.

Andrew Volk, MEd, completed his first degree at the University of Winnipeg in 2004 and completed his Master's of Education on educational bureaucracy at the University of Manitoba in 2014. He worked as a substitute teacher before being hired as a Teacher-Librarian in an elementary school, where he also ran enrichment and technology programs. He is currently a vice-principal in a Middle School and a part-time instructor in the Faculty of Education at the University of Winnipeg. He has published in the University of Winnipeg's *Student Anthology* and in the proceedings of the University of Manitoba's Education Graduate Student Symposium. He lives with his wife and son in Winnipeg.

Diane Wishart, PhD, has been teaching in the Department of Educational Policy Studies in the Faculty of Education at the University of Alberta in Edmonton since 2006. In 2009, her book called *The Rose That Grew from Concrete: Teaching and Learning with Disenfranchised Youth* was published by the University of Alberta Press. This book documents her experiences teaching disenfranchised urban youth who dropped out of school and then became more engaged in their education in an alternative high school setting. Dr Wishart has also published in national and international journals and has presented widely at academic and professional conferences. She lives in Edmonton with her husband, Steven, her daughters, Frances and Sydney, and her son, Alec.

OVERVIEW

Many of the cases in this book illustrate the kind of hot-button issues that spark public debate in newspapers, blogs, and television shows, reminding us that education is rarely the subject of "good news." Indeed, if we are to believe what we read and hear in the media, schools are generally failing and are full of unruly students, corrupt school officials, and questionable sexual behaviour on the part of both teachers and students. Although exaggerated and patently false media reports may be the fodder of staff-room jokes, the effects of such stories are no laughing matter. Repeated media narratives often become accepted as "truths" that can be extremely damaging to the status and reputation of the teaching profession and to the support that schools receive from parents and community members.

Unfortunately, research in cognitive psychology shows that people are extremely quick to accept claims in spite of surprisingly limited information (Kahneman, 2011). These unwarranted certainties, in the form of myths, bandwagons, and moral panics, are often immune to reasoned arguments or disconfirming evidence. In this book, we take a deeper look at some of the unwarranted certainties in education and demonstrate how readers can draw on the rich traditions of the history, philosophy, and sociology of education to avoid succumbing to faulty first impressions or being blinkered by long-held beliefs and unexamined assumptions. We argue that the essential questions posed by the **foundations of education** enable educators to recognize the validity of certainties that are warranted and to challenge those that are not.

Uncertainties and certainties

We are aware that the pursuit of certainties and the fear of uncertainties can consume new teachers and create tensions and frustrations long after teachers have gained experience in the classroom. As Floden and Clark (1988) point out, "Teaching is evidently and inevitably uncertain" (p. 505). The uncertainties that face us as educators are too numerous to list here, but they include concerns about whether we have sufficient knowledge and experience to teach the subject matter we are asked to teach, how we will be able manage our classrooms and accommodate diversity, whether we are teaching what is most worthwhile for preparing our students for the future, and whether we are assessing our students fairly.

The question of whether teachers are debilitated by such uncertainties or are motivated to grow professionally as a result of them has yet to be resolved

(Edwards, Gilroy, & Hartley, 2002; Floden & Buchmann, 1993; Floden & Clark, 1988; Schuck & Buchanan, 2012; Shulman, 2005). However, Helsing (2007) points out that "schools can and should do much more to minimize uncertainty while teachers learn how to reflect successfully on the uncertainties that remain" (p. 1329). She also argues that teacher education programs need to address the messiness of teaching explicitly, because otherwise,

> teachers will continue to feel that the uncertainties they experience are anomalous, indications that they are not teaching well, or are aspects of the job that should and will vanish with time and increased expertise and experience. (p. 1330)

It turns out that such feelings of inadequacy are common among the unacceptably large percentage of teachers who leave the profession within five years of graduating (Karsenti & Collin, 2013). Although this exodus has been blamed, in part, on the fact that teacher candidates are unprepared for the uncertainties of teaching, we think that *certainties*, which are viewed as the major goal of teacher education, have been overlooked in the discussion of teacher attrition.

We argue that greater attention should be paid to myths, bandwagons, and moral panics because such certainties are based on unexamined assumptions, taken-for-granted beliefs, and unsupported theories. To understand these types of certainties, we need to expand our understanding of the complexities of education to include the substantial differences between what we know that is warranted and what we know that is not, as shown in Figure 1.

	UNCERTAINTIES	**CERTAINTIES**
WARRANTED	A What we do not know or what is yet unknowable because of: • insufficient data • anecdotal evidence • lack of appropriate knowledge or skills	B What we know on the basis of: • peer-reviewed empirical research • evidence-based conclusions • verifiable facts
UNWARRANTED	C What we are unable or unwilling to know due to: • anxiety • cynicism • confusion	D What we know as a result of: • **unexamined assumptions (myths)** • **unjustified faith (bandwagons)** • **unsupported fears (moral panics)**

FIGURE 1 Certainties and uncertainties

Warranted uncertainties, as summarized in quadrant A, occur when we confront unknowns, such as how to achieve excellence and equity, or when we try to learn something new, such as how to speak a foreign language or operate a new computer program. Warranted certainties, depicted in quadrant B, arise when we can verify what we know, like the capital of France or the effects of specific descriptive feedback on our students' achievement. Unwarranted uncertainties, shown in quadrant C, occur when we are unwilling or unable to know something, such as refusing to learn how to use new report card software because we are overwhelmed by the technology. **Unwarranted certainties**, found in quadrant D, arise when we rely on myths, bandwagons, and moral panics to inform our teaching despite the fact that they are not supported by evidence.

Overcoming unwarranted assumptions, theories, and beliefs is neither an easy nor an intuitive process. Indeed, teachers often cling tenaciously to what they think works and try to increase the predictability of their work by establishing and maintaining routines rather than experiencing the discomfort and unpleasantness of uncertainty (Floden & Buchmann, 1993; Floden & Clark, 1988). Furthermore, our uncertainties and doubts can make us feel inadequate, especially when we compare ourselves to our own teachers, whom we tend to remember as competent and confident regardless of their actual abilities (Lortie, 1975).

Many of the strategies that have been suggested for coping with uncertainties, such as collaboration among teachers and reflective practice (Helsing, 2007), are also useful for dealing with unwarranted certainties. However, coping strategies may not be sufficient because unwarranted certainties lurk beneath the surface of our awareness and are therefore much more difficult to disrupt. As unconscious and highly resistant barriers to critical thinking, unwarranted certainties, such as myths, bandwagons, and moral panics, pose special problems for education.

Myths, bandwagons, and moral panics

The myths, bandwagons, and moral panics that pervade education are socially constructed, often unconscious certainties that are generally resistant to disconfirming evidence. Since we tend to look for confirmation rather than refutation of what we already know, our assumptions, theories, and taken-for-granted beliefs can become significant barriers to critical thinking (Kahneman, 2011). This tendency may in part explain the large number of seemingly illogical policies and practices that persist in education.

Whether something is labelled as a myth, bandwagon, or moral panic depends on a variety of factors, including our subjective and personal point of view, the amount of public and media interest, and the degree to which the issue is considered to be a threat to society. Figure 2 summarizes the main attributes of myths, bandwagons, and moral panics and highlights both their similarities and differences.

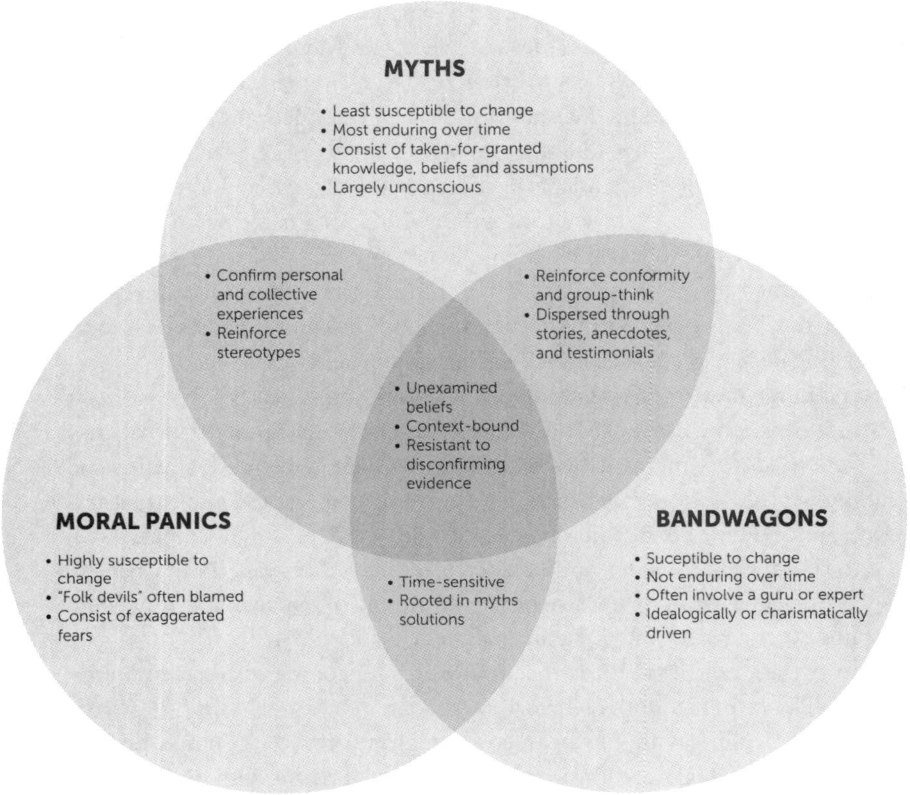

FIGURE 2 Comparison of myths, bandwagons, and moral panics

Myths, which consist of taken-for-granted knowledge, beliefs, and assumptions, are the least susceptible to change of the three types of certainties. Unlike short-lived and emotionally gripping bandwagons and moral panics, myths are enduring and largely unconscious. Like bandwagons, myths are mainly disseminated by word of mouth, including stories, anecdotes, and testimonials which serve to reinforce conformity and groupthink (Janis, 1982).

Bandwagons are often driven by gurus or experts who attract followers with their appealing personalities and convincing ideologies. They are quite susceptible to change and often recur from time to time. Bandwagons in education, especially those which cost money, tend to be imposed from the top down, usually without consultation of those who are expected to put them into practice. Consequently, bandwagons may elicit cynicism rather than excitement as they roll through. Like moral panics, bandwagons are generally rooted in myths and are time-sensitive, over-generalized solutions to problems that may have been manufactured or mis-specified in the first place.

Moral panics consist of exaggerated fears that surface suddenly and with a great sense of urgency. They are the most susceptible to change of the three. Moral panics are trumpeted as threats to the fabric and well-being of society from identified groups or ideas, known as "**folk devils**" (Cohen, 1972). The fears evoked by moral panics are amplified by the media and inflamed by "**moral entrepreneurs**" (Becker, 1983) who campaign for policies or laws to remove these imagined threats to society. Like myths, moral panics reinforce stereotypes, fuel generalizations, entrench personal and collective biases, and establish cultural norms.

We suggest that you refer back to Figure 2 as you read the book and consider the myths, bandwagons, and moral panics that are illustrated in the 30 cases. By doing so, you will soon see that, depending on the circumstances, these three unwarranted certainties can overlap, and at times, the boundaries between them may dissolve completely. This overlapping occurs, in part, because myths, bandwagons, and moral panics are often causally related. As Figure 3 suggests, a myth, such as *boys and girls learn differently* (Gurian & Henley, 2001) can fuel an alarm or moral panic, such as the overblown "boy crisis." The substance of this moral panic is that boys are losing ground academically as a consequence of what some, like Christina Hoff Sommers (2000), believe to be "a war on boys" and undue attention to girls' ways of knowing. Once a moral panic like this is set in motion, a number of bandwagons may be triggered in response. In this example, the responses include policies to recruit more male teachers, arrangements to teach boys and girls in single-sex classrooms, and calls for more books to be written with male protagonists and themes (Weaver-Hightower, 2003). Often moral panics and bandwagons result in the cultivation of a new myth or a modification of one that already exists. In this example, the slightly altered myth becomes: *Boys should achieve the same as girls*. It is important to note that we are not implying that unwarranted certainties are necessarily sequential but rather that examining the relationships among them can be instructive.

Rather than avoiding or denying the unwarranted certainties and the inevitable uncertainties in education, we believe it is better to address them systematically and explicitly. To do so, we turn to the rich traditions of educational

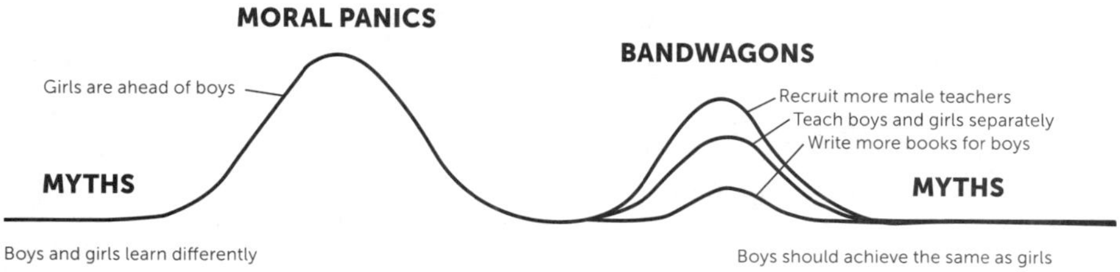

FIGURE 3 Interdependence of myths, bandwagons, and moral panics

thought and methods of inquiry developed by the foundations disciplines—history, philosophy, and sociology.

The foundations of education

Chapter 1 asks the question, "Why do foundations of education matter?" Teams of educational historians, philosophers, and sociologists were invited to answer this question for their discipline. We believe that the question is a timely and relevant one because foundations courses are either quietly disappearing from university syllabuses or are increasingly being relegated to the margins of teacher education. Although much has been written about the importance of the foundations of education in preparing teachers (Butin, 2004; Kerr, Mandzuk, & Raptis, 2011), there are increasing pressures to restructure teacher education to be more technical and rational (Hare & Portelli, 2003) or, in other words, to concentrate more exclusively on methodology. As a consequence, some universities and colleges have drastically reduced or even eliminated foundations courses from their teacher education programs (Christou & Bullock, 2013).

We believe that this trend is short-sighted because teacher candidates need to situate their learning in the roots of educational thought in order to understand and deal with both the inevitable uncertainties and the unwarranted certainties of education. In arguing that teacher education programs need to revive the foundations of education and attend more closely to taken-for-granted certainties, Liston, Whitcomb, and Borko (2009) conclude,

> What ails teacher education today is that it tends to offer programs fueled by a quest for certainty and motivated by a misplaced sense of efficacy and power. We need to understand that the wisdom of practice is much messier than the certainties we provide, much more provisional than the prescriptions we offer, and filled with a degree of human and educational tension that cannot be ignored. (p. 110)

We think that the shared references and specialized language offered by the history, philosophy, and sociology of education enable teachers to converse more clearly and meaningfully about both the uncertain and certain aspects of their practice. Perhaps more importantly, the rich traditions of these disciplines expose teacher candidates to the kinds of critical conversations and intractable dilemmas that can engage them in "substantive inquiry, intellectual debate, and deep reflection" (Butin, 2004, para. 1). The foundations disciplines not only focus our attention on the aims and morals of education, but also provide

> a conceptual lens through which to view teaching and learning, a beginning understanding of schools and school systems, as examples of

> social structures, an awareness of the racial, ethnic, and socio-economic disparities that exist in society and in schools, and an opportunity to critique current educational practices and the gap that exists between what we *say* we do and what we *actually* do in schools. (Kerr, Mandzuk, & Raptis, 2011, p.123)

Although, history, philosophy, and sociology often remain separate and disconnected from the rest of teacher education, we agree with Shulman (1990) that they "must be seen as an integral part of the connective tissue that gives shape and meaning to the education of teachers—as the framework for connecting and integrating the knowledge acquired in the liberal arts and sciences with the practice of pedagogy" (p. 304).

We make the connection between theory and practice explicit by including questions derived from the foundations of education disciplines after each case in the book. An example of this approach can be seen in the following questions about unwarranted certainties:

History

- What valid and reliable sources support our certainties?
- How does context affect our certainties?
- What historical claims underpin our certainties?
- What are the sources of our certainties?

Philosophy

- What assumptions and/or beliefs underlie our certainties?
- Do our certainties make logical sense?
- Do our certainties reflect an open-minded outlook?
- Do our certainties take into account what is **ethically** and morally defensible?

Sociology

- How do social structures, social cohesion, and forms of capital affect our certainties?
- In what ways do our roles, statuses, and identities influence our certainties?
- Which of society's norms and expectations are reflected in our certainties?
- How do gender, **socio-economic status**, and **ethnicity** affect our certainties?

According to Beadie (1996) the most important contribution of foundations studies, beyond helping students recognize the nature of teaching dilemmas, may lie in helping teacher candidates develop the **habits of mind** that will enable them to identify and understand the values that often conflict in educational situations. We think that teacher candidates can develop those skills by applying the kinds of questions that are posed by the foundations disciplines to carefully selected case studies that mirror the reality of life in schools.

Case studies

The case studies in this collection were written by professors from faculties of education, graduate students, and educators from across Canada. Contributors were invited to submit case studies based on actual events they had experienced or had seen reported in the media. The result is a collection of 30 cases that are relevant, engaging, and, at times, provocative. The names and details have been significantly altered to protect the privacy of the individuals and schools involved, and the cases are not attributed to specific authors.

Kindler, Badali, and Willock (1999) explain what we think is the most persuasive argument for using case studies to engage teacher candidates in questioning their certainties:

> When students are asked to solve problems and to make judgments and recommendations in regard to classroom situations presented in case studies, they become challenged to rely on more than intuitive insights and to support and justify their opinions through relevant references to educational theory. The ability to see educational theory as relevant and applicable to solving classroom dilemmas and informing teaching practice is essential for students to develop attitudes of inquiry and an interest in continuing professional development. (p. v)

The notion that case studies enable teacher candidates to make important connections between theory and practice has been described by Shulman (1996) as the key to their value as pedagogy: "Only in the continued interaction between principles and cases can practitioners and their mentors avoid the inherent limitations of theory-without-practice or the equally serious restrictions of vivid practice without the mirror of principle" (p. 201).

The cases presented in this book are designed to provide teachers with opportunities to work between theory and practice or in what Bullock and Christou (2009) call the "radical middle" (p. 77). After each case, readers are asked to make systematic and explicit connections between the issues, situations, and dilemmas that are depicted and the kinds of essential questions posed by the history, philosophy, and sociology of education. As Sykes (1992) points out, this type of foundational approach

> does not presuppose any tidy correspondence between theory and cases, but aims to cultivate analytic skills in the application of ideas and to convey theoretical knowledge in a form useful to the interpretation of situations, the making of decisions, the choice of actions, and the formation of plans and designs. (p. 469)

We think that the case-study approach and the application of discipline-based questions from the foundations of education can help us to understand the complexities of teaching and particularly to make sense of myths, bandwagons, and moral panics. Although some of the cases may appear to be illustrating more than one type of unwarranted certainty, for the purposes of this book, we have categorized each case by what we consider to be the most salient concept. In addition, we have organized the reading of the cases by the four commonplaces of education, as described in the following section.

The four commonplaces

The notion of the four **"commonplaces" of education**—students, teachers, subject matter, and context (or milieu) was used by Schwab (1977) to describe the interconnectedness of curriculum development. Posner (2000) speaks similarly of the four "common features," of which the first three (the teacher, the student, and the subject matter) occur "within the fourth feature of a teaching situation—a social and physical context consisting of rules, facilities, values, expectations, and personal backgrounds which act as resources, constraints, and direct influences on teaching and learning" (p. 3). On the surface, these commonplaces or features may seem obvious, but as Posner (2000) points out, they can serve as important reference points since they "comprise the whole phenomenon we call education" (p. 7).

The commonplaces are understood to be separate, equal, and interdependent features of teaching which need to be kept in balance without any one feature being allowed to dominate, unless there is a particular and defensible intention to do so (Schwab, 1973). The problem with overemphasizing one commonplace can be seen from the example of what happens when we teach only to the interests of students. Such a single focus may not only affect classroom management and the depth to which we can teach the mandated curriculum, but may also lead to wider community concerns about accountability. Furthermore, Schwab (1973) argues that overemphasizing one commonplace over the others is actually responsible for encouraging bandwagons in education:

> Despite the educational bandwagons which bear witness to the contrary, neither child nor society nor subject matters nor teachers is the proper center of curriculum. Indeed, the short merry life of many bandwagon curriculums often has arisen from just such overemphases: the child-centered curriculums of Progressivism; the social-change-centered curriculums of the 1930s; the subject-matter-centered curriculums of recent re-forms; the teacher-centered curriculums which may arise from unionism. (p. 509)

We have used the commonplaces to frame the commentaries and organize the cases because this structure highlights the interdependence of all the commonplaces while allowing us to focus on the most salient features. As you read the cases, we suggest that you keep the four commonplaces in mind and consider how the events might have played out differently if they had occurred in different schools; with different teachers; among students from different backgrounds, abilities, and educational goals; and within different networks of support.

CHAPTER ONE

Why the Foundations of Education Matter

Introduction

As previously mentioned, the history, philosophy, and sociology of education enable teacher candidates to gain critical insights into the teaching profession. In the three sections that make up this chapter, the contributing writers provide a more in-depth look into these disciplines, mapping the unique terrain each covers and offering a rationale for including the discipline in the education of teachers. Each section concludes with four examples of the kinds of essential questions that are typically posed by the discipline. These questions will serve as useful prompts for thinking about the 30 cases presented in the chapters that follow. As you read this chapter, see if you can identify what is unique about each discipline as well as the common threads that weave through all three.

Depending on your comfort and familiarity with the three disciplines, you may wish to consult the Glossary at the back of the book. Perhaps, like us, you are drawn to one of the disciplines more readily than to the others, but you will find as you read this chapter that each discipline helps us understand better the challenges and complexities of the teaching profession and the myths, bandwagons, and moral panics that surround it.

History of education

Half the way down a hill that is shared by Saint Thomas University and the University of New Brunswick stands a relatively small and inconspicuous white building that attracts very little attention. No traffic enters or leaves the building, which stands on short cement stilts at the corner of King's College Road and Windsor Street. A wooden fence encloses the property, and a pathway leads from an opening in the fence to the steps that climb to the front entrance. The several feet of snow that accumulates each winter reveal no footsteps leading in or out of the property.

This old schoolhouse, the Burden Academy building, predates Confederation. It was originally located some 30 kilometres from Fredericton in Burden, New Brunswick, and was relocated to the University of New Brunswick campus in 1966, preserved as part of the same planning that led to the development of King's Landing. Established in the Saint John River Valley, King's Landing was created in the 1960s as a reconstructed historical settlement; it consists of over 70 buildings which transport visitors to nineteenth-century New Brunswick. The buildings on the site were saved from regions that were flooded by the construction of the Mactaquac Dam, opened in 1967. As a consequence of the dam's construction, Burden, along with a number of small villages, is presently at the bottom of the Saint John River.

In a curious, regrettable way, it can be argued that Burden Academy and the many thousands of one-room schoolhouses that once dotted Canada's pioneer landscape find themselves beneath the river Lethe, the river of forgetfulness, or of forgetting, which the ancient Greeks placed in Hades. These one-room schoolhouses, once animated by wafts of smoke emerging from their chimneys as well as sounds of laughter and activity, offered free, public schooling to a relatively underpopulated, vast, and beautiful land. By opening up the doors and windows to these schools and peering inside, we can see the context of past socio-political events more clearly and gain a much-needed insight into the present. The study of the history of education, therefore, offers us a means out of the river Lethe and out of our educational forgetfulness, providing us with a more complete road map to the twenty-first century and making us less susceptible to the educational myths, bandwagons, and moral panics that race along the shore.

Sandwell (2011) provocatively asks teacher candidates to think of history not as a noun but as a verb. In other words, we shouldn't just think of studying history but of doing it. Doing history requires that we pay careful attention to who we are within our contexts and spaces, both as individuals and as part of a collective. In examining each case and story according to the information available and weaving our own understanding about teaching, learning, and above all, humanity into each narrative, we are, in fact, doing history. As Vacalopoulos (1976) suggests,

> Presumably history's highest goal may one day be attained: that of bringing men [*sic*] closer together and facilitating their communication with one another, by helping humanity understand itself and each man [*sic*] himself, even if only those parts inherited from the past. And what, after all, is history if it is not this perpetual search for individual and

social self-knowledge to the end of achieving a better tomorrow? (p. xiv) ("sic" appears in original)

We argue that the purpose of studying educational history is to foster **historical-mindedness**, which Osborne (2001) has defined as "a way of looking, not so much at history, but at the world at large, that derives from a familiarity with the past and with trying to understand and interpret it" (p. 552). In other words, historical-mindedness is a world view of sorts, which we can use for examining, interpreting, and acting upon contemporary educational contexts.

Historical-mindedness is not a new notion. Osborne (2001) revived it from a report published more than a century ago by the American Historical Association's Committee of Seven report entitled *The Study of History in Schools* (1898). The Committee of Seven explained that historical-mindedness could best be understood as a set of dispositions, or attitudes, which it regarded as vital to critical and effective citizenship in a democracy. These dispositions include a detachment from immediate pressures, a willingness to search for comparisons and analogies, a readiness to subject emotions to reason, consideration of multiple perspectives on issues, and the weighing of forces of continuity or change. In the next section, we discuss why these dispositions are as important for teachers as historians.

Why history of education matters

Being prepared to handle the day-to-day realities of classrooms is often an overarching concern for beginning teachers. Although such concerns are understandable, we argue that historical inquiry does not take away from this goal but, rather, is essential to it. Violas (1990) suggests that historical inquiry enables teacher candidates to develop two kinds of knowledge: understandings that substitute for experience, and knowledge of how things came to be in the present time. Through these two forms of knowledge, Violas argues, teacher candidates will be able to link socio-political conditions to educational structures and goals. For example, by studying the history of education, teachers come to understand how social conditions have significantly affected families and the reach of schools, including how certain programs, such as vocational education, and practices, such as home schooling, arose over time.

Murphey (2011, p. 258) notes that historical studies help teacher candidates to query and comprehend the "constellation of forces, ideological and material, that have perpetuated historically constructed differences," which are critical to teachers' understanding of increasingly multicultural classrooms. It is important to note that students in Canadian schools come from all corners of the globe and from countries whose accounts of history may diverge from or even contradict our own. This reminds us that we need to learn how to interrogate historical contexts critically, not only because accounts may differ depending on one's perspective, but also because our own frameworks of meaning can prevent us from seeing the perspectives of others clearly. In order to remove our individual and collective blinders, we must learn to think and read like historians, learning to question contested sources, contexts, and claims and continually seek corroborating evidence (Wineburg, Martin, & Monte-Santo, 2011).

Some of the easiest problems to identify are those related to the validity and reliability of primary and secondary sources. For example, accounts of the same historical event can differ markedly depending on the author's biases and relationship to the event and his or her reason for recording it. Furthermore, the accuracy of any account depends on how soon it was set down, how verbally adept the recorder was, and how much access the writer had to the event or the people who were directly involved in it.

Thinking about the context or what was happening at the same time as historical events helps us to consider the way that these events are recounted, and as a result we can gain a deeper understanding of them. Specifically, the role of human agency and power relationships among elite and marginalized groups may have a determining influence on how an account is written. To that end, Seixas and Peck (2004) argue,

> In the past 30 years, historians have sought ways to understand the historical agency of powerless groups. Labour historians, womens' historians, and other social historians have attempted to take their subjects out of the textbook "sidebars" into the centre of history, and not simply as victims. (p. 114)

We also need to avoid the danger of "**presentism**"—the error of interpreting past accounts as if they happened today and of failing to acknowledge that the very words used to describe an event may have changed in meaning with the passage of time.

The language used in historical accounts provides clues to the sorts of claims being made. Sometimes words are deliberately chosen to act as signals for specific audiences, and at other times, language is chosen to obfuscate the writer's intentions more generally. In addition, post-colonial biases and prejudices can affect whether the accounts of certain groups are missing entirely or are distorted. When this occurs, what is left out may be highly significant and as illuminating as claims that may or may not be supported by reasoned arguments and reliable evidence. This is especially important when one is considering how "curricula and discipline-based texts . . . have been constructed and read throughout different historical periods" (Giroux, 2005, p. 192).

Perhaps the most difficult, and at times, impossible, task of the historian is to establish what is true or accurate, even when reliable accounts are available. Accounts may be carefully analyzed and compared for disparities and filtered through the context of power relationships, types of claims, and purpose of writing, and yet their validity may still be inconclusive. Often, corroboration is not possible and judgments about what a teacher candidate should believe must be tentative at best. As Seixas and Peck (2004) point out,

> Public media are filled with conflicting historical accounts and interpretations of what they mean: Native land claims, the experiences of the inmates of residential schools, the role of Canadian soldiers and the Canadian air force in World War II, to name a few from Canadian history. Students need to develop abilities to assess these accounts and ask questions such as, "What are the problems with these accounts?" and "Shall I take them as is, or do they need revision?" (p. 111)

Given the often unresolved nature of historical inquiry, teacher candidates who have the opportunity to "do history" learn that teaching is particular, sometimes messy, and invariably complex. Memorizing and regurgitating names, dates, or ideas is quite remote from the historian's craft. In fact, historians essentially tell stories that reflect human realities from bygone eras and from which we can generate universal understandings (Buchart, 2011, p. 246). We argue that when teacher candidates engage with stories of events and individuals from diverse historical contexts, they can better prepare themselves for the human realities they too will encounter. Take for example, the reality that in today's saturated market, newly certified Canadian teachers must often leave their urban settings and "do their time" in remote rural areas.

The plight of the rural teacher is perhaps best illustrated by Glegg's (2005) analysis of the case of Mabel Jones, a young British Columbia teacher. In 1927, 19-year-old Mabel Jones assumed her role as the teacher in a one-room school at Nixon Creek, a logging settlement in the Cowichan Lake area of south-central Vancouver Island. A gentle soul, Mabel worked diligently with her seven boys and nine girls across a range of grades and thrived in her first year. A 1928 assessment of her teaching found her discipline and schoolwork to be good and the class's progress to be adequate. Nevertheless, on the 14th of November, 1928, a neighbour found Mabel dead on the floor of her cabin, a rifle by her side. Her suicide note implied her distress was due to criticisms, both personal and professional, levelled against her by two local school trustees who, it was later revealed, hoped to secure Mabel's job for a friend.

Teacher candidates stand to learn much from this narrative about the nature of unrestrained criticism, small towns, and the politics that characterized (and arguably continue to characterize) school board affairs. Insight into the role of the teacher in Canada's small, rural communities and how it has changed over time can go a long way in preparing beginning teachers to handle criticism from others without such tragic results.

Essential questions

By taking an active approach to questioning their own and their collective past, teacher candidates can gain a deeper understanding of it. Apart from learning from specific past events, teacher candidates who have an awareness of history are able to situate their own experiences, to refine their teaching practice while broadening their "conceptual scope" and establish a "range of possibilities for action" (M. Greene, 1973, p. 181). In other words, learning how to interrogate historical contexts through historical inquiry effectively counters an increasing tendency to seek the elusive one "right way" to teach (Liston, Witcomb, & Borko, 2009). Posing essential historically minded questions, such as the following, provides at least a partial antidote for this type of one-dimensional thinking:

- Is the source trustworthy and is the evidence reliable?
- How does knowing the context inform our understanding of the events?
- Are the claims supported by reasoned argument and evidence?
- Can we corroborate the account?

In addition, historically minded questions, such as those above, enable teacher candidates to situate myths, bandwagons, and moral panics. Given that many of the current barriers to critical thinking are variations of time-worn themes, those who examine sources carefully, check the claims and the context in which they are made, and withhold judgment on evidence that has yet to be corroborated are developing habits of mind that are essential for effective teaching.

Philosophy of education

The characteristic problems in philosophy of education and the breadth of thinking—and disagreement—about them can be readily seen by comparing two famous texts which arguably have had an enormous influence on education. The first is *The Republic*, written in about 360 BC, in which Plato sets out the ideal organization of society. The second, written by Jean-Jacques Rousseau in 1762, is *Émile*, in which the author describes the ideal education by way of an engaging narrative about a tutor and his pupil.

The Republic contains the well-known allegory of the cave, in which Plato describes prisoners, chained for life to a wall in a dark cave, who are only able to look forward and not from side-to-side. Behind and above these prisoners is a fire, and the people moving back and forth on a road between the fire and the prisoners are projected as shadows on the wall in front of the prisoners. Plato points out that for such prisoners, the shadows and their movements would be all they know—the prisoners would understand the shadows as real things and assume they represented all of reality.

Plato asks us to imagine what would happen if one of the prisoners were released and dragged up out of the cave and forced to look at the normal, above-ground world that we all take for granted. Likely, the newly released prisoner would reject what he or she saw and would think that his or her previous understanding of reality was truer. It would be painful, if not impossible, to convince the former prisoner otherwise.

One implication of Plato's allegory is that the benefits of education—at least an education into a higher knowledge and understanding of our world—are not available to all. Not everyone can see or be made to see the world as it really is. Most are bound by the shackles of their previous experience just like the prisoners in the cave. A second implication is that students may only be able to see certain aspects of the world when they are *forced* to reject what they already *know* and comprehend.

It is instructive to contrast Plato's educational beliefs with those in Rousseau's *Émile*. Rousseau recounts the education of a young man, Émile, at the hands of a tutor who manipulates the environment in such a way that Émile believes that what happens is the result either of chance or his own agency. Most of Émile's learning takes place as he draws conclusions for himself from things that happen to him and as those experiences teach him how to interact with his world.

For instance, Émile learns about ownership and agreements through gardening. He plants beans and thinks of that part of the garden and the beans as his, until one day he finds that the gardener has ripped up all of his produce. Émile learns that the garden actually *belongs* to the gardener and that if he wants to plant beans he must negotiate with the gardener for a portion of the garden.

In *Émile*, Rousseau promotes an education in which an individual learns to think for him- or herself and can freely enter into society with other individuals. Such a person would act confidently on his or her own knowledge instead of being driven by social mores and societal expectations or being governed by his or her own natural inclinations.

Consider the vastly different sets of beliefs connected to each philosopher's view of education: for Plato there is a body of knowledge, not easily accessible to the layperson, requiring a rigorous, possibly painful, education. For Rousseau, what is important is a deep and confident knowledge of the self, with most other knowledge being either deduced by the pupil alone (yet, often with careful guidance by the tutor) or being acquired later through personal experience. Each philosopher had very different political conceptions: Plato argued for a state in which stability is a key virtue and where each person occupies a role based on what they are most naturally suited for and educated to fulfill. Rousseau, on the other hand, believed that the state must be entered into freely and that education is intended to prepare people to take whatever role they were inclined to take.

As evident from these two examples, philosophers have been thinking about educational questions, if rarely coming to agreement on them, throughout recorded history. Familiarity with philosophy helps us to understand that education is based on beliefs (or assumptions—often tacit, or unstated) about what we know and how we come to know, what is morally permissible, who should decide what is appropriate for others, and what constraints exist. Philosophy involves critical reflection on these and related issues, and it is worth asking what value such inquiry has for people learning to teach.

Why philosophy of education matters

Philosophers down the ages claim that philosophy begins in wonder, that anyone can do it. In reality, however, not every child or student is encouraged to wonder, and this capacity may not develop. As a result, philosophy is considered by some to be a waste of time. It is certainly not everyone's cup of tea, and even philosophers recognize its limitations. Watts (1995) compares Western philosophy to trying to bite your own teeth: reason cannot transcend itself, an insight Eastern philosophy has long acknowledged. Nonetheless, like each tooth, philosophy serves important purposes despite its absolute limitations.

Philosophy is, at one and the same time, a scholarly discipline and a teaching method. The philosopher asks students questions that are still under consideration, and everyone learns as the inquiry proceeds. There are no philosophical facts in the sense of a set of widely agreed-upon conclusions. There are historical facts about philosophers and their ideas, but the questions Socrates asks about truth, justice, beauty, and goodness are still open questions. Though there is a place for leading students through a series of questions toward ready-made answers, that is certainly not how philosophical inquiry works. It proceeds by questioning, but not in the sense of an interrogation; there is no coercion and students are never left with the impression that inquiry is a game of conceptual hide-and-seek with the teacher always the one in the know. Rather, philosophical inquiry is a collaborative process of mutual seeking, ideally one in which teacher and students use viable and challenging points to carry the inquiry along. It is this practice of mutual wonder and collaborative questioning that philosophy of education offers teacher education.

Furthermore, philosophy offers teacher candidates an opportunity to explore questions they may already find puzzling, such as whether certain novels taught in schools should now be seen as biased in various ways (Hare, 1993a). They will also encounter many other intriguing ideas and begin to realize that philosophical discussion is indispensable. For instance, teacher candidates who are exposed to relatively unfamiliar philosophical accounts, such as "teaching for empowerment" (Freire, 1970), "teaching as risking one's own judgment" (Scheffler, 1973), and "teaching to release the imagination" (M. Greene, 1995), may find that those ideas challenge their conventional conceptions of teaching. Through philosophical discussion and reflection, they may not only begin to understand the meaning and significance of those stances, but, as a result, may also proceed with greater confidence to re-think their overall understanding of teaching and its central ideals.

To do so, teacher candidates need time to explore the notion of good teaching and the central **virtues of teaching**, such as humility, courage, open-mindedness, and empathy. They need to think about the kinds of tasks and problems teachers ought to concern themselves with and gradually come to understand that many of the most enduring problems, those that transcend time and place, have little to do with technique or fact. They need to be able to question the assumption that the absence of consensus shows that time would have been better spent on other matters. In other words, philosophical inquiry uncovers complexities in ideas that will be enormously helpful to teacher candidates in reaching a more sophisticated conception of their own professional responsibilities.

Those who are philosophically minded are fascinated by questions that others may find frustrating, but progress in philosophy is never clear and straightforward. Lipman (1991) compares it to sailing into the wind: one can make headway only by tacking back and forth, not by trying to sail straight toward one's destination. Imagine the following scenario. A new teacher faces a group with widely divergent abilities for the first time. She assumes that she has two options: adapt the lesson for students with learning difficulties or cover the curriculum at a pace suited to the majority of students. Neither course of action is justifiable, however, because she is responsible for the best interests of *all* students. If the situation, as she sees it, rests on the unquestioned assumption that she has to choose one option or the other, then eventually a choice will be made. On the other hand, if the teacher is philosophically minded, she will proceed with the knowledge that questioning an assumption can change the nature of the problem altogether. In this case, the teacher will come to understand that the choice—between teaching slowly for students with developmental delays or at the same pace for all regardless of their abilities—only exists because she was assuming that "teaching" means direct instruction. However, if teaching is defined more broadly—as teaching *how* to learn with increasing independence—the opposition between disparate needs dissolves and, with it, the dilemma. In other words, the teacher will come to realize that independent learners who need less direct instruction can leave the teacher more time for those with greater needs. Therefore, instead of sailing straight into a headwind and losing ground, the teacher can tack around the point of greatest resistance. Once again, philosophy of education shows that in some cases, the longest way round is the shortest way home.

Occasionally, public debates erupt that spur us to consider all kinds of philosophically minded questions, such as "What is the nature of good teaching?" "What is the difference between education and indoctrination?" or "What knowledge is of most worth?"; but generally our educational theories are deeply ingrained and influence our teaching without our being aware of them. The importance of philosophical inquiry becomes more evident when we consider the powerful influence of myths, bandwagons, and moral panics on teaching. Philosophers like Dewey (1971) have long understood that we are all affected by philosophical theories that escape scrutiny simply because they are firmly embedded in the intellectual outlook of the day. We argue that teachers need to make their beliefs more explicit and deliberately subject them to intense examination (Scheffler, 1973; Siegel, 1988), developing an ethic of philosophical-mindedness that embodies a number of intellectual virtues such as humility and critical self-appraisal, judgment, and open-mindedness (Hare, 1993b).

Philosophical inquiry makes clear how important it is to subject our presuppositions to critical scrutiny (Nussbaum, 1997). For instance, we ought to consider whether our teaching reflects our ideals or those of the textbook publisher, whether our teaching drifts into bias or propaganda, and whether we continue to see ourselves as students with much to learn. The fact is that many of our beliefs are much less certain than we imagine and may actually be the result of myths that we have never seriously questioned. Although it is notoriously difficult to detect flaws in ourselves that we may readily observe in others, teacher candidates who learn to probe their own convictions, opinions, and habits are more likely to teach with greater understanding, confidence, and humility than those who do not.

The absence of authoritative conclusions in philosophy underlines the need to become one's own philosopher (Dewey, 1971). Teachers who are philosophically minded develop a healthy tendency to raise questions about proposed educational policies, especially when criticism is discouraged, and can resist subtle pressure to go along with the educational experts. Although we can always learn from expert opinion, it is not always easy to distinguish genuine expertise from the persuasive rhetoric associated with educational bandwagons. Consequently, it is important to be able to weigh rival opinions and decide what is most appropriate in our own circumstances. By relying on our own judgment, we can learn to evaluate the merit of arguments and counter-arguments and look for a reasonable balance between the extremes of excessive caution and jumping to conclusions.

When we engage in philosophical inquiry, we are continually faced with what Russell (1973, p. 6) calls "surprising possibilities," whether we are considering contentious ideas or trying to avoid an emotional response to a crisis or a moral panic. Such possibilities help to foster an open-minded outlook that is intimately related to the ideal of good teaching. If our students see us as being open-minded, they will trust that the ideas under consideration are offered in a fair and balanced presentation. If they see us as being open to new and unusual ideas and being prepared to change our beliefs and practices in light of emerging knowledge, logic, and evidence, they will develop confidence in the process of inquiry. If they have opportunities to engage in collaborative inquiry and flexible thinking, following an argument even when it leads to a conclusion they would have preferred not to reach, they may be inspired to adopt an open-minded outlook themselves.

Essential questions

To the casual observer, philosophical inquiry can seem like an ordinary conversation. In a conversation, contradiction is not an impediment. It is common for us to answer "Fine" when asked "How are you?" and in the next breath recite a litany of complaints which contradict the opening statement. Whereas a conversation may go this way and that without any particular purpose beyond a pleasurable exchange, the dialectical process has a direction, however difficult and circuitous. When difficulties arise over, say, the definition of a term, the pleasant banter of conversation ceases. Such conceptual difficulty is the core of philosophical inquiry; it leads to deeper questioning that uncovers assumptions or contradictory claims.

Contradiction flourishes in our age of instantaneous, mass-mediated information; the spirit of contention has become a form of entertainment. When sound bites dominate substance and derogatory remarks undermine reasoned discussion, dispute reigns in a dialogical fight to the finish. Winning matters more than good reasoning, and often the winner is the loudest and most persistent in spite or even *because* of flawed reasoning. We need to recognize the difference between discussion and disputation and, as educators, intervene when the former degenerates into the latter.

Whether one is dealing with contradictions, discussing what knowledge is most valuable, or trying to determine what ethic is exemplified by a complex cartoon character like Homer Simpson (Irwin, Conrad, & Skoble, 2001), philosophical inquiry provides teacher candidates with access to the thinker's universal toolkit. Perhaps the most practical tools to be found inside are essential philosophically minded questions such as the following:

- Which assumptions might be questionable?
- What underlying beliefs should be exposed?
- Are the arguments and counter-arguments logical?
- What relevant conclusions can be drawn?

Questions such as those help teacher candidates to examine their beliefs and practices, use their own judgment, and adopt an open-minded outlook. In doing so, they are more likely to reject false or specious arguments and develop increasing skill in making logical and relevant inferences, as well as imagining the implications of their conclusions. In other words, they will be less likely to succumb to the myths, bandwagons, and moral panics surrounding teaching and learning.

Sociology of education

A letter to the editor that was signed by 80 academics from 22 universities across Canada and published by the *Montreal Gazette* on 30 April 13 was headed "Let's all commit sociology," and it concluded,

> In face of a world that is so self-evidently badly served by reactionary forces, we rededicate ourselves to committing critical scholarship. We also support scientists who document the precarious state of the environment. Like them, we embrace the "sin" of employing data in aid of a proactive public policy that fosters a sustainable and equitable planet. We urge all Canadians to do the same.

This unusual letter and a flurry of angry newspaper articles and opinion pieces were prompted by Prime Minister Stephen Harper's curious statement to the House of Commons on 25 April 2013 that "this is not a time to commit sociology." Mr Harper had been talking about the way the government was responding to the alleged plot to bomb a Via Rail train. His barb was clearly aimed at Justin Trudeau to remind voters of the new Liberal leader's sociologically minded comments after the Boston Marathon bombing, in which he tried to focus attention on the "root causes" of terrorism. Mr Harper's remark may or may not have been politically astute, but his statement provoked outrage among the academic community at home and abroad. Academics from around the world attending the Worldviews 2013 conference in Toronto vowed to commit sociology in "every panel, keynote, and even during their coffee breaks" (Ontario Confederation of University Faculty Associations, 2013) and to show their support for the discipline by wearing a button with the slogan "Keep calm and commit sociology."

But what does it mean to commit sociology? Sociology is the study of how individuals and society interact. Wotherspoon (2009) characterizes this interdependent relationship as follows:

> It examines how social structures (relatively enduring patterns of social organization) and social practices (ongoing social activity) both shape and are shaped by human beings. It is a scientific discipline in the sense

> that it is based on research and theories that attempt, in a systematic and organized manner, to describe and explain important features of social reality. (p. 4)

Berger (1963) probably put it best when he said, "[T]he fascination of sociology lies in the fact that its perspective makes us see in a new light the very world in which we have lived all of our lives. This also constitutes a transformation of consciousness" (p. 21). Like Berger, we believe that sociology has the power to change the way beginning teachers think about themselves, their students, and the society in which they live.

Sociology is a relatively new discipline, which surfaced as a distinct field of study about two hundred years ago. Given the unsettled nature of the times, it is perhaps not surprising that social imperatives captured the imagination of prominent intellectuals. After all, the increase in international trade, widespread dislocation as a result of the Industrial Revolution, and massive upheavals caused by new social and political orders had created challenging social conditions for large segments of the population. Tepperman (2010) points out,

> Sociology began with important cross-national comparisons. [Its] main founders—Marx, Durkheim, and Weber—were all familiar with, and interested in, the variations between societies . . . sociology probably arose out of a desire to explain differences and find patterns in people's social relations, in their ways of doing things and their ways of living together. (p. 1)

Not long after its inception, sociology began to focus on problem solving, looking for ways to deal with difficult societal issues such as poverty, crime, political instability, and social disparities. In time, a common language, a number of theories, and specific approaches to conducting research began to emerge and sociology matured enough to branch into sub-disciplines. One of the sub-disciplines was the sociology of education. For the purposes of this chapter and the book more generally, we will use the terms "sociology of education" and "educational sociology" interchangeably, recognizing the value of both the scientific applications of the former and the policy-related applications of the latter (Saha, 2010). What is perhaps more important than recognizing the distinction between the two is knowing that these sub-disciplines arose from the need to examine the distinct roles that schools, as types of social structures, play in socializing the young and the ways in which they either advantage or disadvantage students, particularly those from different socio-economic backgrounds.

According to Wotherspoon (2009), "sociologists are interested in education because it is so central to human social experience, to our direct and indirect relations with other people" (p. 3). Furthermore, Barakett and Cleghorn (2008) maintain that the sociology of education is particularly concerned with "how individual students come to abide by the norms and values of society at large, and the role that schools play in recreating social structure as this relates, in particular, to the division of labour and the hierarchy of power" (p. 2).

Taking a sociological perspective means examining both the intended and unintended functions of education. The intended functions are those we think of readily when we think of schools—knowledge, skills, values, mental abilities, and so on. The unintended functions of education include the so-called **hidden curriculum**, in which taken-for-granted aspects of schools such as timetables, streaming, and the use of physical space in classrooms may have far-reaching consequences for teaching and learning. For instance, power and authority play out differently in classrooms where students are assigned to fixed rows of desks than in those where students are grouped at tables or in learning centres, where teachers remain in the front of the classroom instead of moving around, and where walls are used only for displaying classroom rules and commercial posters rather than students' work (Horne, 2004; Lawson, 2001; McGregor, 2004; Polites, 1975; Proshansky, 1978; Sommer, 1977; Tarr, 2001). Looking at education sociologically can also help us to understand schools as places where roles, identities, and statuses are rehearsed. For example, some areas in schools are public or "**front-stage**" whereas others are restricted or "**back-stage**" areas. We use "**impression management**" to adjust our behaviour to the expectations embedded in each of these different areas (Goffman, 1959). Furthermore, the shared meanings and social norms developed in schools reproduce society (Anyon, 1981).

We believe that having even a cursory understanding of the sociology of education is essential for beginning teachers, who will work with students from increasingly diverse backgrounds in a wide variety of school settings. For some students, school provides numerous opportunities for success, whereas for others, it is an alienating experience that may not only dampen their curiosity but may also quash their aspirations altogether. Beginning teachers need to be aware of how socio-economic, racial, and ethnic factors can intensify the differences among students and how the sociology of education can help them make sense of this diversity.

Why sociology of education matters

Sociology of education can help teacher candidates develop the critical thinking skills they need to recognize and confront myths, bandwagons, and moral panics while maintaining an awareness of, and sensitivity to, social forces and contexts. Critical thinking skills enable educators to expose the gaps between what we *say* we do in schools and what we *actually* do. In other words, sociology can help us see beyond the rhetoric of commonly voiced claims, such as "schools can meet every child's needs," "effective schools build capacity with external stakeholders," and "sustainable school improvement depends on working with parents as equal partners in the educational enterprise."

While such claims are laudable and even achievable to a certain degree, those with a background in sociology are more likely to recognize the "**loose coupling**" of such unwarranted certainties to the realities of the typical classroom (Butin, 2004: Meyer, 1977; Weick, 1976). Meeting every student's needs is what a quality education should strive to do, but sometimes educators promise more than they can deliver, particularly when time and resources are limited. Building capacity with communities that have a vested interest sounds like a goal upon which we can all agree, but the realities are far more complicated: stakeholders, like professional organizations and special interest groups, often have their own agendas, which may be highly contested within groups and between them. Conflict may erupt between groups if each expects its own agenda to be at the top of the priority list. Although working with parents as equal partners makes sense, some parents don't want to be equal partners in their children's education, expecting schools to do it all whereas other parents expect to have an even greater voice in school decisions.

The sociology of education can also help teacher candidates understand the role of social structures in our lives. By virtue of our membership in social structures such as families, teams, community groups, schools, and classrooms, we are expected to conform to the specific norms of those structures. Such norms control our attitudes and behaviour so that, for example, we soon learn that conduct which is acceptable at a football game is unacceptable in the classroom or at a concert. In other words, as Sam Sommers (2011) argues, "situations matter." In addition, schools, like other social structures, resist our efforts to change them and can even go so far as to sanction group members who try to do so. It is not uncommon for teachers who try to use unconventional teaching methods to be reminded subtly or even overtly by their colleagues to fall into line and stop confusing their students.

In addition, sociology of education provides teacher candidates with a means of labelling and better understanding many aspects of the human condition that play out in schools or in the broader school community. Basic sociological concepts such as "**alienation**," "**marginalization**," "**power**," "**authority**," and "**identity**" not only illuminate our *own* experiences at a deeper level but also help us make sense of our students' experiences. For example, teachers who have experienced and understand the concept of alienation are more likely to recognize when one of their students feels a sense of "**powerlessness**," "**meaninglessness**," "**normlessness**," "**social isolation**," or "**self-estrangement**." Teachers who have experienced "**sociological ambivalence**" and understand the concept are more likely to recognize when one of their students is struggling with the conflicting expectations of contradictory roles or other identity issues. In other words, the language of sociology can help beginning teachers *name* what they see in the classroom, in the hallways, or the playground so they can understand it better. That is what Tepperman (2010) means when he says that the language of sociology allows us to "label the real world so that we can foreground it for further discussion" (p. 2).

Furthermore, the sociology of education enables teacher candidates to become more aware of how schools may privilege some students while inadvertently disadvantaging others. For example, "**tracking**" or "**streaming**" can provide enriching opportunities for some students and yet stifle or limit the learning of others. Similarly, curriculum that tends to place a strong emphasis on linguistic and mathematical intelligence can favour students who enjoy reading and writing and have an intuitive number sense, while students with other strengths do not have as many opportunities to have those strengths acknowledged and valued. Although schools increasingly provide students with opportunities to develop and grow through enrichment programs, band and choral programs, international travel, and high-level music, debating, and athletic competitions, it is a fact that the students who are most likely to be able to take advantage of such opportunities are those who were already privileged when they started school (Davies & Guppy, 1998, p. 138). The sociology of education, then, reminds educators of the importance of socio-economic factors and encourages them to challenge current ways of doing things so that they don't continue to reinforce disparities and put up insurmountable barriers for students who are already disadvantaged.

Finally, the sociology of education, in taking a scientific approach to gathering and analyzing data, enables teachers to examine more closely how social factors are related to academic attainment and other educational indicators. Research in the area of gender and education leads us to ask why female students are outpacing their male counterparts in Kindergarten to Grade 12 classrooms as well as in post-secondary institutions (Davies & Guppy, 1998) and to wonder whether the increased emphasis on collaboration, reflection, and literacy has indeed made classrooms more "girl-friendly." When the data gathered in response to concerns about the generally low academic performance of visible minorities (Boyd, 2002, 2008; Davies & Guppy, 1998; Thiessen, 2009) are analyzed closely, we come to understand that the results are highly dependent on which groups are being surveyed. For example, Asian students, who are classified as "visible minorities," have very high rates of high school completion and post-secondary participation and knowing this fact helps us to make more nuanced and thoughtful decisions. The awareness that the research literature has established a relationship between socio-economic status and academic attainment provides us with a greater understanding of the advantages that parents with higher socio-economic backgrounds and education levels confer on their children even before they start school and how these advantages accumulate throughout a student's school career.

Essential questions

We think that teacher candidates need to employ evidence to understand social relationships and structures. In the poem "Under Which Lyre," written in 1946, W.H. Auden (Mendelson, 1976) cautions, "Thou shalt not sit/ With statisticians nor commit/ A social science," and some, like Prime Minister Harper, apparently agree with the poet's satirical advice. However, if we are to expose the pervasive myths, bandwagons, and moral panics that create invisible barriers to critical thinking, we need to continually commit sociology. We need to ask important sociologically minded questions, such as these:

- How do social structures, such as schools, enhance or inhibit learning?
- How do norms, roles, and identities affect teaching and learning?
- In what ways do gender, socio-economic status, and ethnicity limit or expand educational opportunities?
- What is the role of human, social, and financial capital in education?

Teacher candidates who develop the habit of systematically interrogating their experiences from a sociological perspective are more likely to develop a sophisticated understanding of their experiences. Sociological perspectives expose societal fault lines and generate complex debates about the very nature of schools and their role in society. Furthermore, teachers who apply sociologically minded questions to their educational experiences are better able to develop strategies for managing the dilemmas that often arise from the myths, bandwagons, and moral panics that characterize teaching and learning.

Conclusion

The preceding three sections and the essential questions that conclude each one are intended to help you read the cases in this book through the lenses of historians, philosophers, and sociologists of education, using what is sometimes referred to as historical-, philosophical-, and sociological-mindedness. In doing so, you will become more familiar with the rich traditions of each of these disciplines and discover how they can help you to sort out the confusing and often mixed messages you may receive from the media, your colleagues, and your supervisors.

CHAPTER TWO
Myths

Introduction

In the previous chapter, we considered some of the essential questions raised by the foundations of education that help us to interrogate myths, bandwagons, and moral panics. In this chapter, we focus specifically on the unwarranted certainty of myths—what myths are, which myths pervade education, and how we can use the questions raised by the educational foundations to avoid their negative effects. The myths highlighted in this chapter are illustrated by 10 cases that were inspired by actual events. After each case, we offer questions about the facts of each case, its historical, philosophical, and sociological implications, and how the case can be applied to teaching.

What are myths?

The word "myth" carries the connotation of fiction or even falsehood, but as Jay P. Greene (2005) points out,

> Myths aren't lies. They're beliefs that people adopt because they have an air of plausibility, people want to believe they're true, and they are consistent with at least some pieces of evidence. But of course, myths aren't true—or at least they're not the whole truth. (p. 16)

Myths gradually acquire what satirist Stephen Colbert calls "truthiness"—the conviction that something is true because it intuitively makes sense or *feels right*, not because it has been shown through evidence, logic, intellectual examination, or facts to be true. Whether the source of a myth is true or not, Segal (2011) points out

> the tenacity with which myth is held counts even more. Myth does not hold a tighter grip when true than when false. If anything, the grip is tighter when myth is false, for adherence to the myth flies in the proverbial face of the evidence against it. (p. 590)

Myths, and the often misguided beliefs that give rise to them, permeate every aspect of education. They are enduring, persistent, and resistant to change and are rooted in a collective mythology of teaching that Lortie (1975) calls the "**apprenticeship of observation**." This informal and often unconscious apprenticeship originates in the time we observe our teachers for the 13 or so years we spend in school as students. Such experiences have a profound influence and, when coupled with often stereotypical portrayals of teachers in the media, suggest that teacher candidates begin their "anticipatory socialization" into teaching long before they ever set foot in a university class.

Clifton (1989) contrasts that unexamined body of knowledge, or what he refers to as the "**encyclopedia of mythology**," with the "**encyclopedia of knowledge**," which is based on research and scholarship. Although faculties of education might be expected to value scholarship over lore, Clifton (1989) contends that teacher education programs are steeped in mythology. Nuthall (2005) echoes that sentiment, arguing that the ethnographic and empirical research that underpins educational theory and practice are essentially based on myths. He argues that ethnographic research, being mainly derived from teachers' perceptions and self-reports and empirical research, consisting primarily of large-scale studies of so-called best practices, simply amount to studies of myths in action. Moreover, as Kerr, Mandzuk, and Raptis (2011) argue, teacher education programs are increasingly dominated by practice teaching and methods courses while foundations courses and other learning experiences that might challenge ingrained assumptions and beliefs are marginalized.

Myths may be benign and simply serve to maintain the status quo, but a number are quite insidious, for they shift the blame for poor performance onto the students, their families, or their community; in fact, it is often misguided myths that fuel the public discourse about education. As Jay P. Greene (2005) cautions,

> The people promoting these myths may not be fools or liars, but the myths themselves do real harm to children. They cause us to misunderstand the nature of the problems in our schools, to continue engaging in practices that short change students, and to resist the adoption of effective reforms that would improve education. (p. 2)

Gregory (2007) observes that such myths "haunt real classrooms like ghosts and invisibly distort all students' and teachers' notions about what education is for, how it should be conducted, and what kind of experience it should provide" (p. 8). Consequently, Nuthall (2005) points out,

> well-intentioned teachers can be completely unaware that they are favoring boys over girls (Alton-Lee et al., 1991) or majority over minority students (Spindler, 1999) or teaching content that the students already know (Nuthall, 2001b). (p. 22)

Myths are by nature self-confirming. Much of what we take to be common knowledge or common sense is actually the result of a "**confirmation bias**." In other words, whether we are prepared to admit it or not, we tend to look for information that confirms our beliefs or theories and to discount anything that contradicts them (Kahneman, 2011). For example, if we believe the myth that girls are better readers, we may not notice that some of the best readers in our class are actually boys. So fixed are some of the beliefs that we may unfairly ascribe to students and parents motives and behaviour that do not fit our preconceptions.

The inspiring true story of high school teacher Jaime Escalante and his class, recounted in the 1988 movie *Stand and Deliver*, demonstrates the lengths to which some educators will go to confirm their biases. When Escalante's students, who were from one of the poorest barrios of Los Angeles, all pass an Advanced Placement Calculus examination the results are rejected on the assumption that the students must have cheated. They have to fight for the opportunity to re-take the test and prove that their strong performances are actually the product of high expectations, hard work, and effective teaching.

Ullucci (2007) contends that it should not be surprising that myths are contested only when something extraordinary comes to light:

> While many of these beliefs remain unspoken and unchallenged, they form the bedrock on which we build educational policies and practice. Such beliefs can be considered a form of grammar: those taken-for-granted, unconscious structures that form the basis of the "way things are" (Tyack & Tobin, 1994). (para. 2)

As a result, the way things are is remarkably similar to the ways things were in the last century. Over a hundred years ago, elementary schools changed from being predominantly non-graded one-room schoolhouses, such as the ones described in Chapter 1, to being the easily reproducible graded egg crates we have today, in which boys and girls still learn mandated subjects together in self-contained classrooms, taught by a single teacher. Our high school system is virtually unchanged from 1906, when the "Carnegie unit" was first introduced to differentiate subject matter and to provide an accountable method of awarding credits in preparation for admission to post-secondary institutions (Tyack & Tobin, 1994). With few short-lived exceptions, these structures and the myths on which they are based have proven to be notoriously difficult to disrupt in spite of a number of creative and determined efforts. Such innovations as ungraded schools, flexible use of time and spaces, integrated subject matter, and team teaching have not lasted long because, as Tyack and Tobin (1994) point out, "Reformers believe that their innovations will change schools, but it is important to recognize that schools change reforms" (p. 478). It is evident that change requires more effort and a longer time to effect than many reformers might anticipate.

What myths pervade education?

Myths permeate what are known as the four commonplaces of education—students, teachers, content, and context (Clandinin & Connelly, 2000; Schwab, 1977). As mentioned in the Overview, these commonplaces are understood to be separate but interdependent features. For example, a teacher's efforts to make content more meaningful and relevant may affect student engagement, student achievement, and classroom dynamics and even lead to structural changes in the learning environment. In other words, the myths portrayed in the cases that follow would undoubtedly look different with different players and under other circumstances in different schools and communities. Although myths pervade each of the four commonplaces, the cases in this chapter illustrate those that arise in relation to the commonplaces of students, teachers, and context, which we have used to organize the discussion that follows.

Students

Normalcy

One of the most enduring and misleading educational myths is that of the "**normal child**." The details may vary, but when teachers are asked to describe a normal child, they usually portray a young person who bears a remarkable resemblance to the majority of teachers, that is, White, able-bodied, and a native English-speaker (Ullucci, 2007). Students who live in poverty, come from non-English-speaking homes, have unfamiliar ethnic backgrounds, or have physical and mental capacities that deviate from our conception of normalcy are sometimes seen as less desirable and, more importantly, *someone else's* problem. Teachers have come to expect that any student who does not fit the profile of the normal child will be appropriately labelled and treated by specialized staff (often in segregated spaces) until they are *cured*, thereby *earning* a place in the regular classroom.

The myth of the normal child affects how teachers perceive their students. Within the first weeks of school (or even earlier), teachers judge how close students are to being normal and make assumptions about their ability. In addition to information gleaned from their colleagues, teachers' perceptions are bolstered by myths that certain student characteristics, such as body build, gender, race, ethnicity, given name, attractiveness, dialect, and socio-economic level correlate with achievement (Tauber, 1998).

Teachers may or may not communicate their expectations overtly, but students certainly pick up on even subtle cues such as increased smiling, nodding, and leaning towards those considered to be the most desirable students (Bamburg, 1994). In their classic study, Rosenthal and Jacobson (1968) illustrated the power of the "**self-fulfilling prophecy**." Merely telling selected teachers that a group of their students (who actually had been chosen at random) had performed in the top 20 per cent on an IQ test resulted in those students outperforming a matched group of students who had not been labelled as having high academic potential.

The case "This Suit's for Wearing" highlights the struggles of a group of diverse students who are enrolled in the same Performing Arts class. Their teacher, who appears to ground his pedagogy in the myth of the normal child, questions his expectations when he begins to think about these students as individuals. As you read this case, consider the ways in which teachers' beliefs about what is normal affect their students.

Gender

Notions about gender remain highly contested even though our understanding of human sexuality has deepened and our laws are changing to reflect society's broadening sensibilities. Nevertheless, from the moment of birth when many hospitals place blue blankets on boys and pink ones on girls, we make our different **gender expectations** apparent. Despite the fact that research has demonstrated that most gender stereotypes are the result of sociological or cultural imperatives rather than basic biological or anatomical differences, many of the myths surrounding gender are entrenched and persistent. Consequently, students whose behaviour differs from our expectations for females and males may be poorly understood by their peers and teachers, and the pressures on them to conform may have damaging consequences.

There are many overt and subtle ways that gender stereotypes are socialized in the hidden curriculum of schools in spite of educational policies and human-rights legislation that mandate the equal treatment of boys and girls. As Lynch and Feeley (2009) point out,

> Even when schools have explicit gender equality policies, they can inadvertently reinforce a culture of hegemonic masculinity and femininity.

> Throughout the hidden curriculum, stereotypical images of "good, quiet girls" and "tough, naughty boys" emerge in school discourses, wall displays, stories, and through the attitudes of some teachers. (p. 56)

Two of the cases in this section deal specifically with gender expectations. "When I Grow Up I Want to Be . . ." examines the impact of explicit and confining expectations for females in a small fundamentalist rural community. For members of this society, gender expectations are extremely clear, have a religious basis, and are not open to debate. For others, like the teacher who has been hired from outside the community, gender differences are regarded as being more fluid, existing along a continuum that is influenced by biological and sociological factors.

However, it is not only females who are subject to rigid identities, power imbalances, and marginalization. Gosse (2012) argues that narrow social expectations for males contribute to the "punishing process" of becoming a man:

> Boys in school are subjected to homophobia, racism, classism, and shame as a means of policing their burgeoning identities, and stifling anything that might be construed as "feminine", so that being studious becomes considered "gay" or "sissy" or even "White". Both girls and boys, and men and women, enforce these behaviours in implicit and explicit ways. (p. 18)

The case "Who Cares?" explores the tensions surrounding males who are headed towards careers as caregivers, traditionally viewed as a female occupation in Canada, and the conflicts experienced by a transgender lesbian teacher. As you read this case, think about how unexamined assumptions continue to prevent both males and females from stepping outside normative gender assigned roles.

Ability

Research that has exposed the powerful influence of teachers' expectations on achievement helps us to understand why students develop adaptive or maladaptive responses to academic challenges. Dweck (1975) has shown that two different theories about the nature of ability, "**entity theory**" and "**incremental theory**," highly influence achievement motivation in students.

Entity theory is the belief that intelligence is a fixed trait that cannot be developed. Teachers who subscribe to this theory tend to blame students' failures on their lack of ability. As a result, students respond by using less sophisticated problem-solving strategies, demonstrating less task persistence, and displaying more negative emotions. This is essentially a deficit theory, in which students' academic weaknesses, usually conflated with other factors such as socio-economic status, come to define them. Consequently, teachers all too often expect very little from students from low socio-economic families. Such a view supports the widely held belief that poverty is the result of presumed moral and intellectual deficiencies and that the privileges enjoyed by the economically advantaged are, therefore, justified. As Gorski (2008) points out, such myths allow schools to ignore systemic conditions that perpetuate the cycle of poverty:

> If we convince ourselves that poverty results not from gross inequities (in which we might be complicit) but from poor people's own deficiencies, we are much less likely to support authentic antipoverty policy programs. Further, if we believe, however wrongly, that poor people don't value education, then we dodge any responsibility to redress the gross education inequities with which they contend. (p. 34)

Incremental theory, on the other hand, views intelligence as a malleable quality with the potential to be developed. Teachers who believe in this theory tend to encourage students to blame their failures on lack of effort. As a result, students may increase task engagement, demonstrate sophisticated problem-solving strategies, and display more positive emotions. The problem with this meritocratic theory, however, is that it implies that if students from low-income families would simply work harder they would have equal opportunity to succeed in life and in school. Ullucci (2007) notes the fallacy contained in this myth:

> This myth supports the notion that schools are neutral places, where structural inequities do not exist and fairness is the name of the game. Teachers who support the notion of meritocracy set up a worthy/unworthy dichotomy. Because all students have equal chances to excel, students who do succeed within the system are worthy of the benefits they receive. Children who fail do so of their own accord, not because of bias in the system. (para. 14)

The case "Flipping Burgers" illustrates how myths about the nature of ability can affect teachers' approaches to assessment and students' achievement motivation. As you read this case, consider the effects of low expectations on students and the double-bind in which some students are placed when we focus too much attention on effort and not enough on unequal educational opportunities.

Teachers

Constructivism

Rooted in the philosophies of Socrates, Rousseau, and Dewey, **constructivism**, or the idea that students learn by constructing their own knowledge, is now a widely understood explanation of how students learn (Abdal-Haqq, 1998; Nuthall, 2005). Elizabeth Murphy (1997) points out that this understanding has a profound impact on the way we teach:

> How we perceive knowledge and the process of coming to know provides the basis for educational practice. If we believe that learners passively receive information then priority in instruction will be on knowledge transmission. If, on the other hand, we believe that learners actively construct knowledge in their attempts to make sense of their world, then learning will likely emphasize the development of meaning and understanding. (para. 3)

Nevertheless, Hyslop-Margison and Strobel (2007) caution that the claim that knowledge is constructed "amounts to little more than an educational slogan in the absence of conceptual understanding and clarification" (p. 73). They point to an influential article by Phillips (1995) called "The good, the bad, and the ugly: The many faces of constructivism," which raises important questions about the uncritical adoption of constructivism as an approach to teaching.

Phillips (1995) characterizes the active participation of learners as a *good* implication of constructivism because when students are more engaged in the subject matter their learning improves. The *bad* implication is that the knowledge that is being constructed may be an exercise in reinforcing misinformation, biases, and incomplete understanding. Furthermore, Nuthall (2005) argues that simply organizing teaching so students construct knowledge does not necessarily mean that knowledge is transferred to the learner:

> Student talk has replaced teacher talk, so that it is now assumed that when students talk together about a new concept or procedure they are "mutually constructing" knowledge (Wells, 2002). What has changed is the concept of what constitutes an effective "learning activity". What has not changed is the mythical belief that engaging in learning activities (such as listening to the teacher talking, discussing the results of an experiment, or writing a report of an investigation) transfers the content of the activity to the mind of the student. (p. 922)

The *ugly* implication of constructivism, according to Phillips (1995), is that constructivism has become a type of educational sectarianism rejecting all other methods of teaching regardless of the learning context. Direct instruction (or lecturing), for example, is often dismissed as having no place in a constructivist classroom even though it may be the most effective teaching method when students already have prior knowledge or practised skills (Hyslop-Margison & Strobel, 2007).

In the case "Missing in Action," the teacher reflects on the good, the bad, and the ugly of constructivism and questions whether it is the best approach for all of her students. As you read this case, think about the tensions between theory and practice and what teachers can do when the two are not connected.

Digital divide

The term "digital natives" was coined by Prensky (2001) to characterize students who grow up with technology and who "think and process information fundamentally differently from their predecessors" (p. 1). Using the same metaphor, Prensky (2001) labels those who come to technology later in their lives as "digital immigrants" who are "in the process of learning a new language" (p. 2). Helsper and Enyon (2010) note that this metaphor locates those born before 1980 "within the past, unable to fully understand the natives" and characterizes them as "not going to the Internet first for information; printing things out as opposed to working on screen; and reading manuals rather than working online" (p. 504). Although popular, the metaphor has come under widespread attack for a number of reasons, including the obvious one that we should always be suspicious when people of any particular age are considered to be a homogenous group (F. Sullivan, 2012).

Bayne and Ross (2007) argue that binary opposites such as those suggested by the digital native metaphor are simplistic and misleading. They point out that this metaphor carries with it some hidden assumptions, including what amounts to a racist understanding of what it means to be an immigrant who is barely tolerated. Furthermore, they point out that the metaphor creates a hierarchy in which students are placed in the commanding position, thus de-privileging teachers, who are expected to follow where the digital natives might lead while at the same time being incapable of doing so.

There is no empirical evidence to support the implication of this metaphor that there is a big discontinuity between the generations. Indeed, it has never been established that a significant proportion of youth are actually expert in technology. Moreover, Helsper and Eynon (2010) found that "breadth of use, self-efficacy, and education are more important than age as an explanation of how people become digital natives" (p. 504). The generational argument makes the unwarranted assumption that those who come to technology later in their lives are unable to achieve the same fluency as those who are younger no matter what they do. Helsper and Enyon (2010), who reject that claim, point out that adults, "specifically, teachers, can speak the same language as their students, if they want to" (p. 516), and like their students, multi-task, go to the Internet as a first port of call for information, and use technology to carry out a wide range of activities.

Furthermore, the assumption that students are now *wired* differently and that the brains of digital natives are physically different from those of digital immigrants is unsubstantiated. This argument hinges on recent research on "**neuroplasticity**," the brain's ability to reorganize itself by forming new neural connections throughout life in response to changes in the environment. However, just how that works and whether neuroplasticity affects younger brains differently than older brains are not well understood.

In the case "Just in Time," a teacher confronts differences in technology skill that he considers to be a generationally based. As you read this case, consider how unwarranted certainties about teaching digital natives and digital immigrants might affect teaching and learning with technology.

Rewards

Rewards, both tangible and intangible, are common features of everyday life in classrooms, in the form of smiles, head nods, stickers, pizza parties, bonus marks, increased attention, and praise. Some classrooms are even structured as token economies in which students receive tokens (check marks, stars, chips, and so on) which can be exchanged for prizes. However, Mader (2009) points to a substantial and consistent body of research that questions the motivational benefits of such efforts to increase desirable behaviour (Giroux, 2000; Maher & Tetreault, 1994; Moffatt, 2006; Pink, 2009; Shor, 1997). In particular, research has found primarily negative effects of external incentives on "**intrinsic motivation**." Richard Ryan and Edward Deci (2000) define intrinsic motivation as "doing something because it is inherently interesting or enjoyable" in contrast to "**extrinsic motivation**," which is "doing something because it leads to a separable outcome" (p. 55). They point to numerous studies which have found that intrinsic motivation results in high-quality learning and creativity whereas extrinsic motivation tends to disappear when the reward or incentive is withdrawn (Kohn, 2010; Marinak & Gambrell, 2008).

Although psychologists have generally warned that external rewards, such as money for attendance, co-operation, or achievement, undermine the joy of learning for its own sake (Guernsey, 2009), the line between extrinsic and intrinsic motivation is not always clear. Scholarships, academic awards, honour rolls, sports trophies, band trips, and even praise are all extrinsic incentives, dependent on certain types of performances. Yet educators are more likely to defend these as contributing to rather than diminishing intrinsic motivation. Furthermore, as Schwartz (2009) points out, not all people respond to extrinsic incentives in the same way.

A report of the mixed results of recent experiments (Allan & Fryer, 2011) demonstrates that the effect of incentives on motivation is indeed a complex question. The experiments, which were conducted by Fryer (2010) in four major American cities, distributed more than $6.3 million to some 38,000 students in 261 schools for behaviour ranging from attendance and reading to grades and test scores. Interestingly, this research found that incentives were effective when students were rewarded for things they could control (such as improving their attendance or co-operation or increasing the amount they read) but were less effective when they were rewarded for things they didn't know how to control (such as improving their grades and test scores). The belief that external rewards have negative effects on interest and intrinsic motivation were not substantiated. Furthermore, rewards have been found to be effective in schools when they are combined with performance feedback; when the students have no initial interest in a task; when the task is demanding and complex; and when the students have a choice of the task and/or the reward (Pierce, Cameron, Banko, & So, 2003).

In "Who Pays?" a teacher questions whether extrinsic incentives would be a valuable strategy for students who may not otherwise complete high school. As you read this case, think about whether paying students to learn can sometimes be justified.

Context

Multiculturalism

The idea that all cultures should be encouraged and accepted has been federal government policy for over 40 years. It is enshrined in the *Canadian Multiculturalism Act* of 1988, and is a taken-for-granted assumption of school policies across Canada. Eiserman (2009) notes that, although Canadians are "intensely proud of our multicultural policies, most of us have never actually read the Act" (p. 68) or examined its assumptions. Originally a political solution to questions of French sovereignty, Aboriginal rights, and pressures from minority groups for greater inclusion, **multiculturalism** is intended to ensure that all Canadians are protected equally under the law and are able to participate equally in Canadian society.

A number of critics (Ghosh, 2008; Simpson, James, & Mack, 2011; St Denis, 2011) argue that the underlying assumptions of multiculturalism are seriously flawed, engendering a naive belief that there is racial equity and harmony in Canada. Simpson et al. (2011) blame multiculturalism for normalizing the myth that colonialism and racism do not exist in Canada, and St Denis (2011) abhors "the use of multiculturalism discourses to manage and silence competing interests within the nation." Ghosh (2008) adds to these criticisms:

> [F]ailing to recognize Canada's racist history and portraying a raceless and colour-blind society condones and continues White privilege (white racism). In education, we cannot be fair to all citizens by being colour-blind because Canadian society is not colour-blind; it privileges certain ethnic groups. Fairness, not colour blindness, is a fundamental principle of justice. (p. 28)

Although the majority of Canadians support the basic principles of multiculturalism, there is nonetheless an inherent dilemma at its core—purporting on the one hand to give individuals from all groups equality of opportunity, while on the other hand guarding the retention of the rights of diverse groups, regardless of the inequities that a culture may contain within it. Nevertheless, DeFaveri (1995) reminds us that the tension between cultural assimilation and cultural retention cannot be resolved through mere tokenism:

> It is fraudulent to acknowledge diversity of cultures within a society while assuming that culture deals only with clothing styles and cooking recipes and has little to do with ways of perceiving the world, moral judgements, and public goals. (p. 273)

Two cases, "Whose Culture, Who's Teaching?" and "Unmasking Hallowe'en," underscore the need to enter into a dialogue that goes beyond "trying to 'add and stir' diversity into the classroom" (McCreary, 2009, p. 7). The first of these two cases explores concerns of Aboriginal people about multiculturalism, which, in considering all cultures to be equal, essentially ignores their unique rights and history. The second case exposes the tensions that exist when a school's efforts to implement neutral education in the name of multiculturalism collide with the expectations of families that want to retain majority cultural celebrations at the school. As you read these cases, consider whether the standard of fairness is met in debates about multiculturalism.

Secularism

In Canada, a distinction is made in matters of religion between what is acceptable in the public and the private sphere. In the public sphere, laws, government policies, and institutions are expected to adhere to "**secularism**," that is, to exclude religion or religious beliefs. For example, the British Columbia *School Act* (1996) stipulates that public schools are to be conducted on "strictly secular and non-sectarian principles" and that "no religion, dogma, or creed [may] be taught in a school." In the private sphere, individuals are guaranteed the right to religious freedom, as enshrined in the *Canadian Charter of Rights and Freedoms* (1982) and the *Canadian Multiculturalism Act* (1988).

As Canadian society becomes more pluralistic, it is increasingly apparent that religious beliefs can no longer be confined to the private sphere. Recent court decisions upholding the presence of books in schools which show children with same-sex parents, the wearing of the *hijab*, *bourka*, or *niqab* in school, and the carrying of a *kirpan* suggest that a more inclusive approach to the role of religion may be evolving. As cited in Clarke (2005), Judge Mackenzie of the British Columbia Court of Appeals observed,

> Strictly secular in the School Act can only mean pluralist in the sense that moral positions are to be accorded standing in the public square irrespective of whether the position flows out of a conscience that is religiously informed or not. The meaning of strictly secular is thus pluralist or inclusive in its widest sense. (p. 359)

Nevertheless, it can be argued that public schools have *never* really been strictly secular. Education, first introduced and sustained by Christian missionaries, still retains many vestiges of its origins in public schools. Furthermore, as Blumenfeld (2006) reminds us, "Society marks time through a Christian lens" (p. 199). For instance, our current year dates from the birth of Jesus, the academic year and its holidays are based on Christian festivals, and the work week is scheduled around the Christian Sabbath. Until recently, Bible readings and recitations of the Lord's Prayer were a daily feature of most elementary schools, and though the practice is hotly debated, Gideon Bibles are still being distributed free in many Grade 5 classrooms. Although some educational jurisdictions include religious celebrations of other religions in their calendar and readings from other faith literature, a visit to public schools around Christmas or Easter reveals that Christian symbols, activities, and music remain privileged. Although some defend such practices as neutral seasonal markers, Blumenfeld (2006) argues,

> While some of the religious significance has diminished over time as traditional Christian religious practice has entered the public square, on critical analysis, the clearly religious meanings, symbolism, positionality, and antecedents of these practices betray claims to mere secularization. (p. 206)

In "No Space for God Here," a teacher and his administrator are locked in an ongoing debate about the nature of secularism and whether the rights of the minority are infringed upon by the use of the Bible as a resource in a high school English class. As you read this case, consider the role that religion should or should not play in public schools.

Conclusion

The deeply rooted myths to which we have become "acculturated" have significant consequences for our practice, "shaping our definition of reality, not only what it is but what it should be" (Sarason, 1996, p. 14). As individuals, it would be a daunting task indeed to try to uncover and counter the overwhelming number of myths that pervade education. Fortunately, we can draw upon the rich traditions of history, philosophy, and sociology and the essential questions posed by each of these disciplines for guidance.

Looking at myths from the perspective of history helps us to situate our beliefs in context and to locate the sources of our unwarranted assumptions and beliefs. For example, by comparing multi-age grouping to the one-room schoolhouse of the past, we can gain insights about the benefits and limitations of both. Furthermore, being grounded in educational history helps us to determine whether educational reforms are just recycled ideas from the past or are truly worthy of our serious attention. When we adopt a historical stance to question the validity and reliability of myths, we serve as models of inquiry for our students, become more confident about our ability to explore issues in an unbiased way, and are less likely to accept myths uncritically.

Philosophy encourages us to question our assumptions and expose them to serious scrutiny. By developing philosophical-mindedness, we subject myths to tests of logic, determining whether myths are the result of misunderstood facts or culpable fictions. For example, we might consider whether assigning a zero for the late submission of an assignment is logical in terms of the principles of fair assessment or whether there are more appropriate consequences for this behaviour. Furthermore, philosophy challenges us to explore our notions of good teaching and its central virtues. As we become more aware of what is truly important to us as teachers, we may feel compelled to pay increased attention to the myths that conflict with our values.

Taking a sociological stance means examining the social implications of the myths that underlie our practice, especially those that involve our assumptions about gender, ethnicity, socio-economic status, race, religion, sexual orientation, and identity. We need to determine which individuals and groups are privileged by our beliefs and which are disadvantaged. Once we have identified the dynamics of power in our classrooms, we can take action to disrupt the most negative effects. For example, we might reflect on our classroom seating arrangements and deliberately create opportunities for marginalized students to develop social capital with those who have more stable and integrated social networks.

In order to develop historical-, philosophical-, and sociological-mindedness, it is essential to have opportunities to practise the critical thinking skills embedded in each of these disciplines. That is why, in addition to a question about the case and a question that asks you to apply what you have learned to your own practice, we have included three foundations-based questions. We think that, by examining the myths illustrated in the cases from a foundations perspective, you will be better positioned to apply this type of thinking to other myths that you will encounter in your own practice.

THE CASES

This Suit's for Wearing

It was Tuesday morning, and as usual Miriam, Noor, Alejandra, and Ngoc were meeting in their favourite corner of the Valley Secondary School library. All four girls had found their way to the school because of their common interest in the performing arts and to the library, where they found comfort in one another's company. Their meetings had drawn them closer over the past three months, and the corner suited them well. There was a table large enough to accommodate them comfortably, and because they were so often found there together, they quickly became known as the "corner girls."

The girls enjoyed their corner and found they could still hear each other without having to raise their voices and catch the unwanted attention of Mrs Cruikshank, who was vigilant in maintaining a well-run library with a quiet working environment. On this occasion, the group was meeting to help one another make sense of their assignment on homonyms. The task was somewhat challenging for them. It not only involved understanding how a word can sound the same as another and have a completely different meaning, but also required students to demonstrate their understanding in the form of a skit. Their teacher, Mr Dyer, didn't hold out much hope that the corner girls would actually be successful given that they were mostly new to the school, were non-native speakers of English, and had remained aloof from the other 30 members of the class.

The girls had been placed together in a Grade 6/7 split, since the school didn't know what else to do with them. Some of the four girls struggled more with English than the others, and a few had serious "family issues." On occasion, one or another of the girls had an emotional outburst or displayed rude behaviour. No one really knew what went on in their homes after school, and no one dared to probe.

Although Miriam and Noor spoke English well enough to get by, they had been categorized as "slow learners." Some of the staff wondered whether their learning difficulties were actually linguistic rather than cognitive, but Miriam's behaviour seemed, at times, to be symptomatic of ADHD. In any event, the school counselling department was booked for months in advance and it was highly unlikely that any more diagnostic tests would be arranged to make a proper determination.

Noor, on the other hand, had undergone a series of formal and informal tests and was found to have dyslexia in addition to some auditory processing difficulties. She was also observed to take more time than usual in thinking through what she should do in simple situations where neither language nor reading seemed to be a factor.

Ngoc, who had come to Canada as a young child, was the daughter of boat people who had received little formal education in Vietnam. At home, she had no access to technology or books since both were beyond her family's reach. She was often restless, and although she seemed to relate well to the other corner girls, she remained distant from the rest of the class.

Of the four, Alejandra, a daughter of Nicaraguan parents, was the best "adapted" and the most adaptable. Her teachers had identified her as being well-read and being gifted academically, but she had annoyed the other students by frequently challenging her teachers. Some of her peers obviously felt threatened by Alejandra's precociousness, intelligence, and talent. When they began to call her a "geek," "freak," "brain bore," and "know-it-all," she realized that she was out of favour with her classmates and requested a move to Mr Dyer's class. When cyber-bullies got to her on Facebook, she was resourceful and confident enough to use a message-blocking system to prevent them from spreading derogatory messages about her.

Morris Dyer enjoyed the support of his superiors. They praised him publicly as a "quality educator" who could be counted on to maintain high educational standards even with increasingly diverse students under his charge. He was highly enthusiastic about evidence-based teaching and, if requested, could print out a complete numerical profile of any student he had taught in the past five years. When he took on the Performing Arts course in addition to his regular load, Morris simply continued to teach in the same way, breaking down the course into measurable outcomes that he could assess through so-called objective tests, quizzes, and well-defined performance tasks. He was aware that most of the outcomes in this course might be better assessed with rubrics and anecdotal comments, but he had always found these to be too difficult, time-consuming, and subjective for the kind of data analysis he preferred. Morris liked to be able to defend his grades as being standards-driven, norm-referenced, and accurate.

However, he was beginning to wonder whether his approach to teaching and assessment was going to work as well as it usually did, given the nature of this course. Although he had been very confident about his data-based teaching in the past, he was no longer sure he could rely on the validity of his assessments when used with such a diverse group of learners, including the "corner girls." He also began to wonder whether he had fallen out of step with current thinking on assessment and was inadvertently causing some of his students to disengage from their own learning. Anxious to find out, he scheduled back-to-back performance assessments. Tablet and stylus in hand, he was ready to keep score.

As he tallied the results, he felt both pleased and frustrated at the same time. He was not surprised to find that most of the class had easily grasped the point about homonyms and had creatively acted out the words assigned to them. The corner girls had been assigned the word "suit" and were expected to show three different meanings: (1) a two-piece matching garment, (2) a combination of playing cards, and (3) the process of trying to win a woman's affection with a view to marriage. Alejandra and Miriam had not only understood the object of the lesson, but had also performed delightful pantomimes, complete with costumes and music. However, the other two members of their group, Ngoc and Noor, either didn't understand what they were supposed to do or were stubbornly resisting the opportunity to participate in any approved or expected ways. They barely took part in their group performance, and even words of encouragement from the other two had little effect. Morris realized that his usual assessment methods were inadequate for grading Ngoc and Noor fairly: on the basis of the performance, he really didn't know what they had understood.

As he began to think more carefully about these apparently disengaged students, he saw them clearly for the first time as individuals with very different needs instead of just being one of the corner girls. He realized the time had come to re-evaluate his teaching methods, his expectations of his students, and his approach to assessment.

Questions

The Case

At the beginning of the case, Morris Dyer assumes that his class will meet quality standards if he teaches the same content in the same way to everyone. Why does he begin to question these assumptions?

History

In the past, schools segregated students on the basis of various differences. How do schools continue to segregate students today? Justify your response.

Philosophy

What do you think it means to be a "quality educator"?

Sociology

In what ways do Morris Dyer's evidence-based teaching practices advantage or disadvantage certain learners in his classroom?

Implications for Practice

Whether we like to admit it or not, the myth of the normal child affects our perceptions of our students. How will *you* challenge this myth in your own practice?

When I Grow Up I Want to Be . . .

It wasn't Martha's day to tidy the entry way, but like all of the other girls in her fundamentalist community in rural Saskatchewan, she took pride in making sure that everything was in its right place. This was women's work and no one expected any of the boys to spend their time or energy on tidying. In fact, Martha had been taught that it would be unnatural if they did.

It was Friday and the heady smell of yeast was wafting through the building. The women and the older girls had been up early baking in the community-hall kitchen, and Martha could hardly wait to sink her teeth into the warm, buttery buns at lunch. She looked forward to being able to join the older girls who cooked together in the mornings. Martha was already caring for the little ones at lunchtime and after school, and she looked forward to the pleasures of motherhood. She loved reading to the little children and playing house with them and had been praised for sewing neat stitches by her grandmother.

Martha was soon joined by Jenna, Maris, and Flora in their multi-grade classroom at the back of the church. They couldn't wait to tell her what had just happened.

"Oh, Martha, you should have seen Stanley and Ernie racing through the playground and sliding into that huge puddle that Miss McCaffrey warned us to stay away from!" laughed Jenna. "Look out the window—their mom is hauling them off to get a bath and she looks like thunder. I guess they'll be late for school again today!"

"Only a bunch of silly boys could get into so much trouble between breakfast and school time," said Martha, turning to Jenna for agreement.

Jenna smiled and added that the boys would be lost without the girls to keep them in line.

Jenna was an excellent student who was taking most of her high school courses through distance education. She was the class monitor and quickly told Maris to get out the writing journals and the rest of the girls to take down the chairs that were perched on top of the tables. With Jenna in charge, the classroom would be ready in time for Miss McCaffrey's arrival. Before long, the rest of the boys and girls had arrived, kicking off their shoes and padding along the shiny floors into the classroom, with their teacher close behind them. The classroom was noisy and bustling as the boys and girls found their seats on opposite sides of room, ready to start another school day.

The students liked Miss McCaffrey, but when she first arrived, they had been warned not to be too welcoming. The education committee had hired Sandra McCaffrey in spite of the serious concerns of some of the long-time community members. They openly expressed their fears that the young unmarried teacher was too worldly. They worried about what kind of role model Sandra would be—

wearing trousers, her short hair uncovered, living alone, and travelling freely around the world. However, with the high turnover of teachers they had experienced in the past five years, the education committee finally persuaded the community to give Sandra a chance. After all, she had come well recommended and she seemed to have a positive and respectful attitude.

Although they reluctantly agreed to accept her as a teacher, the community decided to set some limits. They would not, for example, invite her into their homes or ask her to attend community events. Parents were comforted in knowing that anything untoward that happened in the school would be repeated around the dinner table at suppertime.

Sandra knew she was under a microscope and was mindful of how even her casual comments might sound out of context. However, she was also fully aware that her own beliefs, experiences, and outgoing personality couldn't be completely excluded from her teaching. She realized that, as an outsider, breaking through the community's protective wall could well prove to be the hardest part of her job. It would take patience to build relationships with her students and their parents, but unless she was successful, it was going to be a very lonely year and a very short career with the school.

At first, few of the children would make eye contact with Sandra. However, as fall turned into winter, most of the children had dropped their wariness. The younger students, especially, no longer treated her like a stranger and were beginning to contribute more freely to class discussions.

Sandra was surprised to learn how little her students knew about the modern world and how little curiosity they had about it. Perhaps this was because they had extremely limited access to the Internet, were not permitted to watch television, and only saw movies that had been vetted by the education committee. Sandra's students also had very little exposure to alternative narratives about women's and men's roles. Their ideas about relationships between the sexes were drawn solely from their community and the books that had been approved for their tiny school library. Sandra found these books to be anything but stimulating. They were usually set in the frontier past and showed women as being dependent on men, neither making their own decisions nor questioning the status quo. Since her students were very interested in learning about vehicles, nature, and geology, Sandra decided to show them pictures from her trips to Asia, Africa, and Europe, where she had spent time on holiday and taught in overseas schools. In this way she hoped to broaden her students' outlooks without overstepping the boundaries established by the community.

However, she soon wondered whether this had been such a good idea. At the end of the day in early December, Jenna shyly approached her desk to ask if they could talk privately about something *very important*. Jenna had started to stay after class to help Sandra tidy up the classroom, and after a few weeks they had settled into a friendly routine. Sandra was beginning to think that Jenna just might be the one to unlock the door to the community and let her in. However, as Jenna looked around furtively, checking over her shoulder to make certain she wouldn't be overheard, Sandra could tell that something was disturbing her student's usual calm. Jenna jumped right to the heart of the matter.

"Miss McCaffrey, I love my family, but I really want to study biology when I grow up and I want to travel the world like you did! No one has ever gone to university from our community, but I can't stop thinking about it. I'm not like the other girls—I know I am not cut out to spend my life in the kitchen!" Jenna reached out and grasped Sandra's hand, pleading, "Please, will you help me?"

Sandra was visibly shocked. She had no inkling that Jenna questioned her future role as a woman in her community. Sandra wondered how she could possibly help Jenna to realize her dreams without jeopardizing her own position as a teacher. Whatever else happened, Sandra knew that she and Jenna would have to tread very carefully as they began their first conversation about the possibilities that lay ahead.

Questions

The Case

Given what you've read in this case, in what ways might Sandra be or not be a good "fit" for this community?

History

Traditionally, women's roles have been clearly defined in religious communities. In what ways might changes in these roles threaten the stability of these communities? Explain your response.

Philosophy

In this case, Sandra is caught between upholding the values and traditions of the community and helping one of her students to break free of them. As a teacher, to whom is she most obligated—the community or the student? How would you justify your position?

Sociology

In this case, Jenna does not want to conform to the social norms of her community. How do social norms affect girls' career aspirations, more generally?

Implications for Practice

In a tight job market, new teachers often have to consider teaching in remote and alternative settings. What kinds of things will you need to think about if you accept a position in a school where the traditions and values are very different from your own?

Who Cares?

Long before entering the classroom at Brantford Secondary School, a large urban high school in a medium-sized Ontario city, Kate Turnell was concerned about how she would be judged as a teacher and as a staff member. After all, she wasn't a traditional Science teacher by any stretch of the imagination. Kate was a lesbian, and she presented herself as a gender-non-conforming individual. She wasn't feminine in appearance; she didn't wear jewellery, dresses, or even make-up. She wore her hair short, combed straight back in a blunt cut, and usually wore men's clothing, preferably suits with a masculine cut. She was androgynous in appearance and was sometimes even taken for a man. Before coming out as a lesbian in university, she had presented herself as gender-conforming and had not stood out in any way. She was drawn to Science as a largely male educational discipline in which society expected few feminine women to be engaged.

Kate realized that she did not fit most social expectations of her gender, and so she anticipated that her legitimacy as a teacher would be questioned by her students and perhaps even her colleagues. She was surprised that her first teaching assignment included an all-male Biology class. She was even more surprised to learn that almost all of her students planned to become caregivers, a career path that Kate had always associated with women. Many of these students were of South Asian and Caribbean descent, and she quickly discovered that they were influenced by very different cultural norms about masculinity than she was. The families of her students came from a long tradition in which both men and women viewed school, and particularly Biology, as gateways to various caregiving professions, such as nursing and physical therapy. From the students' point of view, boys and men could and should be caregivers, and this did not appear to conflict in any way with their own notions of masculinity or their cultural identities. If masculine boys and men could be caregivers, Kate's students seemed to be willing to accept that lesbians (and a woman who dressed more like a man than a woman) could teach them what they needed to learn. As a consequence, she found that she was able to build positive relationships with most of her male students.

To fulfill their provincial service-learning requirement, all of Kate's Biology students had elected to volunteer in health-care facilities. Recognizing an opportunity to engage her students more deeply in their learning, Kate framed her major assignment as an inquiry in which students were expected to investigate biological questions related to patient health. The students enthusiastically developed projects that covered the major concepts of their Biology course and allowed them to become more aware of the health challenges faced by patients and their caregivers. Kate was gratified to see that the completed assignments demonstrated her students' grasp of the concepts and was moved by the very real compassion her students revealed in their responses. Kate began to recognize how many of her assumptions about males were being driven by her own cultural experiences and how little she had questioned her own beliefs about gender norms. In fact, Kate was surprised to discover that her all-boys Biology class was teaching her to be more comfortable in her own transgender identity.

Kate was careful not to bring up issues of sexual orientation in her classroom (although she guessed that her students suspected she was a lesbian). She didn't wear a wedding ring or tell her students anything about her family. Most heterosexual teachers were quite open about the presence of husbands, wives, and children in their lives. Kate realized that the stories that gender-conforming teachers provided about their lives outside of the school day contributed to their ability to develop learning relationships with their students. Because they had no personal information about her, Kate's students were often curious about her private life. Even though the topic of her sexual orientation was never brought up directly, her students would ask who she lived with and whether or not she had a boyfriend or girlfriend. Her responses to these kinds of questions were courteous but intentionally vague, and throughout, she was conscious of the fact that she was presenting an unusual role model for most of her students.

In spite of the warm relationships she seemed to be developing with her Biology class, Kate was disappointed to learn that homophobia was nevertheless still present in the class: someone had carved "Miss Turnell is a dyke" on one of the desks in the classroom. Not knowing what else to do, she decided to speak to her principal, Evelyn Bowden, about how to handle the situation. Kate asked to meet with Evelyn privately and took the opportunity to come out officially as a lesbian (although she was fairly certain that her principal already knew). Kate hoped that Evelyn would support her and take the opportunity to address the issue of homophobia in the school head on. Evelyn was clearly uncomfortable with the conversation, and though she expressed concern and promptly arranged for the words on the student's desk to be removed, to Kate's disappointment, nothing else happened. No proactive efforts were taken and soon it was as if the hateful incident had never occurred.

Kate got the feeling that Evelyn and most of the staff simply didn't know what to make of her. As a result, many of them tended to keep their distance. Kate found this curious and disheartening because at this point in the year, she had expected more from her colleagues. It seemed as if both staff and students saw her as being ageless and sexless. In fact, she felt that she was often put in the same gender category as the adolescent boys in her classroom rather than the other adult female teachers in the school. As she had predicted, this turned out to be problematic for forming social and professional relationships with the rest of the staff, particularly her female colleagues.

Although it was still relatively early in the year, Kate was beginning to wonder if she was going to make any lasting friendships at the school. She was going to have to give this some more thought if she wasn't going to remain marginalized at Brantford.

Questions

The Case

Although this case highlights how typical gender expectations are challenged, how might Kate actually be reinforcing gender stereotypes?

History

In what ways have schools changed to accommodate teachers with diverse sexual orientations? In what ways is it business as usual? Explain your response.

Philosophy

Kate is intentionally vague with her students about her sexual orientation. How much about their private lives should teachers share with students? Why do you think so?

Sociology

How do our taken-for-granted and unconscious assumptions about gender influence our educational practices?

Implications for Practice

In what ways do the gender positions of other teachers affect you and your interactions with them?

Flipping Burgers

It was the first week of August, and Elizabeth Chaput, a first-year teacher, had just been hired to teach Grade 6 at Millbrook Community School, an inner-city K–8 school located a short drive from her apartment. Her principal, Dianne Halworth, thoroughly impressed by Elizabeth's portfolio, professionalism, and ability to teach in both English and French, chose Kevin Gartner, one of the school's veteran teachers, to be her mentor. Dianne, who was well aware of the stresses involved in beginning to teach, had helped to develop the school board's mentoring program. She was concerned about the rate of teacher turnover and the need to retain more new teachers. After all, close to 40 per cent of new teachers chose to leave the board (and often, teaching) within five years!

Kevin had taught many of the same students the previous year, when they were in Grade 5. He had just moved to the intermediate level from the elementary grades, where he had taught for most of his career. As the Grade 7 teacher, he would teach these students again the following year, barring any unforeseeable changes. He felt that he knew these students very well and offered Elizabeth his opinion on them at every possible opportunity.

However, Elizabeth did not always welcome Kevin's opinions, nor did she believe that they were necessarily accurate. Furthermore, she wanted to get to know her students—particularly their interests and strengths—in her own time, without being biased by her mentor's opinions. As school policy dictated, she had examined her students' school records, but she did so with the aim of identifying the need for accommodations.

The first month of the school year was a torrent of activity. Long days and often longer nights were spent planning, writing a journal, reflecting, and grading. By the end of the first week, Elizabeth felt that she needed her own administrative assistant just to deal with the paperwork involved in teaching.

However, as the weeks sped by, her concerns were increasingly directed to the unhealthy attitudes that some of her students had developed towards their grades. It wasn't just that some students were more anxious about the marks they received than about learning, but Elizabeth suspected that some had internalized their low grades and that the effect was paralyzing them. She remembered studying about **learned helplessness** in her teacher education program, and now she was actually witnessing it firsthand.

"Ms Chaput, I can't do math!" exclaimed Muktiar. "I'm just not smart enough. I've always been a C student in math and that's the best I'll ever do."

Unfortunately, this lack of confidence was not limited to just one student, nor was it confined only to mathematics, as Elizabeth would soon discover.

The problem came to a head in early October when the annual school-wide public speaking competition was announced over the intercom. Each student would be expected to write a three-minute oral presentation and present it before his or her classmates. When Elizabeth began to discuss the project with her class, there was a great deal of groaning. The students knew that the best speeches from each class would be presented in front of the school, and a further competition would be held to decide which speeches moved on to the regional, then district-wide event. When students all around the room announced how poorly they had done in the competition last year, Elizabeth realized she would have to do something to counteract what had clearly become a pervasive sense of discouragement.

She discussed her concerns with Dianne, who agreed that her students could meet the provincial oral language requirements in a different way. The next day, Elizabeth proposed that the class collectively write and perform a play together for the school instead of participating in the public speaking competition. The students were thrilled with the idea and decided to adapt "The Three Little Pigs" to address the theme of bullying. Each student took part in writing and performing the play in front of the whole school.

Elizabeth was impressed with her students' efforts and delighted with their enthusiasm. On the basis of that success, she was emboldened to develop a more comprehensive plan to deal with learned helplessness in her classroom. She decided she would respond to students' work with comments only. She would record a grade in her daybook, but her formal reply to students would only be in the form of anecdotal comments about what the students had done well and what they could do to improve. If her students wished to revise and resubmit assignments on the basis of her comments, she promised to re-evaluate them. Dianne approved Elizabeth's approach but emphasized that the young teacher would need to be diligent in recording all grades and grant any parent's request for more information on their child's progress. Over the rest of the term, Elizabeth's workload increased dramatically. At the same time, the students were revising their work and resubmitting it more often. On one occasion, a student submitted the same writing assignment for assessment seven times! Not only did Elizabeth notice that the students took more interest in learning but also that their grades were improving. After several attempts, many assignments that started out as C's could now justifiably be graded as A's. Behind the scenes, Elizabeth ensured that all student progress was marked in her daybook, and student portfolios were kept in a filing cabinet that the students managed themselves.

At the end of term, Kevin offered to help Elizabeth enter her grades with the district-mandated report card software. Over lunchtime, they sat in Elizabeth's classroom, with Kevin at the computer and Elizabeth perched on a stool beside him. He suggested that he would call out the student's name and subject, and she would call out the grade.

"Michelle Lacerte: Language Arts, Writing," said Kevin.

"A," Elizabeth replied.

Kevin winced, shrugged, and began again, "Language Arts, Oral."

"A," Elizabeth replied.

As the pattern emerged, Kevin became so agitated that he couldn't even bring himself to enter any more of the students' grades. Instead, he turned to Elizabeth and asked her to look more closely at the summary sheets that she had prepared.

"These are not A students, Elizabeth," he said as patiently as he could. "I know you want these kids to feel good about themselves, but let's face it, they are going to be flipping burgers for a living and they will have to face reality sooner or later.

Honestly, I think I know more about these students than you do. After all, I have been teaching a lot longer than you have, and I know which students are going to succeed academically and which will not."

He was about to continue, but Elizabeth cut him off. She explained that she had spoken with Dianne and had records of the students' work to justify the grades that they had achieved.

Kevin stood up quickly. Unable to contain his anger any longer, he exploded, "These students will have a rude awakening next year, and every year after that. And when their parents come complaining to me next year about their kids' grades being so low, I'm going to send them right back to you."

"Please do," Elizabeth replied, as coolly as she could. "I'll make sure they know how well their kids can do when they are given half a chance."

Kevin fumed as he left the classroom, "Boy, are you naive! Unless you wake up and realize where these kids come from, you'll be another one with a rude awakening!"

Questions

The Case

How does Elizabeth address learned helplessness in her classroom, and what are the positive and negative implications of her approach?

History

Historically, teachers assumed that students from higher socio-economic backgrounds would always outperform students who were more disadvantaged. From your own experience, what evidence do you see that teachers are still making these kinds of assumptions?

Philosophy

What are the virtues of a good mentor?

Sociology

This case illustrates ways in which mentoring programs can fail to achieve the desired outcomes of supporting new teachers. How do you think age, experience, status, and other sociological factors affect this professional relationship?

Implications for Practice

In your practice, you are likely to encounter students who have internalized low expectations. How will you recognize these kinds of students in your own class, and what will you do to help them?

Missing in Action

Samantha Fynes was in her fifth year of teaching at Melrose Middle School, located in one of the outlying suburbs of a large metropolitan area. She was looking forward to teaching her fractions unit, knowing that last year's students had said that this unit was their favourite. Typically, Samantha's unit planning involved sequencing the essential concepts and then mapping out possible tangential ideas to be explored. In this way she could ensure that the essential concepts would be taught in order but she would be prepared if students opted to explore other related ideas. So far, none of her classes had explored all of the areas she prepared, but it was worth the extra preparation to know she was ready to help students explore the ideas that were most interesting to them.

As usual, she began by asking the students to brainstorm a list of ideas that she would later use to help them draft inquiry questions. Although Samantha found that students were fairly predictable in the eventual inquiry questions they would come up with for learning about fractions, she found the free-flowing activity of brainstorming areas of interest to be the most enjoyable part of the process. It helped her to get to know her students' interests and learning needs better and to decide which learning activities would most actively engage them in meaningful learning.

Essentially, Samantha believed that meaningful learning must be "uncovered for oneself" rather than being revealed by someone else. She knew that direct teaching, supported by lots of worksheets with an emphasis on finding the one right answer, was what her students knew best, but she disliked that approach and rarely used it. Not only did she believe that this style of teaching interfered with a child's unique learning journey, but it also inhibited students' abilities to generate their own questions, and that, in her opinion, reduced them to passive and disengaged recipients of meaningless information.

Consequently, Samantha intentionally kept her teaching plans loosely structured. Her goal was to empower her students to make their own decisions about what and how to think. Her commitment to the inquiry process, however, did not mean that she expected students to figure everything out for themselves. Once she determined that the students had understood the essential concepts, she allowed them to pursue their own interests freely, usually in collaborative groups. Knowing the importance of keeping middle-grade students on track, Samantha scheduled conferences with the students to help them determine the format and timing of the research checks and evaluations.

Samantha saw her primary role as facilitator whose function was to create a learning environment that encouraged students to ask and pursue their own questions. It was not easy to create a classroom climate in which students felt safe and supported in generating their own research questions, but Samantha believed that it was worth the extra effort if students developed greater confidence in their own thinking abilities. She believed that the inquiry approach was especially suited to the diverse life experiences of her students—some had never left the city while others had just arrived in the country. Some of her students' parents contacted her regularly about homework or school events, whereas other parents had had relatively no contact with the school. Samantha knew that her students' varied backgrounds would mean that there would be diverse interpretations of concepts, and she was excited by the possibilities this opened up for class conversations and inquiry.

Lately, however, she had become uneasy about an emerging pattern in class discussions about how the more abstract concepts related to real-life situations. Early in the unit, most of the students seemed eager to share their ideas; for example, one boy connected fractions to his favourite Bollywood music video, while one of the girls made connections to sections of a graffiti mural that she passed every day on the bus. Another student related fractions to her cousin's elaborate sixteenth birthday party while one of the more troubled students in the class disturbingly connected fractions to the number of his Dad's beer bottles that were routinely lined up on the kitchen counter each morning.

Although these classroom discussions were interesting, Samantha increasingly found them to be exhausting because she needed to simultaneously co-construct concepts with her students while trying to help them make some sense of each other's incredibly varied life experiences. She could see that most of the students didn't appear to know what to make of the graffiti mural example and was a little concerned when some parents had complained that it had been inappropriate for Samantha to allow the beer bottle anecdote to be told in class.

Feeling increasingly disillusioned with how things were going, Samantha felt relieved when the essential concepts had been collectively developed. The students were now ready to work through the inquiry process in smaller groups, depending on their areas of interest. This shift in learning was also timely because Samantha was noticing that the same students always seemed to be contributing during whole-class discussions, while others remained silent, distracted, or even disruptive.

Although Samantha had hoped that group work would provide an environment where *all* students would feel more comfortable about sharing their ideas, that is not what happened. Unfortunately, the same students who dominated the whole-class discussions were now controlling their group work by abruptly interrupting or even mocking other children's contributions with eye-rolling and smirking. Even worse, some of these students would take the group's work home to get help from their family. Consequently, after receiving hours of individualized help the night before, they would return to class the next day boasting to the other group members about the extra work that they had managed to do. In the end, the gap between the children who were dominating class discussions and group work and those who were becoming increasingly marginalized was growing wider each day.

In truth, the entire process had become a nightmare. The motivated students who worked at home or during breaks progressed quickly during the inquiry process while many of their less motivated peers struggled even to develop relevant inquiry-based questions. Furthermore, once they settled on their questions, these students seemed to require just as much support to move to the next stage of the inquiry process, that is, *if* they were still willing to persevere. Although some continued to work diligently, an increasing number seemed to be giving up and were now spending their class time either staring vacantly into space or distracting others. By all accounts, they were producing little work, and Samantha gradually came to understand that the inquiry process simply wasn't working as well with this class as it had worked in the past. Although a small number of parents were telling Samantha that their children were more engaged than ever in their learning, most were complaining that their children were feeling discouraged and "worn down" by Samantha's approach to teaching and learning; in fact, one family had already met with the principal requesting that their child be transferred to another classroom.

Samantha knew that she needed to adjust her teaching practices, but she didn't know exactly what to change and where to start. However, she believed that whatever she did, she would remain committed to the inquiry process and to honouring children's self-generated questions. Feeling exhausted and close to tears, she tidied her desk, locked her classroom door, and headed home to think more about how she could address her students' learning needs and remain true to her own beliefs.

Questions

The Case

At the end of this case, Samantha begins to question whether her approach to teaching is meeting all of her students' needs. As a strong believer in constructivism, how might she have responded more effectively at different stages of the process to keep *all* of her students engaged?

History

The enthusiasm for constructivism has waxed and waned over time. What do you think contributes to its *current* popularity?

Philosophy

What should good teachers do when faced with evidence that their deeply held beliefs about how to teach may not be working as planned? Justify your response.

Sociology

In what ways might students with greater social capital be advantaged in a constructivist classroom?

Implications for Practice

What strategies might you integrate into your teaching that might help *all* the children in your class succeed?

Just in Time

Stephen Horowitz moved to the West Coast at the end of July to take up his new position at Greenwood School. In addition to teaching Grade 7 Math and Science, he had been hired to head up the school's technology focus team and had time built into his schedule to help teachers with their use of technology. Stephen felt completely comfortable in both roles. He had been using technology in a variety of forms for most of his life, and he had previously taught both subjects as a middle years teacher in his hometown. Considered a rising star in his district, Stephen had been commended for integrating technology seamlessly into his own teaching. He was brimming with ideas for infusing technology into the curriculum and was looking forward to sharing these ideas with his new colleagues.

As he began the school year, Stephen had lots of questions about the school's technology infrastructure and the technologies that teachers were already using. However, the first thing he noticed after being introduced to the staff was the relatively high number of older teachers in the school, several of whom seemed to be close to retirement and, perhaps not coincidentally, how little technology integration was actually happening at Greenwood. Given the gap in age and experience between Stephen and the rest of the staff, he wondered whether his older, more experienced colleagues would even be open to being mentored by a younger and newer staff member. Dismayed, he doubted whether these "digital immigrants" were even teachable and whether it was even worth his while trying to involve them in any long-term educational technology initiatives. However, it was soon clear that their involvement was non-negotiable.

Grace Yamamoto, the principal of Greenwood, was committed to ongoing school-based professional development, and she took a hands-on approach with the school's five focus-team leaders. She insisted that each teacher, even the late-career teachers, sign up for at least one of the focus groups: assessment, early literacy, education for sustainable development, behaviour management, or technology. No one was allowed to opt out. Stephen soon realized, as the technology group leader, that he would have no choice but to take the older teachers into account in whatever plans the group might make.

When Stephen accepted the position, he assumed that he would be able to build on initiatives that had already been started before he arrived at Greenwood. However, he soon discovered that only one project had been started the previous year. It was essentially just a checklist with staff members' names down one column and basic technology tasks across the top. The intent was for staff to check off the tasks they could do well, so that if someone else needed help, they could refer to the chart and ask the right person. As Stephen looked across the list, he mentally checked off every one of the tasks, but he quickly saw that few of the other staff felt that they could check off any. It looked to him as if no one at Greenwood was really integrating technology the way that the district and the province expected so he braced himself for a lot of resistance, particularly among the older teachers.

In October, Grace informed Stephen he would be playing a key role in the implementation of the new provincial Literacy with Information Technology Initiative at the school. Along with organizing and delivering professional development, he and the technology group would also be responsible for allocating funds to buy interactive whiteboards and organizing the necessary training for using them effectively. It was a very exciting prospect, but it was also somewhat daunting when Stephen considered how the older teachers, like Maggie Bertrand, would manage this new technology. Maggie was a 35-year veteran of teaching who had never really embraced technology of any kind. She routinely complained that her computer, TV, or DVD player was not working when it simply wasn't plugged in.

Stephen decided to conduct an audit of the technology situation at Greenwood so that the technology group could make informed decisions before recommending any purchases. It was clear from his audit that major changes could not be rolled out all at once. At Grace's suggestion, the technology focus team decided to start with those who were most excited about the purchase of the interactive whiteboards. These teachers would be the first to have their classrooms upgraded and to participate in just-in-time training with Stephen. Watching their colleagues turn morning routines into research opportunities and reluctant learners engaging in remedial learning in the form of games spurred excitement through the school. A group of teachers took to spending part of their lunch break in the classrooms where the whiteboards had been installed, playing with the software and sharing ideas. Grace was pleased to see a steady stream of requests from formerly uninterested teachers to have whiteboards installed in their rooms. She could also detect an increase in the amount of technology of all kinds being used in the classrooms as a result of teachers having scheduled time to work with Stephen.

For Stephen's part, he was surprised to see that some of the teachers who seemed most interested were older, more experienced teachers like Trevor Sagitt, Maggie's Grade 5 teaching partner. Although he had not had much experience with technology, Trevor was just as enthusiastic as the youngest teachers on staff and was often more thoughtful about the benefits and limitations of technology. Of course, there was still a small group of teachers, including Maggie, who didn't want interactive whiteboards in their classrooms, no matter how many demonstrations or engaged students they saw.

Much to his relief, Maggie ended up retiring at the end of Stephen's first year; gradually, the rest of the teachers seemed to accept the fact that integrating technology was not just a passing fad they could wait out. However, there were still many questions and problems for Stephen to deal with along the way because some teachers didn't take the time to learn how to use the technology properly. It was frustrating to Stephen when teachers told him that their computers had no sound when the volume was simply turned down, or that their flash drives didn't fit into their computers when they had them upside down, or that they wanted to use computer programs that couldn't be installed because they were more than a decade old. Stephen was tempted to write off the "digital immigrants" as simply being too old to learn, but then people like Trevor made him think again.

Over coffee one day, Trevor and Stephen talked about how best to support teachers at various stages in their careers. As he listened to Trevor talk admiringly about his colleagues and the kinds of changes they had adapted to over the course of their careers, Stephen began to wonder if he had been too hasty in judging his colleagues on the basis of their age. It suddenly dawned on him that he should approach those who were new to technology the same way that he approached his own struggling students. He would build up their confidence by assessing their learning needs and then scaffold complex tasks so that they could proceed from a solid foundation.

Stephen's admiration grew as he observed Trevor and some of his more experienced colleagues as they began to take more and more risks with technology. He realized that an important part of his growth as a technology leader would be his willingness to question his unwarranted assumptions about learners and learning.

Questions

The Case

Before Stephen's arrival, very little had been accomplished at Greenwood in the area of technology integration. How did the principal turn this around, and what kinds of challenges might still lie ahead?

History

We sometimes forget that pens and pencils were once new technologies. How has our definition of technology changed, and what can we learn from past experiences with technology in the classroom?

Philosophy

By the end of the case, Stephen begins to question his assumptions about his older colleagues and becomes more open-minded about them. What can you do to become a more open-minded teacher?

Sociology

More than ever, teachers are following the lead of their students when it comes to technology. How do you think this affects authority relationships in classrooms? Justify your position.

Implications for Practice

Given that new technologies will likely continue to be introduced with increasing frequency, what will you do to keep current?

Who Pays?

Eli Janzen was a new teacher at Ralston Heights, an inner-city alternative high school in Atlantic Canada. Most of the students at the school were older, between the ages of 16 and 21, and had come to the school after having a range of academic and social difficulties in other schools. Some students hadn't attended any school for months or even years, and most had attended many different schools because their families were transient. By the time they arrived at Ralston many were either living on their own or in group homes and were used to moving from place to place.

Eli had accepted a teaching position at Ralston because he couldn't find a job anywhere else; in fact, recent government cutbacks to school funding had left many of Eli's graduating class unable to find jobs as teachers. However, in the short time he had been at the school, he had grown attached to many of his students and now couldn't imagine teaching anywhere else.

Carolyn was one of those students. She had arrived at school that morning in tears and it wasn't the first time. Carolyn had left home two years before, shortly after her fifteenth birthday. Her father struggled to raise her and her sister but he didn't manage well on his own. Carolyn didn't manage well either; she soon became pregnant and decided to move in with her boyfriend. Once the baby arrived, Carolyn's schoolwork just didn't get done. The school helped her find child care, but Carolyn didn't always want to drop the baby off, especially when he was fussy. Her boyfriend had complained loudly about the baby's crying that morning, and that is what had set Carolyn off.

As Carolyn pushed the now peacefully sleeping baby down the hall in his stroller, Eli recognized an opportunity to engage Carolyn in a discussion about her math homework. He knew how important it was for her to complete her assignments and get a high school diploma. Generally speaking, there were fewer opportunities for women to earn good wages, but for Carolyn, getting a good job would be even more difficult without a high school diploma.

"How's your homework coming along?" Eli asked her.

"It's too hard," Carolyn replied.

"Come to my classroom and we'll start it together," Eli suggested.

"Why bother?" Carolyn looked up at her teacher in exasperation. "I'm never going to graduate, now that I have a baby."

Eli knew that at the rate Carolyn was going, graduation was going to be a long shot. She had no parent encouraging her and almost no help from her boyfriend. As Eli headed for his classroom, he wondered how he could motivate her to keep going. Attending school was especially difficult for students who were coping with young families, drug use and addictions, homelessness, violence, or depression. The program at Ralston recognized those problems and tried to be flexible enough to meet the needs of its students while still maintaining academic standards. This flexibility allowed Eli to tailor his courses to his students' individual needs, but he still struggled to find approaches that worked well for all of his students.

Most of the Ralston students who were over 18 were receiving financial support from the government, but in order to collect their monthly cheques, they had to maintain minimum attendance and academic standards. Cheques were not released unless teachers affirmed that students had attended regularly and had completed their assignments satisfactorily. As far as Eli could tell, many of his students wouldn't complete their work otherwise.

Unfortunately, many of Eli's students were not old enough to qualify for government support. Carolyn, at 17, was one of these. Although she might respond to the government incentive, Eli doubted that she would stick around, and, in her case, a month just might be too long for her to wait. He wondered whether the school might adopt the idea he had heard about in which students, like Carolyn, were given weekly monetary rewards for doing their schoolwork. Maybe, if she wasn't worried about money, she might be motivated to stay in school.

As the school day ended, Eli gathered up his books and headed off to the staff meeting, hoping for once it would start on time. He had promised to meet his wife for dinner before his parent–teacher interviews. Staff meetings tended to go on for a long time as they discussed every student issue that had arisen over the course of the week, but he was pleased to see that student motivation was first on the agenda. Eli was anxious to discuss the idea of extending monetary incentives to younger students.

Jan Holder, one of the resource teachers, began, "I think it comes down to either intrinsic or extrinsic motivation. Our students need external motivators until they develop that intrinsic desire to learn. You have to give them praise and other things because they've had so many difficulties in their lives, they just don't have that internal drive to do well in school."

Steve Parsons, the principal, agreed: "Lack of internal drive is common among the students we have. A lot of them haven't experienced academic success, and they don't see the benefits of an education beyond getting a piece of paper. They may be smart, but it doesn't help that there are such huge gaps in their learning from missing so much school along the way."

Eli said, "What about providing some kind of incentive, like money for completing assignments?"

"No way," Steve said quickly, shaking his head. "We can't afford that . . . and anyway, learning should be its own reward. That's what we want to foster, isn't it? Our students can do it. We just need to help them get there."

Eli considered whether these students really would become intrinsically motivated eventually or whether that was just a pipe dream. He thought back to his own experiences in school and didn't recall any strong internal desire to learn. He couldn't blame lack of motivation on a troubled childhood or lack of parental support, because he had both encouragement and support in abundance. As he reflected on his own education, Eli realized that intrinsic motivation had come later, once he decided to become a teacher. He had needed an authentic purpose for learning before he had experienced the shift from "grade grubbing" to being actively engaged in learning.

Maybe his students would have the same kind of experience, but he suspected that Jan had it right. His students needed extrinsic rewards to keep them motivated and in school so they could reach the point of being intrinsically rewarded by learning. In the meantime, without cash as a reward, Eli resolved to find other ways to make learning more authentic and personally rewarding. He would continue to advocate for his students and do his best to show them that learning was not just about getting a job.

Questions

The Case

What makes Eli think that paying students to learn will improve their life chances? Is his argument convincing? Why or why not?

History

At different points in time, cognitive psychologists have either encouraged or discouraged the practice of rewarding students for academic achievement or good behaviour. Where do you stand on this sometimes thorny issue, and what support can you find in the literature for your position?

Philosophy

Is it morally defensible to pay students to learn? Why or why not?

Sociology

Some argue that high schools, as they have been traditionally structured, disadvantage students like Carolyn who come from lower socio-economic backgrounds. In what specific ways are such students denied the opportunities afforded to their more advantaged peers?

Implications for Practice

What do you think are the advantages and disadvantages of giving students external rewards? What would you need to think about before adopting such an approach in your class?

Whose Culture? Who's Teaching?

The three-day August retreat for teachers and administrators of the Upper Niskawa School District began with the acknowledgment that it was taking place on the traditional territory of the Niskawal'ly in the easternmost part of the Artiv'na'ypl River region. The organizers hoped that this retreat, designed to promote better cultural understanding, would help to heal some of the rifts in the district.

During the retreat, participants immersed themselves in discussions about a variety of educational topics, as well as cultural activities, such as morning treks to cook breakfast on the riverbank; eating bannock, reindeer meat, and berry sauce; woodcarving and working on a giant dream catcher; and personal storytelling about sweat lodges and peace pipes.

The speakers included a young Indigenous father who spoke passionately about what it was like to be colonized, a grandmother who recounted the horrors of living in a residential school, and a pair of teenaged sisters who talked about the problems of living alternately with their father on the reserve and their non-native mother in the city. The topic for two of the afternoon sessions, "Accommodations," was especially well-received. The facilitators highlighted the actions that teachers, students, staff, and community members could take to help students and teachers feel included, respected, and valued and gave participants opportunities to practise their new skills.

However, the retreat had not been *all* sweetness and light. Early on, there had been verbal scuffles over the topics "Who are we?" and "Who do we want to be?" Decibel levels rose steadily as attendees grew more and more comfortable with close-up debate and conflict. Generally speaking, everyone seemed to take the sharp exchanges and nervous laughter in stride; however, as the days wore on, deep concerns about Canada's immigration policies and self-government initiatives came bubbling to the surface.

And there had been lunchtime arguments—not just discussions but open disagreements—about whether any group had sovereignty rights or decision-making power over themselves and/or other groups in the region and in the district. Tempers occasionally flared about some of the cultural assumptions that undergird Canada's judicial, financial, and educational systems. There were also conflicting views about how school districts might integrate local culture into provincially developed public school curricula.

However, the most heated exchange occurred during a plenary session on the subject of who should teach the new Indigenous language course. Connie, the granddaughter of an elder, was adamant that only elders or teachers who had been personally prepared to teach by elders should be allowed to instruct Indigenous languages. Pitted against Connie, and just as articulate and insistent, was Armand, the school district's human resource specialist who was responsible for staffing.

When the moderator called upon Armand to respond to Connie's concerns, he stated emphatically, "There can be no favouritism in our staffing complements. We have no choice but to abide by the union contract. If we have to assign a certified non-Aboriginal teacher—or even two—to teach Indigenous language courses, that is what we will do. None of the elders hold valid teaching certificates or seniority in our district, and that is contrary to the terms of our agreement."

Armand's statements sent a chill through the plenary session, but several heads nodded in agreement. The audience was clearly divided on the issue. On Connie's side were teachers of Indigenous background who broke into quiet conversation among themselves and stared disapprovingly at Armand as he regained his seat. Several White teachers, who were also on Connie's side, left no doubt about their convictions, muttering loudly,

"Yet another example of why neo-colonialist attitudes must be identified and changed."

"After all, Canada's First Nations were here first."

There were others who, sympathetic to the district's commitment to Indigenous education, could also see the pragmatic side of this thorny issue. After all, there were contracts to honour, and student numbers, staffing ratios, and teaching loads to consider. It became increasingly clear that matters involving language and culture did not always co-exist easily with financial and legal imperatives.

As the moderator brought the discussion back to the floor, the speakers who followed captured the strong discomfort evoked by Armand's comments.

"We would die, our culture would just die out—if we were to allow ourselves to think only inside the box like you administrators almost always do."

"Armand talks a big line, but when it comes to preserving *our* cultural heritage, he doesn't stand *with* us!"

"Our language IS our culture! We're the only ones who can preserve and promote it. If we were to give away something as critical as this, we'd simply be helping Indigenous individuals, families, and communities commit cultural suicide."

Finally, the moderator called for a nutrition break and walked around with others outside the lodge where she hoped participants would refresh their outlook, cool down, and prepare for the next session. By the end of the retreat on Friday, the mood had lifted and everyone joined together in a winding "circle of hope" organized by local band members. As the musical instruments, food, and backpacks were loaded back into vehicles for the return trip, hugs and handshakes were exchanged and participants headed home for the long weekend and the beginning of another school year.

The following Thursday, a letter from the district office appeared in faculty mailboxes. The letter, signed by Armand, announced the assignment of two seasoned teachers in the district, one Indigenous, the other White, to teach the two sections of the district's Indigenous language course. The letter stated the teachers had been assigned according to seniority and because their teaching loads required "topping-up." With budget shortfalls looming, Armand made the case that this was the only way the district could offer the course, considering the limited resources available.

As Connie quickly scanned her copy of the letter, she could feel her blood pressure rising. She knew that neither of these teachers was fluent and that both would have trouble teaching the language effectively. Connie marched down the hall to the staff room and as she waved the letter and raised her voice, she brought the conversations to an abrupt halt.

"Has everyone seen Armand's letter? There's a copy in each of your mailboxes. After our retreat last week, I can't believe that he has just gone ahead and appointed those two teachers! What happened to consultation? All we get is cultural oppression!"

"Armand just doesn't listen!" she continued angrily. "How can we let people who don't even speak the language teach this course? I can see it all now—they'll just give the kids busy work. It's not like we don't have elders available who know the language and who would be thrilled to pass it on to our kids. Let's hire *them*!"

Connie's voice strengthened as she concluded, "Join with me *now* and stand up for your beliefs! We can't stand by and watch our culture being destroyed. You know and I know that language is absolutely essential to our survival as a people!"

A chorus of support cheered Connie on, but no one knew what would happen next as language, legalities, and the bottom line came crashing together.

Questions

The Case

With whom do you sympathize most, Connie or Armand, and for what reasons?

History

The *Canadian Multiculturalism Act* (1988) is intended to ensure that all Canadians are able to participate equally in Canadian society. Based on what happens in this case, is that even possible? Explain.

Philosophy

In this case, Connie makes a passionate plea for allowing non-certified elders to teach the Indigenous language course. Should all teachers be certified? What might be the consequences if we opened up teaching to non-certified persons? Justify your response.

Sociology

Much of what happens between school districts and cultural groups involves issues of power and authority. Explain how these two concepts play out in this case.

Implications for Practice

What would *you* do if *your* teaching load was "topped up" by having to teach a language you didn't know very well?

Unmasking Hallowe'en

It was recess at Middleboro Elementary School, and the chilly prairie air which had crept across the school yard was causing the leaves to yellow and the school children's cheeks to redden. The teachers at Middleboro had been thoughtfully planning fall activities and celebrations, some in relation to seasonal changes and others in relation to ongoing classroom inquiries. In particular, they had been considering various field trips for the 31st of October in order to minimize the focus on—and distractions of—Hallowe'en. The teachers had worked diligently over the past few years to make school celebrations more inclusive of different cultures, particularly since the community's immigrant population, especially families from the Philippines and India, was continuing to increase. They came to understand that Hallowe'en falls one day before the Filipino celebration of All Saints' Day, an extremely important holiday in which families honour their loved ones who have passed on. Knowing this, many teachers questioned whether the Canadian tradition of organizing garish Hallowe'en parties at school might be considered cultural insensitivity by these communities. In fact, some of the teachers argued that school-based Hallowe'en celebrations privileged and perpetuated a narrow North American perspective that simply disregarded the values and traditions of immigrant families and their children.

With this in mind, the teachers made alternative plans for October 31st. The Kindergarten classroom teachers planned pyjama parties highlighting the various stories they had been reading. The Grade 3 class planned a trip to the Art Gallery to see a photo exhibit of their city which complemented their current community study, and the combined Grade 1 and 2 class planned to go on a nature hike in an urban forest to support their study of animals and their habitats. By all accounts, the children were looking forward to their field trips and special events.

The new principal, Jennifer Bassaraba, supported the teachers' rationale for changing their approaches to Hallowe'en. As she was accustomed to doing, Jennifer engaged in a casual conversation with some parents of Kindergarten children who were outside the school, waiting for the bell. One of the parents, Kim Petrowski, who was excited about her child's first school experiences, asked Jennifer about the school's plans for Hallowe'en. Jennifer, proud of her teachers' thoughtfulness in honouring both the curriculum and multiculturalism, explained the school's alternative plans for Hallowe'en this year. Jennifer explained to Kim the stress that Hallowe'en usually creates for young children, the economic inequities that become more apparent, and the cultural privileging that Hallowe'en perpetuates.

Kim, who was also the vice-chair of the parent council, asked, "So, when did the school district pass a policy to ban Hallowe'en?"

"Oh, it's not a policy," said Jennifer quickly. "Teachers are simply using their professional judgment to accommodate our new children and their families. As you may or may not know, we have many new families in our community who don't celebrate Hallowe'en. It is not a part of our curriculum, so the teachers think that the classroom time is better spent on more relevant and inclusive activities. We aren't banning Hallowe'en, we are just trying to minimize the disruptions that it causes while doing a better job of including our families who do not celebrate it."

The conversation was interrupted by the school bell, and the children and parents entered the building to greet their teachers. Jennifer replayed the conversation in her mind as she walked through the school and thought that it had gone well enough. She made a mental note to talk with her teachers at the staff meeting the following week about sending a letter home to families with more information about the school's plans.

Two days later, Jennifer received a phone call from Greg Leung, the school district superintendent. "Jennifer, Greg here. What's going on over there at Middleboro? I have a parent—Kim Petrowski—up in arms because you've banned Hallowe'en at the school. She's called one of the trustees and claims she's got a petition going."

"What? We haven't banned Hallowe'en," Jennifer retorted. "We're just not planning outrageous parties and costume celebrations."

"Yeah, yeah. That's what she said and that's exactly what she's upset about. She says that you're 'depriving her child' of Hallowe'en. She sees it as a fundamental part of the Canadian experience," Greg responded rather flatly.

"Greg, the staff here had many conversations about this before my arrival. The teachers are not only trying to minimize the disruptions that Hallowe'en brings, but they are also trying to respect our new Canadians by not forcing them to participate in an event that some might not understand and may even find inappropriate."

"I hear what you're saying," Greg replied, "but Mrs Petrowski feels that this is an opportunity to teach new Canadians about Canadian traditions and for children to learn about proper nutrition."

"Seriously? You've got to be kidding me!" Jennifer was shocked by the arguments she was hearing.

"Look," continued Greg, "Mrs Petrowski is not going to let this go. If you can believe it, she has even threatened to contact the media over this. You need to make this to go away and go away fast!"

Exasperated, Jennifer took a deep breath and asked, "What would you suggest, Greg?"

"Mrs Petrowski says that the parent council wants to organize a school-wide Hallowe'en celebration. They want a dance, costumes—the works! She said the parent council will organize it all. They just want the teachers to support it and for the kids to attend."

Jennifer felt her heart starting to race. "Look, the teachers here are adamant about this. When I started at Middleboro this year, they made it plain that the status quo simply won't fly. Furthermore, Mrs Petrowski's position is Eurocentric and condescending to our school's immigrant families. It bothers me that just because her voice is the loudest, she is being allowed to speak for everyone." Jennifer was getting angrier by the moment.

Suddenly, Greg interrupted, "Look, Jennifer, I've got to get to a meeting. Call me when you've got this resolved."

Jennifer hung up the phone and dropped her head into her hands. She wondered how this could have spun out of control so quickly. She believed, along with the teachers, that schools should do more than just *tolerate* the cultures and customs of new Canadians. Like them, she worried that the parent council's perspective was narrow-minded and did not represent the views of the larger Middleboro community. On the other hand, as a new principal at the school, she knew that she was expected to collaborate effectively with *all* of the parents. If she disregarded these concerns, it would likely be more difficult for her to establish herself in the community.

But what was she to do? She needed to find a compromise that would respect all the parties involved—whether they were part of the vocal minority or not. Unfortunately, she did not have the luxury of time.

Questions

The Case

Kim Petrowski disagrees with the decision that the staff has taken to downplay Hallowe'en. What are her arguments for keeping this tradition? What are the counter-arguments?

History

Historically, the celebration of Christian holidays has been taken for granted in Canadian schools. What has happened in Canadian society to make us question the appropriateness of this long-standing tradition?

Philosophy

Are Middleboro's attempts to be inclusive to cultural minorities fair to everyone? Why or why not?

Sociology

Kim Petrowski threatens to take her concerns to the media. What role should the media play in decision making by school boards? Why do you think so?

Implications for Practice

Imagine you teach in a school that has decided on alternative activities to traditional holiday celebrations. What kinds of activities might you plan that would be pedagogically defensible yet appealing to students?

No Space for God Here

Urgel Patak, principal of a suburban high school in a working-class community with a fairly large immigrant population, normally looked forward to solving the day-to-day problems that came with his position. However, as he stared at the email on the screen, he had a sinking feeling that he knew who it was about before he even looked at the words. Resigned, he clicked it open to view yet another carefully worded complaint from a parent:

> Dear Principal Patak:
>
> We thought that we would bring to your attention the unusual teaching resources that are being used in Mr Greenwood's Grade 12 English class. According to our son, Mr Greenwood has, on numerous occasions, had the students engage in serious "Bible study." We don't want to tell you how to do your job, but we feel that he may be overstepping the boundaries of his course. We would be very interested in hearing your views at the next parent council meeting.
>
> Best regards,
> Sylvia and John Stanton

He reached for the phone and muttered to himself, "What am I going to do with 'Bible Bill'?"

Bill Greenwood's reputation was the stuff of legend; he was an award-winning teacher whose students had won numerous essay-writing contests. However, as soon as Urgel had transferred to the school as vice-principal, he began to hear whispers about what was going on in Bill's classroom. Of course, at the beginning, these were only of fleeting interest to him in his role as vice-principal, since Bill was evaluated by the principal, Janice Vonn. When Janice retired and Urgel was promoted, Bill became his responsibility and was now becoming a major source of frustration. Janice had light-heartedly warned him to handle "Bible Bill" delicately. At the time, Urgel had chuckled about the nickname, but now that he was in charge, he wished Janice had handled the situation more effectively at the time. He wondered if this teacher was actually using his position to proselytize and, if so, as principal whether he would have to put a stop to it.

However, Urgel's first meeting with Bill had not gone as expected. He called Bill into his office for a conversation and tried to explain that, as an English teacher, religion should play no part in the courses that he taught. It wasn't long before Bill Greenwood began smiling in a way that Urgel would grow to loathe in the next three years.

"Now, Urgel," he prodded, already knowing the answer, "what subject area did you teach when you were in the trenches?"

"Math . . . I taught Math," hesitated Urgel, knowing that Bill would use this against him.

Bill threw up his hands and gazed skywards. With the air of delivering a well-rehearsed speech, he began, "Let's start with the basics—you need to understand that it is virtually impossible to teach Western literature without grounding the students in some basic religious teachings. In past generations, this wouldn't have been necessary since students would already have internalized this knowledge through family and church influences. However, as you can well appreciate, these influences have all but dried up. But, without this background, a true understanding of literature simply isn't possible."

"Yes, I see what you mean, Bill, but I think there are other ways of getting that information to students without using the Bible," replied Urgel.

Bill hardly seemed to hear Urgel's comment before sailing on, "Okay, let me give you an example. This year, Grade 12s are studying Margaret Laurence's *The Stone Angel*. Ever heard of it? The book is extremely relevant to the Canadian experience, but it's chock full of biblical phrases and references. It's essentially a re-telling of the Genesis tale of Hagar. Yet, if I just casually mentioned this, the students wouldn't have the foggiest idea of what I was talking about! Isn't that ironic? When the book first came out, it was banned due to an uproar of narrow-minded fundamentalists who thought it was obscene. Now, I'm getting the reverse response from you, of all people."

The conversation continued in this vein with Bill rebutting any of the points that Urgel tried to make. The meeting ended in a stalemate, and Urgel decided to let it go for the time being. However, it wasn't long before he had to call Bill back into his office. This time, Urgel pointed out that some parents were concerned that Bill's approach privileged Christianity and didn't reflect the ethnically and religiously diverse population the school served.

"The last time I checked, Statistics Canada reported that the population of this area was still 75 per cent Christian which is a pretty significant majority!" Bill retorted. "But the fact remains that children from non-adherent Christian homes and minority groups have no other way of learning what the majority of the population has believed for centuries or what drives the culture that they live in unless I teach it to them."

Urgel persisted, "That may be true, but the beliefs of the minority groups in our community have to be respected, Bill. They just don't want their children to be exposed to the Bible."

"This has nothing to do with their beliefs! Today's parents are mainly concerned about us teaching whatever will help their children get a job."

"Wait a second, Bill. We can't just ignore community concerns, can we?"

"Well, the community is your department. Just let me teach and you can worry about how to spin it."

In the coming weeks, Urgel "invited" Bill into his office on several more occasions, all to no avail. Urgel even tried to corner him about spending public money on Bibles, but Bill simply laughed and reminded Urgel that he hadn't asked the school for a single penny since he had received a free set from the Gideon Society.

Finally, Urgel decided to raise the issue of legalities, feeling this argument would put the matter to rest. He asked for a meeting and waited for Bill to appear.

"Urgel, we've been through this so many times before. I'm starting to feel a little persecuted," said Bill in exasperation.

"Well, Bill, I think we're talking unconstitutionality on your part. I think you're violating the requirement to maintain the separation between church and state."

"First of all, Urgel," Bill spoke slowly and deliberately, "we do not live in a country that makes such a distinction. You are thinking of our neighbours to the south—and boy, it's good to see that religion doesn't influence politics down there," he said sarcastically. "Second of all, I have something to show you." From under his arm he brought out a thick black book.

"You're not going to quote scripture to me are you, Bill?" Urgel chuckled, trying to make light of the situation.

"No, I'm not going to quote scripture, but I will read you something that we all have to pay attention to, regardless of our beliefs." With that, he tossed a copy of the province's *Consolidated Education Act* on the table and pointed to subsection C on page 27, which he had already flagged. "As you can see, it says that it's 'the duty of a teacher to inculcate by precept and example respect for religion and the principles of Judaeo-Christian morality.' Isn't that exactly what I am doing? I'm just doing my job, Urgel. Now will you please just let me get on with it?"

After Bill left, Urgel slowly sunk into his chair, groaning loudly, "I don't know what I am going to do about this situation. Maybe *I'm* the one who just doesn't get it."

Questions

The Case

How might Urgel have handled this situation more effectively?

History

What is the place of religion in public schools, and how has that changed in your province over the years?

Philosophy

Urgel and some of the parents think that Bill Greenwood may be guilty of indoctrination. What is indoctrination, and how would we know if such fears were valid?

Sociology

In what ways might our beliefs about religion have an impact on our professional identities as teachers?

Implications for Practice

If you have a student who brings a religious perspective into every interaction, what might you do to help this student adjust to the secular nature of public schools?

CHAPTER THREE

Bandwagons

Introduction

In the previous chapter, we focused on the phenomenon of myths. In this chapter we turn our attention to bandwagons—what they are, which ones pervade education, and how the foundations disciplines can help us recognize them and manage their effects. The bandwagons highlighted in this chapter are illustrated by 10 cases that are based on real events. Each is followed by five questions: first, a question about the facts, then, three questions that consider the historical, philosophical, and sociological implications, and finally, a question about how the case can be applied to your own practice.

What are bandwagons?

The literal meaning of bandwagon is a vehicle used to carry musicians in a parade. The phrase "to jump on the bandwagon" originated in the mid-nineteenth century when Dan Rice ("Bandwagon effect," 2013), a popular American circus clown, used a bandwagon to draw attention to Zachary Taylor's presidential campaign. When people began, literally and indiscriminately, to join politicians on board simply because other people did, the term began to take on a pejorative meaning. Today bandwagon means an idea or cause that people support because it is popular or likely to be successful.

Often, educational bandwagons are driven by well-paid, self-proclaimed experts, or gurus. They use emotional appeals and exaggeration to persuade teachers and administrators to purchase educational materials and the often expensive professional development that accompanies them. Bandwagon leaders often seek out influential "believers" to endorse their innovation as a means of attracting more followers. Once a critical mass of teachers climbs on board, counter-claims and contrary evidence are drowned out in the chorus of acclaim.

The heightened attention paid to bandwagons can sometimes make bystanders feel that the parade will pass them by if they don't join in. As a propaganda device, bandwagons can be used to create a false impression of widespread support, playing on the desire of people to be on the winning side and their fear of being isolated if they are not. This strong desire to belong or conform to the wishes of a group can lead to the social psychological phenomenon known as **groupthink** (Janis, 1982). Groupthink occurs when people ignore rational decision making because of their loyalty to the group and their overwhelming desire to preserve harmony in it, sometimes with disastrous consequences.

Whether they are affected by groupthink or the charisma of influential individuals, educators at all levels are susceptible to the allure of educational bandwagons. Consequently, districts and schools can waste scarce funds on materials or professional development that sound promising but may actually make no discernible difference or may even have the opposite effect to what was originally intended. The failure of so many bandwagons to deliver on their promises serves to reinforce the personal and professional cynicism of some teachers, prompting them to make such disparaging remarks as, "What goes around comes around!" or "Been there, done, that!" before they even know any of the details (Pennington, 2009).

We think that the level of enthusiasm for innovations depends partly on what stage teachers are at in their careers (Stroot et al., 1998). Katz (1995) identifies four developmental stages of teaching that shed light on how professional teachers may be expected to respond to bandwagons: Stage I (year 1): Survival; Stage II (year 2): Consolidation; Stage III (years 3 and 4): Renewal; and Stage IV (year 5 and up): Maturity. It is important to note that while Katz (1995) aligns these stages with the number of years of teaching experience, she cautions that this relationship is not fixed because some teachers have extensive experience before certifying and others, because of personal characteristics or circumstances, may take longer to move through the stages.

Teachers in the Survival stage, who are concentrating all their energy on getting through the day, the week, or the year, may not even recognize bandwagons as they race by, but teachers in Stages II and III may be ready and willing to climb aboard. Teachers in these middle stages are becoming more comfortable with routines and procedures and are beginning to look for new and exciting ideas that will help them solve specific problems in their teaching. Teachers in Stage IV are the most likely to question bandwagons and reflect more deeply on their effectiveness. As a consequence of these differences, tensions among teachers at different stages can be expected to arise, given what Katz (1995) reports about the attitudes of teachers towards professional development:

> Training sessions and conference events that Stage II teachers enjoy may be very tiresome to the Stage IV teacher. Similarly, introspective, in-depth discussions enjoyed by Stage IV teachers may lead to restlessness and irritability among the beginning teachers in Stage I. (para. 14)

Depending on the finesse with which bandwagons are rolled out, the support of the administration, and the stage of teachers' careers, educators may embrace bandwagons enthusiastically or ignore, subvert, or even reject them. Certainly, there are those who refuse on principle to conform, but the majority of teachers, at one time or another, have been persuaded to embark on the latest bandwagon, in spite of the lack of any evidence to confirm that the new ideas or approaches are worthy of the effort.

To try to help educators recognize educational fads or bandwagons for what they are, Kevin Murphy and Lori Sideman (2006) describe three distinguishing characteristics: "the fast growth trajectory, the tendency to promise more than they can deliver, and the intensity of reactions" (p. 293). Furthermore, they suggest that educational fads take the following invariably self-destructive path:

> 1. They emerge suddenly and capture popular attention;
> 2. They attract a dedicated core of "true believers" whose fervor and uncritical acceptance of the new idea or approach fuels both its growth and controversy over its value;
> 3. These true believers trumpet this new idea as a general solution to a wide range of problems;
> 4. These claims become the focus of bitter disputes; and
> 5. The idea, approach, or solution collapses as suddenly as it arose, and is replaced by a new fad or fashion. (p. 283)

Although many educational fads follow the same path, not all consist of unreasonable ideas, approaches, or solutions. In fact, as Elder and Paul (2007) point out, "even reasonable ideas can be transformed into bandwagons by flawed or superficial understanding of the basic ideas" (p. 6). Certainly, great ideas can appear to be bandwagons when there is insufficient professional development or weak administrative support to sustain them.

Indeed, many worthwhile educational initiatives never get beyond what Fullan (2001) describes as the "**implementation dip.**" This term aptly describes the point at which a bandwagon typically flounders—when the initial enthusiasm has worn off and there are no immediate or visible signs of progress. As the innovation appears to stall, public pressure mounts for tangible results and new and different solutions to what are often intractable problems. At this point, educators may feel compelled to cut their losses and abandon the initiative rather than spend further resources and effort on trying to make it work. The pressure for results may also serve to elevate new ideas to the implementation stage far more quickly than is prudent, leaving teachers frustrated and confused as they struggle to remain on board. Although educators may lament when their favourite ideas fall by the wayside, they can take solace in the fact that most worthwhile innovations will come around again, albeit as freshly painted bandwagons.

What bandwagons pervade education?

Although some educational bandwagons have enough momentum to evolve into productive practices that become widely accepted, the vestiges of many failed bandwagons may remain long after disconfirming evidence has caused them to be repudiated, as Ravitch (2003) points out:

> Many failed and forgotten innovations continue to live in schools where they were introduced with great fanfare and subsequently forgotten. I have often heard it said that some schools are like archeological digs; one can dig down and find layer after layer of school reforms and obsolete programs. New ones get added, but old ones do not get subtracted. (para. 10)

As a consequence, Henig, Hula, Orr, and Pedescleaux (1999) caution, "The addition of new programs on top of old ones may result in disjointed or fragmented sets of experiences for students."

Although lists of educational bandwagons are compiled regularly (Elder & Paul, 2007; Nikiforuk, 1994; Pennington, 2011), such catalogues are rarely identical since bandwagons are to some extent in the eye of the beholder. Most attempts to consider the bandwagons that pervade education range from particular strategies and tools such as digital "clickers" or portfolio assessment to broader approaches or arrangements like "**open classrooms**," "**whole language**," teaching to learning styles, and "**brain-based**" **teaching**. Similarly, in the rest of this chapter, we consider a range of bandwagons, from the general to the specific, which are illustrated by 10 cases. These cases are organized for discussion purposes around the three salient commonplaces we discussed in the previous chapter—students, teachers, and context. Each case is followed by questions to help you consider the facts of the case, its historical, philosophical, and sociological implications, and how the case relates to your own practice.

Students

Full inclusion

Full inclusion has emerged, at least in part, as a response to the negative impact of the myths of normalcy and ability discussed in the previous chapter. Educators, parents, and elected officials have fought against the assumptions embedded in these myths and have argued persuasively that disability is socially constructed. Consequently, they insist that *all* children benefit from being placed in regular or so-called mainstream classrooms. Kochhar, West, and Taymans (2000) point out that being in a regular classroom promotes greater acceptance of disabled students by their peers, more balanced relationships, and greater gains in academic knowledge. Indeed, advocates of full inclusion point out that, as students become more successful in regular classrooms, parental expectations increase, and students become more capable of achieving.

Certainly, support for inclusion is fuelled by strong legal, moral, and pedagogical imperatives, but the issue remains highly controversial and confusing. Hornby (2011) lists "definitions, rights, labelling, peers, aetiology, intervention models, goals, curricula, reality, finance, means and ends, and research evidence" (p. 323) as just some of the sources of controversy and confusion. The definition is confusing because inclusion is used to mean a variety of accommodations. Some jurisdictions maintain separate facilities for students with special needs such as hearing impairment and blindness along with provisions for mainstreaming. However, other jurisdictions educate *all* children together except for temporary withdrawal from the classroom as necessary. According to Hornby (2011), perhaps even more confusing is the fact that inclusive education is often conflated with "**social inclusion**," which is more broadly concerned with bringing about a fair society in which all socio-economic, racial, and ethnic groups are equally valued.

While the definition remains elusive, the courts are moving away from mandating inclusive placements as a matter of right or law and are increasingly ruling that students with disabilities should be educated with their non-disabled peers *to the extent possible* (Douvanis & Hunsley, 2002). However, as Hornby (2011) argues, the pursuit of legal rights with regard to placement fails to recognize that "the right to an appropriate education that meets children's specific needs is more important than the right to be educated alongside their mainstream peers" (p. 334). Even previously strong advocates of full inclusion, such as Warnock (2005) question whether the regular classroom is the best place for all students: "[T]here is increasing evidence that the ideal of inclusion, if this means that all but those with the most severe disabilities will be in mainstream schools, is not working" (p. 32).

Parents of children with special needs may argue that anything less than full inclusion is detrimental to their child's social, emotional, and cognitive development. Meanwhile, parents of so-called average students worry that their children have less of the teacher's time and attention and achieve less when students with special needs are fully integrated into regular classrooms. In "Alone in a Crowd" the tensions between the ideal of inclusion and the reality of the classroom are highlighted when a teacher and a class try to accommodate a student with special needs. As you read this case, consider what options are available to the teacher and the school as they try to stay on board the full-inclusion bandwagon.

Single-sex education

Single-sex schools have remained a constant feature of the educational landscape of private schools in Canada and the United States. However, they are found less frequently in Canadian public schools and until recently, they were explicitly excluded from public-school districts in the United States by federal law. In the 1980s, single-sex classrooms began to appear in public schools in some Canadian provinces, including Ontario and Manitoba, partly in response to the underrepresentation of girls in so-called gateway Math and Science courses that are needed for entry into some high-paying professions. More recently, the increase in the number of single-sex classrooms has been driven by concerns about the underperformance of boys (Demers, 2007).

Underlying the current movement to establish single-sex classrooms and schools are several myths about gender differences, some of which were discussed in the previous chapter. According to Halpren et al. (2011), these myths are given credibility by pseudoscience based on "obscure and isolated findings about brain maturation, hearing, vision, and temperature sensitivity" (p. 1707). Nevertheless, Salomone (2006) notes that the highly controversial revival of support for single-sex education has

> generated an unusual political alliance among social conservatives touting "hard-wired" differences between boys and girls, political conservatives interested in a free market of parental choice, feminists seeking to close the gender gap favouring boys particularly in math and science, and urban educators and activists concerned with the plight of minority students and particularly African American males. (p. 781)

Summaries of the academic literature on single-sex education (Department for Children, School and Families, 2009; T. Thompson & Ungerleider, 2004) suggest that there is little evidence to support the movement to single-sex classes and schools. Recent research (Ivinson & Murphy, 2007; Jackson, 2002; Salomone, 2006; A. Sullivan, 2010; Warrington & Younger, 2001) points to some advantages for girls and disadvantaged minority boys, but these effects are extremely difficult to replicate or to disentangle from other factors, such as social class and prior achievement.

Perhaps of greater concern, as Halpren et al. (2011) point out, is that "there is evidence that sex segregation increases gender stereotyping and legitimizes institutional sexism" (p. 1706). Given that other types of separation, such as racial segregation, facilitate prejudice and perpetuate racist attitudes, this may not be a surprising conclusion but it is one that warrants further examination. Segregated arrangements, according to Bigler and Eliot (2011) are "harmful because they provide an artificial world in which gender differences are reified as legitimate bases for disparate treatment, and males and females are both left unprepared to negotiate egalitarian relationships" (para. 2). In fact, they point out that research on state-sponsored single-sex programs in California found that pedagogy that was purportedly designed to accommodate the so-called inherent differences between the sexes actually reinforced rather than broke down traditional gender stereotypes. Proponents, on the other hand, argue that "coeducational education has not eradicated sexism or broken down the silos of virility (considered a male attribute) and sensitivity (an attribute traditionally associated with women)" (Demers, 2007, p. 2) and that it may be time to reassess the benefits of single-sex education.

The case "Be the Change" explores the question of single-sex education and the need to foster egalitarian attitudes. As you read the case, consider how schools can successfully advocate for females and males without having to compromise the aspirations of either sex.

Teachers

Technology

Technology bandwagons are highly visible, compelling, and controversial. Though technology is promoted as a means of preparing students for the demands of the digital workplace and the increasingly competitive global knowledge economy, few question whether it actually helps students learn. However, the myth of the digital native (discussed in the previous chapter), which characterizes young people as being hard-wired for technology, may be fostering an unwarranted assumption that "we need to use technology for everything" (Mercer, 2012, p. 19).

According to Levin (2010), technology in schools is touted as being beneficial for students, but these benefits have yet to be realized:

> For fifty years we have been hearing that changes in technology would fundamentally change the provision of education. This argument was

> made about television, and then about computers, and now about personal devices such as notepads or iPads and social networking. But fifty years of history shows that the promise has never been achieved. (p. 4)

Indeed, Mercer (2012) argues that it is time to consider some of the hidden costs of the race to implement technology in schools: "Early indicators seem to show that we might be shortening attention spans, reducing the importance of actual knowledge, de-emphasizing the importance of expertise, and making depth of analysis difficult for our students to achieve" (p. 19).

In their extensive review of the literature on information and communication technologies (ICT), Ungerleider and Burns (2002) found that "[t]here are simply too few studies of sufficiently rigorous design to permit informed policy choices. This is especially troubling given that the use of ICTs requires significant expenditure of scarce resources" (p. 19).

Nevertheless, administrative decisions, like those to replace textbooks, library services, or even teacher-librarians with Internet-accessible electronic devices, continue to be made without solid research or evidence that these are beneficial changes. Although smaller districts are moving more slowly to adapt their facilities, in larger centres many "libraries have changed to a 'learning commons' model, with computer labs and/or smart boards and new seating arrangements so that students, teachers and teacher-librarians can work collaboratively" (People for Education, 2012, p. 19). Achterman (2010) points out that the elimination of school librarians is particularly short-sighted given the key role they play in helping students develop media literacy and in guiding school communities to exploit technologies effectively. Nevertheless, the trend across Canada is either to dramatically reduce trained staff in school libraries or to eliminate school libraries altogether (Coish, 2005).

Two of the cases that follow illustrate ways that technology can affect teachers and schools. "Let Them Eat Cake!" looks at the effect of technology on teacher-librarians and school libraries, while "The Future Is Now" raises concerns about the security of student information. The latter case also illustrates how a teacher who has yet to hop aboard the school's technology bandwagon may become marginalized in a school that embraces technology unequivocally. As you read these two cases, think about the benefits and limitations of technology and whether it promises more than it can deliver.

Journal writing

As discussed in the previous chapter, constructivism, which seeks to engage students actively with content in a personal way and enable them to learn through self-discovery, is widely accepted by educators. Not surprisingly then, the notion that authentic learning is self-directed underlies a number of bandwagons in education, including journal writing.

Students in any subject or grade from Kindergarten to Grade 12 may routinely be expected to make connections to previous experiences and to share their innermost thoughts, beliefs, and values about course material and classroom events in a journal. In the higher grades and particularly in university, journals are more likely to be "written documents that students create as they think about various concepts, events, or interactions over a period of time for the purposes of gaining insights into self-awareness and learning" (Thorpe, 2004, p. 328). When students enter a professional school, they may be expected to use a journal to become increasingly critical and reflective in their thinking, treating it like a "paper mirror" (Hubbs, 2005).

Spalding and Wilson (2002) point out the following benefits of adopting this approach:

> (1) journals serve as a permanent record of thoughts and experiences;
> (2) journals provide a means of establishing and maintaining relationships with instructors;
> (3) journals serve as a safe outlet for personal concerns and frustrations; and
> (4) journals are an aid to internal dialogue (Colton & Sparks-Langer, 1993). (p. 1396)

In addition, Hubbs and Brand (2005) note that when students slow down and record their observations in journals, they have more opportunity to make meaning, identify key aspects of their experiences, gain greater understanding of their circumstances, and question the foundations of their beliefs.

Nevertheless, some researchers (Fendler, 2003; Hubbs, 2005; O'Connell, 2011; Ruitenberg, 2011) express serious concern about the use and the occasional overuse of reflective journals in university courses. Among these are ethical and legal questions surrounding privacy, trust, and confidentiality, especially when journals take on "a disturbingly confessional nature" (Ruitenberg, 2011, p. 43). There are also doubts about the efficacy of this form of pedagogy, since training and evaluation guidelines are often absent and the quality and authenticity of journal entries may not be well monitored. In other words, the act of journal writing may lead not to self-discovery but to students writing what they believe their teachers want to hear, making journals "exercises in reconfirming, justifying, or rationalizing preconceived ideas" (Fendler, 2003, p. 16).

In "Blurred Reflections," a young professor is forced to re-examine his use of reflective journals. As you read this case, consider whether writing in a journal increases the likelihood of becoming a reflective practitioner.

Sustained silent reading

"Sustained silent reading" (SSR), also known as "uninterrupted sustained silent reading" (USSR), "drop everything and read" (DEAR), "sustained quiet reading time" (SQUIRT), and "daily independent reading time" (DIRT), has been a regular feature of classrooms from Kindergarten to high school since it was first introduced by Lyman Hunt, Jr over 40 years ago (Hunt, 1970). SSR provides students with regular opportunities to read books of their choice in silence and without interruption. Teachers model the intended behaviour by reading silently at the same time. Since the purpose of SSR is to encourage rather than to assess reading, no formal records or reports are kept (McCracken, 1971). Teachers may allot up to 30 minutes for each daily session, depending on the age of the students and their familiarity with books and independent reading.

Underlying the widespread implementation of SSR is the assumption that the more students read, the better readers they will become (Krashen, 2001). Advocates (Krashen, 2001; Pilgreen, 2000; Trelease, 2001) conclude that SSR provides the same or better benefits for students in the area of comprehension and motivation as traditional reading-skills classes. In addition, promoters argue that SSR increases reading fluency, provides greater access to a wider variety of books, improves social equity, and exposes students to positive models of reading behaviour (Gardiner, 2001; Pilgreen, 2000).

However, the *Report of the National Reading Panel* (National Institute of Child Health and Human Development, 2000) challenges the assumptions as well as the research supporting SSR:

> Despite widespread acceptance of the idea that schools can successfully encourage students to read more and that these increases in reading practice will be translated into better fluency and higher reading achievement, there is not adequate evidence to sustain this claim. (pp. 3–28)

The influential findings of the report are highly controversial and have been severely criticized for weaknesses in methodology. In particular, critics pointed to lack of definitional clarity, omission of key international studies, over-reliance on short-term studies, and incomplete accounting of students who were already advanced readers (Garan, 2008; Krashen, 2001).

Like many other enduring approaches, there are wide variations in how teachers implement SSR, making generalizations and meaningful comparisons difficult. Nevertheless, there is a growing understanding that "reading alone does not improve reading skills" and that key elements of SSR need to be modified to address "the perceived gaps in the traditional model" (Surrey School District

Research and Evaluation Department, 2010). Such modifications include "scaffolded silent reading" (ScSR), "independent reading" (IR), and "read, relax, reflect, respond, and rap" (R5), in which there is more teacher involvement in the selection of books, monitoring of progress, and setting of goals, as well as opportunities for students to respond to the books they read independently. Even strong promoters of SSR (Garan, 2008) recognize that there is room for improvement, particularly by engaging students in critically important meaningful conversations, or so-called accountable talk, about what they read (Michaels, O'Connor, Williams Hall, & Resnick, 2010).

In "DEAR Me!" a teacher struggles to make sustained silent reading engaging for her students. As you read the case, consider whether the time spent on SSR is justifiable.

Accountability

Accountability bandwagons roll through education regularly, at least once a decade in the past 50 years, according to Linn (1998). Especially in uncertain economic times, people want assurances that schools and teachers are fulfilling their responsibilities:

> Educators are under pressure to show the public that what they are doing is working, and governments everywhere have seized on education as a cornerstone of their political agendas. Government response has been fairly consistent across countries: more centralized curricula and formal student testing. (Earl, 1999, p. 4)

In the United States, the federal government has offered huge financial incentives to persuade the majority of the states to adopt the Common Core State Standards Initiative for English Language Arts and Mathematics. These **standards** are tightly aligned with federally funded "high-stakes" standardized tests, which "are increasingly seen as a means of raising academic standards, holding educators and students accountable for meeting those standards, and boosting public confidence in schools" (Heubert & Hauser, 1999, p. 1). However, Popham (2000) points out the inherent fallacy of such notions:

> When standardized achievement tests are employed to ascertain educational quality it really is like measuring temperature with a tablespoon. Tablespoons have a different measurement mission than indicating how hot or cold something is. Standardized achievement tests also have a different measurement mission than indicating how good or bad a school is. Standardized achievement tests should be used to make the compar-

> ative interpretations that they were intended to provide. They should not be used to judge educational quality. (p. 400)

Similar trends are evident in Canada, but curricula are provincially mandated and standards are monitored through restricted testing of certain subjects in certain grades, administered, in some cases, to just a sample testing group. The marks on provincial tests do not usually make up a large enough percentage of the students' final grades to alter their life chances significantly, except in Ontario, where students must pass the Ontario Secondary School Literacy Test (OSSLT) to graduate from high school.

Critics of high-stakes testing (Kearns, 2011; Linn, 1998; Meier, 2002; Ravitch, 2011; Rubin & Kazanjian, 2011) point out that there is no evidence that testing improves student achievement. They argue that the negative consequences of restricting teachers' autonomy, narrowing the curriculum, devaluing and eliminating subjects that are not tested, and potentially harming minority and immigrant children far outweigh any benefits. Furthermore, Meier (2002) contends that the uncritical adoption of standards and standardized tests inevitably leads to increased **standardization** of all aspects of education, including mandated scripted lesson plans for low-performing schools, standardized textbooks that conform to the common standards, test preparation materials, and even the design of teacher preparation.

Two of the cases that follow illustrate some of the effects of the accountability bandwagon. The first case, "A Test of Wills," considers the impact on immigrant students when their Social Studies teacher fails to "teach to the test." The second case, "Teaching for Dummies," examines the assumptions underpinning mandated curricula and standards tests. As you read these cases, think about how you will decide which outcomes you will teach and to whom you will be accountable for teaching them.

Context

Community involvement

Community involvement is being increasingly emphasized in provincial government documents, district strategic plans, and school outreach efforts. Parents have always had a place in schools as volunteers—cooking hot dogs, contributing to bake sales, and driving students to field trips or sports tournaments. However, the community-involvement bandwagon anticipates a greater role in governance and decision making for parents (Wotherspoon, 2009) and a greater support role for community members, especially businesses (Sanders, 2001).

Community involvement is a particularly productive form of **social capital**.

Like physical capital and human capital—the tools and training that enhance individual productivity—social capital refers to benefits for individuals and ultimately for society. Unlike the other forms of capital, however, social capital is neither tangible nor transferable, residing as it does in the relationships, networks, and communities of which an individual is a part. The trust that builds up in communities as a result of social capital facilitates the kind of coordination and co-operation that is evident in effective schools.

Putnam (2000) identifies two distinct, but not mutually exclusive, dimensions of social capital—"**bonding**" and "**bridging**." Bonding is located in "relations among family members, close friends, and neighbors" (Woolcock, 2001, p. 13), in other words, the close inward-looking relations between like-minded individuals. Bridging, on the other hand, is located in relations among "more distant friends, associates, and colleagues" or, in other words, the more outward-looking relations between people with different interests and goals.

Whether it is bonding or bridging, "social capital cannot be understood independently of its broader institutional environment" (Woolcock, 2001, p. 13). In schools, Putnam (2004, p. 3) argues, educators need to differentiate between social capital generated "inside the walls," including the bonds that are forged among teachers and administrators and the social capital developed "outside the walls," including the bridges that link schools to the broader community.

The benefits of social capital generated by parent involvement have been widely documented (Leithwood, Fullan, & Watson, 2003; Noguera, 2004; and Tennent, 2005). In fact, the evidence suggests that test scores and dropout rates are predicted more accurately by measures of community-based social capital than by measures of teacher quality, class size, or spending per pupil (Fung, 2004; Shirley, 1997; Warren, 2001). However, the increased interest being shown by corporations (Robertson, 1998) can make it difficult for schools to find a balance between community involvement and interference. As Wotherspoon (2009) points out,

> The focus on parental involvement has divergent and sometimes contradictory roots, signifying from various standpoints the expansion of democratic possibilities or the subordination of education to narrow political and economic influences in a context in which public investment in education is falling behind. (p. 100)

Two of the cases that follow consider the effects of community involvement in education. In "Corporate Takeover," a principal who draws on social capital "outside the walls" of his school finds that his social capital "inside the walls" may be negatively affected. In "Over the Rainbow," the effect of social capital is felt by two community outsiders when their attempts to make the classroom a place where it is safe to talk about sexual orientation collide with the beliefs of a tightly bonded religious community. As you read these two cases, think about how social capital will affect *your* teaching.

Conclusion

So many captivating bandwagons roll through education that at times it is a challenge to distinguish between them and genuine evidence-based reforms. In order to gain the necessary perspective, we need to turn once again to essential questions posed by the foundations of education. By taking historically, philosophically, and sociologically minded approaches to scrutinizing bandwagons, we can ensure that we remain true to what is fundamental and enduring in education and yet remain open to adopting innovations that support teaching and learning.

The history of education offers illuminating insights on bandwagons. Ravitch (2003) reminds us that "many proposals that claim to be innovative are merely a revival of some failed idea from the past" (para. 33). Hansot and Tyack (1982) argue that having a sense of history is the key to making sense of new ideas, approaches, and solutions:

> Some people complain that it takes too long to implement new ideas, while others grumble that there are too many foolish notions moving through the system at high velocity. Part of the apparent contradiction may dissolve if one observes that the most significant *problems* have a long history but that proposed *solutions* tend to recycle as educational entrepreneurs reinvent old remedies. (p. 16)

They further suggest that educators would benefit from interrogating each innovation through a historical lens

> to see why it was introduced, how well it worked (under different conditions, to be sure) and why it either disappeared from sight or was so buried under some other name in some obscure corner of the bureaucracy that it had to be rediscovered. (p. 17)

The philosophy of education helps us to ask penetrating questions about what credible evidence there is to support the claims being made by promoters of bandwagons. Clear evidence based on methodologically sound research that is also relevant to the Canadian educational context can be difficult to obtain. Much of what passes for evidence and is widely circulated by colleagues, bloggers, and highly influential professional journals is actually personal opinion rather than empirical research. Furthermore, it is important to remember that popular educational publications are market-driven and often tend to inflate, simplify, or even over-generalize original research findings to appeal to their wide readership (Cahill, 2005). In other words, educators need to seek evidence and ask hard questions about their relevance and reliability before adopting or rejecting proposed initiatives.

The sociology of education helps us to recognize and understand the roles and motivation of bandwagon promoters and the effect that such individuals have on the social fabric of schools (Clifton, Long, Cranston, & Mandzuk, 2013). Recognizing that innovations may be expected to hit an implementation dip and are often followed by a back-to-the-basics movement, essentialist reforms, or even retrenchment helps us to understand the dynamics of change in schools (Ravitch, 2003). We need to ask ourselves honestly whether we are attracted to new ideas, approaches, or solutions because of the appealing form in which they are being presented and the charismatic qualities of the proponents or because of their intrinsic merit.

In this chapter, as in the previous chapter, each case is followed by five questions that will help you to examine the case more deeply, to further develop your skills in asking historically, philosophically, and sociologically minded questions, and to apply the facts of the case to your own practice. We think that essential questions drawn from the foundations disciplines will help you to develop the skills you need in order to know when it is time to jump on or off a bandwagon and to be prepared to justify why you have done so (Kerr, Mandzuk, & Raptis, 2011).

THE CASES

Alone in a Crowd

It was 8:30 on a Tuesday morning and 11-year-old Darlene already looked stressed, covering her ears to drown out the noise as she inched along the hall with her back against the lockers to avoid touching any of the other students. When she finally arrived at her own locker, she stopped in front of it but waited for the other children to clear the area before trying to dig out her materials. Watching from a distance, Jim Fenton, her teacher, started to make his way toward Darlene to offer her a few words of support, but his progress was slowed by the students still rushing to class before the bell rang.

Unfortunately, by the time he reached Darlene, she had already kicked over Gavin's backpack, which he had placed too close to her locker for comfort, and a red liquid, probably fruit juice, was pouring out and down the side of his bag.

Flushed with anger, Gavin turned to Darlene and yelled, "Why did you do that? I didn't touch you! I was just getting my stuff! Now everything is wet and you've wrecked my lunch and my homework is dripping wet! You are such an idiot!"

Two of Gavin's friends had already arrived with a stack of paper towels and had begun to clean up the mess while he tried to rescue his homework. Although a few of his classmates were quietly snickering in the doorway, most of the students in the class ignored the incident and busied themselves with their usual morning routines as they waited for the announcements to begin.

Darlene, fighting back tears, angrily threw her coat and boots into her locker shouting, "I'm not an idiot. You're an idiot. You're all idiots!"

Jim and various support staff had been working with Darlene to help her cope with the challenges she experienced with sensory overload, particularly from sound. One of the strategies she was supposed to use was to navigate the crowded school halls only *after* things had quieted down. Although she had repeatedly been advised to wait at the front entrance for Paula, the class educational assistant, Darlene often sneaked by her.

Today, Darlene had been particularly anxious to get to class because she and her group were ready to begin painting their project. Having spent weeks researching different art techniques, Darlene had excitedly brought her favourite books to share with the others. While Jim and Paula had both given Darlene a number of opportunities to share her growing interest in watercolour painting, they were also trying to help her understand that she needed to consider other people's ideas too. Thinking about others had always presented a huge challenge for Darlene, and Jim and Paula were quite sure that Darlene was going to continue to struggle in this area; in fact, unbeknownst to her group members, Darlene had already assigned them all "painting jobs," and she had also chosen each of their colours.

After discussing the morning's locker incident with Darlene and the other students involved, Jim and Paula circulated around the room, discussing project goals with each group. Paula kept an eye on Darlene. Things seemed to start off well; group members appeared interested in Darlene's art books, and she compromised when it came to choosing colours. The members of Darlene's group even appeared to be enjoying each other's company as they worked diligently on the assigned task.

Unfortunately, the co-operative mood was broken when Tara spilled some water on the work table, which threatened to ruin the map they were working on. This, along with the classroom activity and the growing noise of group work proved to be overwhelming for Darlene. She reacted by throwing her prized art books across the room while yelling, "Now everything is ruined. I hate this group. You're stupid people and I hate every single one of you!" The room fell silent as the books hit the wall and dropped to the floor. As her group members scrambled to wipe up the water, Darlene closed her eyes and began to mumble to herself as she had been trained to do, "It's okay. Everything's okay. It's okay." Paula coaxed her out of the classroom and into a more private place as Jim carefully picked up the books. He gently encouraged the rest of the students to return to their small-group discussions, now more subdued in the wake of Darlene's outburst.

After spending close to an hour outside in the frosty, mid-January air at lunchtime, the students returned to the classroom, ready to put the morning's events behind them. When Darlene, who had spent the lunch break alone in the library reading her art books, met them outside the classroom, she couldn't help noticing that her classmates were not smiling at her. When she tried to talk to some of them, they ignored her and walked away. Jim was aware of what was happening and could tell that Darlene was confused by the way the others were acting toward her. Jim had to begin the Language Arts lesson, and he put an extra effort into redirecting everyone's attention to the story they were reading together.

Later that afternoon, during the locker break, Darlene, once again, tried unsuccessfully to talk to a classmate.

Jim had a hunch that this wouldn't go well, but before he could intervene, she was screaming, "Why aren't you talking to me? I didn't spill the water. I didn't ruin things. Why isn't anybody talking to me? Everyone is so stupid!"

"If we're so stupid, Darlene, then why don't you just leave? Leave and never come back, okay?" one of the students shot back angrily.

Jim calmly escorted a sobbing Darlene back to the library, where he tried to explain how her words had upset the other students. She spent the rest of the afternoon alone with Paula, but she was too agitated and bewildered to accomplish very much.

At the end of the day Jim met with Scott Raeburn (one of the school's vice-principals), Paula, and other members of the support staff to debrief the day's events. Jim was exhausted, upset, and worried. He explained that although there were occasional encouraging moments of success in the classroom, Darlene's erratic behaviour was disturbing the other children and was having a negative effect on the overall learning environment.

"Darlene's outbursts seem to be escalating in frequency and intensity," Jim continued. "Not only that, but each episode erodes the potential for developing positive relationships with the other students a little more. To make matters worse, Darlene now has every reason to believe that her classmates don't like her and hope she doesn't come back!" Frustrated, he admitted, "I no longer know what to do. I just can't get there fast enough to intervene, and Darlene gets so easily overwhelmed. With her short fuse, she just can't control her emotions."

Paula nodded, adding, "I think some of the students are willing to try and include her but they *are* becoming more fearful of her outbursts."

"It's not just the kids who are treading on eggshells," Jim replied. "I'm tied up in knots worrying about the next episode, and I can't help thinking that I am short-changing the rest of the class."

The group concluded that Jim needed more educational-assistant time for his classroom. He appreciated the extra help, but feared that Darlene would continue to be overwhelmed and temperamental and that she would be increasingly isolated by her peers.

"You know," he reflected, "I wonder if our school's philosophy of inclusion is missing the boat by focusing only on differentiation of *instruction* and never on differentiation of *space*."

Just then, Jim was called to the office—Gavin's mother wanted to speak to him and a school administrator about how her son had started his day and she wasn't happy in the least!

Questions

The Case

What strategies did Jim use to support Darlene in the classroom? How effective were the strategies?

History

What has happened to change the ways that schools treat students with special needs?

Philosophy

Is the regular classroom always the best place for students with special needs? Why or why not?

Sociology

Darlene is clearly marginalized in Jim's classroom. What are the signs of her marginal status, and how might she be better integrated with her peers?

Implications for Practice

What would you do if you believed that your school's policy on inclusion was compromising your ability to teach *all* of the students in your class?

Be the Change

Tammy Borden's Social Studies classroom at Winterburn High School was warm and inviting—the desks were arranged in a semicircle so all her students could see each other and she could walk around during class discussions. She loved teaching high school, especially when her students were engaged with the content. Even some of the quieter students were animated when they discussed topics like youth criminal justice, education for sustainable development, and human-rights issues around the world. She was struck by how many of them held strong beliefs, especially when it came to justice and equality for all. Tammy didn't always agree with every position her students took, but their ability to develop a sound argument had grown since the beginning of the term. Tammy wanted her classroom to be a place where students felt encouraged to think critically. There were posters all around the room with inspirational messages and words of wisdom from world leaders like Mahatma Gandhi, Nelson Mandela, and Martin Luther King. Her favourite was the one with a photo of Gandhi and the message, "Be the change you want to see in the world." As she prepared for her lesson on the effects of globalization on identity, she wondered about what other kinds of diversity she might celebrate in her poster collection.

Later that day, Tammy was 10 minutes into her lesson when she noticed that Jessica's head was slumped forward, and then jolted back upright as she struggled to stay awake. In 10 years of teaching, Tammy had seen many 15-year-olds fall asleep in class, but not Jessica, who had always been a high-achieving and highly engaged student. Tammy wondered what was going on in Jessica's life. This was the third day in a row that Jessica was not her usual self in class. She hadn't raised her hand once to answer a question, and her homework wasn't getting done either. As she finished her presentation and prepared the class for some independent work, Tammy wondered if she needed to spice up her lessons a bit to better engage her students.

Once the class started working on their assignment, Tammy strolled over to Jessica's desk.

"Hi, Jessica, you seem tired this week. Is everything all right?" she said.

"Yeah, I guess so, Ms Borden. It's just that I've had early morning basketball practices all week," Jessica replied.

Tammy recalled a conversation at a recent staff meeting. At the time, she hadn't paid much attention when they were deciding that the girls would practise in the morning and the boys would practise after school. It had seemed like a logical way to allocate gym time. Now she could see why the coach wanted the boys' basketball team to practise at the end of the day instead of first thing in the morning.

Jared, who was on the boys' team, turned around in his desk and muttered loudly enough for everyone to hear, "Well, at least you aren't taking really tough courses like computer science and physics."

Tammy knew Jessica would be fine. The basketball season was short, and she might just have to coast through her courses for a while; but Tammy began to wonder whether Jessica wasn't taking computer science or physics this year just so that she could pursue extracurricular activities like basketball. The exchange between the two students nagged at Tammy for the rest of the day. Were boys facing the same kinds of decisions that could affect their future careers? Was the school culture inadvertently sexist? Maybe it was questions like these that had prompted the principal, Marilyn Price, to schedule a meeting to discuss the idea of establishing single-sex classes.

Later that day, as Tammy scraped the ice off the windshield of her car after school, she glanced up and noticed a group of older boys playing hockey on the outdoor rink. She could see Jessica there, too—laughing with a couple of girls who were watching the game. Tammy waved at them before getting into her car. Boys and girls seemed to be naturally respectful of each other at Winterburn, and perhaps that was why Tammy had never entertained the idea of single-sex classes before. However, her recent experience with Jessica made her wonder if she had been looking at the situation from the right perspective.

As she walked into the office the next morning, there was a heated discussion about single-sex classes already in full swing between Angus McDowell, one of the math teachers, and Marilyn.

"There is no solid evidence to suggest boys or girls do better in single-sex classes," Angus said. "I don't want to waste a whole day talking about it."

"It isn't a waste," Marilyn replied. 'We are getting pressure from parents and some of the teachers to try and address some of the imbalances that affect girls in higher-level Mathematics and Science courses and boys in English Language Arts and History."

"Well, in my experience, when students don't perform, it's because they don't work hard enough. Funny thing is, we only start to hear complaints about gender bias around report card time. Why don't we just explain to parents that their kids need to take greater responsibility for their own learning and just do their homework?"

"Come on, Angus, you know you are oversimplifying things!" countered Marilyn.

"I'm already doing lots in class to make sure the girls feel included," Angus pressed on. "After all, we do puzzles and games and lots of other fun stuff."

Tammy wasn't sure that these were activities that could be classified as catering particularly to girls' needs, but she decided to hold her tongue rather than go head-to-head with Angus on this point.

Instead, she said, "But you can't deny that girls aren't getting a fair shake in the timetable so we could and should do something about that. We should at least consider single-sex classes before we reject them outright."

"Well, separating students by sex won't help the timetable," he protested. "Look, we know that schools already reinforce gender differences in many subtle and overt ways. How is separating them going to change that?"

Maybe he had a point, Tammy wondered, as she walked back to her classroom. Maybe segregated classes weren't the answer after all. Sometimes, when Angus resisted every new idea that came along, he turned out to be right in the end. But that didn't mean they should ignore the issue. As her eyes fell on the poster of Gandhi, his words reminded her that she could start in her own classroom to make the changes she wanted to see.

Tammy realized that she had a responsibility to both the boys and the girls to help them recognize and break out of the gender-role stereotypes that prevented them from taking advantage of the full range of opportunities available to them. Thinking about that, she suddenly realized that there were no females represented in her inspirational poster collection. The diversity she had been missing was gender! She obviously needed to raise her own consciousness as well as those of her students.

Tammy decided she would begin to ask more pointed questions in her class discussions so that students would relate the effects of globalization and gender equality to their own experiences as high school students. As she considered the benefits of challenging her students to engage in a conversation about gender issues in their lives, she wondered if this might help them to understand better the broader concepts they were studying. She couldn't wait to get started.

Questions

The Case

At the beginning of this case, Tammy wonders if single-sex classes might be more effective than coeducational classes, but by the end she isn't quite sure what to think. What factors have contributed to her indecision on this matter?

History

What are some of the historical reasons that boys-only and girls-only schools were established in Canada? Are some of those reasons still justified? Explain.

Philosophy

In which environment—single-sex or coeducational classes—are the interests of boys and girls best served? Justify your response.

Sociology

In what ways might the structural arrangements of schools, such as timetables, course offerings, and leadership opportunities, advantage either boys or girls?

Implications for Practice

What would you do if you were concerned that too many of your female students were limiting their opportunities for life after high school? Explain.

Let Them Eat Cake!

Streamers and balloons hung from the empty library shelves at Terry Fox Junior High School. Snacks and a punch bowl sat on one of the long tables in the middle of the room. It was a day that Brina Notabendi had been dreading for months. She looked around the barren library and revelled in the last few minutes of calm before the doors crashed open and a sea of students, parents, and staff poured into the room. Well-wishers queued up to pat her on the back, while others buzzed around the food and drink.

Eventually, the principal, Lynnette Hoggett-Horst, stood up on a wooden chair and then, placing her forefinger dramatically to her lips, exhaled a loud "shhhh." Barely suppressing a giggle, she chirped, "I don't suppose we'll hear much of that in this room anymore. Sorry Brina." She "steepled" her hands and made an exaggerated bow in the librarian's direction. A smattering of chuckles came from the crowd.

"I just wanted to thank everyone for coming for Ms Notabendi's last day. As you are all painfully aware, although I fought like a trooper, I couldn't very well get special dispensation for our school when all the other school libraries in the district were being closed as well."

She motioned for Brina to come over. The librarian's immediate reaction was to hold her ground, but she knew she had no choice but to make her way over to her principal's side.

"You know, Breen," said Lynnette, putting her arm around the librarian's shoulders with sudden and unaccustomed familiarity, "you've had a good run at this school. You must have seen many changes in your day."

At this point, Brina decided to use the principal's unwitting opening to share her opinions before she left. She cleared her throat and began, "Actually, I've seen a lot of changes. For example, the year I arrived they were placing the whole card catalogue on a computer . . ."

"Ah, yes, a foreshadowing of the future." interrupted the principal.

Undeterred, Brina carried on. "Yes, and undoubtedly, some changes have been good. But some were pretty short-lived, weren't they? Shall I share a few?" Her eyes glinted as the grinning crowd encouraged her to proceed.

"I remember when Mrs Hoggett-Horst decided to rename the library with the Orwellian title of 'Learning Commons Area.' Then she shipped in a number of computer banks and couches. I guess the students weren't relaxing enough!"

"One of my better reforms that brought students back to an otherwise dead and unused space," came the principal's unrepentant retort.

"And do you remember when there wasn't room for everything you ordered, Lynnette?" Brina needled, unabashedly using the principal's first name.

"Now that's a little foggy."

"First, you wanted us to remove all the non-fiction books. When I balked, you suggested that I liquidate all publications before 2001—as if they had an expiry date!" Brina chortled. "Remember that books aren't like hairdos!" she added pointedly, gesturing to Lynnette's closely cropped head and receiving a few guffaws for her audacity.

Brina's face turned serious as she continued, "Unfortunately, the biggest change that I've seen in my career is still ongoing. I remember when the government's new Digital Education Renewal Training program was introduced—DERT as we librarians jokingly referred to it, because it essentially used technology funding as an excuse to bury libraries—slashing resources and terminating personnel. I guess the last laugh was on us; we never thought it would succeed in convincing our board and *certain* principals," she glanced sideways, "that laptops could and should replace libraries or that librarians' work hours should disappear or that the board would start replacing retiring librarians with *information technologists*."

"Now, Breen," said Lynnette soothingly, "the schools need those people to manage the new workstations."

"Yes, and let's not forget they were hired at much lower salaries. These people have no expertise beyond computer troubleshooting, and yet if you look around the province, you will see that over the half the school libraries are now being managed by technologists rather than trained librarians," she retorted.

Switching gears, Brina went on, "Then there was the time you referred to trips to the library as 'lost instructional time.' We couldn't believe it! We thought you'd lock the washrooms next!" The room shook with laughter.

Lynnette chuckled through clenched teeth, "What a memory! I guess librarians are like elephants, white or otherwise. You just can't fight progress! And remember, as the board says, libraries aren't really closing—they're just getting a make-over. I, for one, think it is long overdue. Schools of the twenty-first century will have to equip students with the skills they need to be successful beyond high school. This room will soon house serious media equipment . . ."

"But what about the books?" interrupted Brina.

"Now, Brina," Lynnette said, putting her hand firmly on Brina's shoulder to show who was in command, "as you well know, no book will be thrown out. Instead, they will all be reallocated to various classrooms throughout the building. After all, books belong in the hands of children, not hidden away on some dusty library shelves."

"Let's see," Brina calculated swiftly, stepping away from Lynnette, "you can fit in about 100 books per classroom. That should interest the students for at least three weeks." Taking a deep breath to hide the churning emotions she was suppressing, she continued, "The purpose of a library is to *centralize* books for all readers, not to break up the collection so teachers can squirrel away books in their classrooms. How will this benefit the majority of our students? It just doesn't make sense!"

Lynnette had had enough and so she cut the debate short, "Breen, I am truly sorry to see your day ending. I've always found our discussions to be so stimulating."

In response, Brina pulled out her last "party favour." "Stimulating, eh? Well, I hope you find it 'stimulating' to learn that I have been hired as Bright Academy's chief librarian."

Even Lynnette's frenzied waving could not silence the crowd's uproar.

"You see," Brina said, as the audience quieted down, "I believe that the next great leap won't be to more and better technology. Everyone's got that now. No, the competitive advantage in the future will go to schools who can afford to have a librarian to guide students through the world of misinformation and make the library into a hub of learning. Students left to wander through the Internet like the Wild Boy of Aveyron will simply be out of the race."

"Wild boy, eh? I'll bet that Aveyron Board doesn't have the technological advances we have!" concluded the principal triumphantly.

Brina smiled inwardly at her former principal's ignorance of the history of education and the famous book she had referred to.

Lynnette curtly changed direction, "Now, let's turn to more pleasant matters," she said, plunging the knife into the cake.

For the first time, the librarian gazed closely at her goodbye cake, a multi-layered confection in the shape of a large thick book. She noticed that Lynnette was wearing a malevolent grin as she carved it up and distributed overly large pieces to grasping hands. Before long, disappointed students at the back of the line were told there was no more, while many of the huge slices sat half-eaten in the garbage.

Brina shook her head. "Ah distribution—if people just knew what they were wasting while others starved."

Questions

The Case

What were some of the early warning signs that the library at Terry Fox Junior High School would ultimately close?

History

In the past, libraries and books were at the heart of the educational enterprise, but with the ascendance of new technologies and media, they are now vanishing from schools at an alarming rate. Is there still a role for libraries and if so, what is it? Explain your response.

Philosophy

Is it morally defensible to close a school library? Why or why not?

Sociology

How are the social norms and culture of a school likely to change if the library books are allocated to classrooms and the library is replaced by access to the Internet?

Implications for Practice

Given the tenuous future of school libraries, how will you ensure that your students develop the research skills they need?

The Future Is Now

Ricardo Perez had moved to the Maritimes over a year previously from Ontario, where he had been living since his arrival in Canada from Mexico as a teenager. He had been employed as a classroom teacher for three years in two different school districts in the Ottawa area, and during that time he had gained valuable experience as a middle years teacher. However, after Ricardo's wife, Mabel, received a sizeable promotion, her second since their marriage, the young couple's decision to move was a relatively easy one. The downside was that Ricardo would have to leave a permanent position in Ontario at a time when teaching positions were becoming increasingly scarce.

In his first year on the east coast, Ricardo found work as a supply teacher in one of the mid-sized cities. The work was sparse to begin with, but it became more and more regular as Ricardo was seen to be both reliable and competent. Some weeks he worked every day; often, he would even have a sequence of days with the same class. In this, his second year, he was delighted to have been hired for a one-year term appointment at Greenbriar Elementary School to replace a Grade 5 teacher who was scheduled to be on medical leave for the entire year.

Greenbriar was one of the early adopters of the Ministry of Education's Twenty-first Century Learning, or 21C, initiative. The initiative had grown out of a media firestorm about the province's lack of competitiveness in the wake of a particularly dismal showing on the PISA (Programme for International Student Assessment) tests. The purpose of the initiative was to draw attention to skills that would be considered most valuable in the knowledge economy of the future. Schools were being directed to place greater emphasis on core language, science, and mathematics and to make every effort to integrate technology into all aspects of the school.

Greenbriar had already begun moving in that direction, and the staff wholeheartedly supported the Ministry's initiative. Midway through the previous year, the administration and staff had applied for a technology grant and been awarded a substantial sum. The funds were to be used to develop a new technology infrastructure to link the administrative, educational, and support operations in the school, including all of its forms, records, grades, curriculum maps, and even cafeteria purchases.

The grant enabled the school to outfit each classroom with an interactive smartboard and to buy enough laptops for four class sets. All the wireless networking capabilities of the Internet were upgraded and audiovisual equipment and document cameras were bought for teachers to share. Ricardo could see the value of most of these purchases, particularly at the classroom and administration levels, but he remained troubled by the pending implementation of biometric scanning in the school cafeteria.

Greenbriar was to be the first in Canada to become a "cashless" school. The program, already piloted in the United States, made some rather bold claims about eliminating lunchroom bullying in the school. It was argued that without cash being used to buy food from the cafeteria, bullies wouldn't be able to steal money. In addition, the program offered reassurance to parents and caregivers who might be worried that their children's lunch money might get lost. As an added bonus, there would be shorter line-ups since a fully automated lunchroom would mean that staff wouldn't have to waste time on cash transactions.

To enrol in the program, students would be asked to create a unique electronic thumbprint, which would be saved on the school server and linked to a parent or caregiver's account number. To load money onto the student's account, they would simply log on to the server with their own account number and private password. Once the account was loaded with funds, a student would be able to make purchases in the cafeteria by simply scanning his or her thumbprint onto the biometric scanner. The system would perform the match, and the right amount of money would be withdrawn from the family's associated account.

For his part, Ricardo was appalled at the entire prospect of the cashless school. He couldn't get past his aversion to having fingerprints taken. He had always associated fingerprints with images of criminalization and incarceration, but at least when prints were made with paper and ink, they could be destroyed. It was not so clear whether electronic fingerprints could *ever* be expunged from this system. Although the school community was being assured that students' prints were being saved on secure servers, well-publicized breaches had shaken Ricardo's confidence in the security of *any* electronic data. In fact, he had lots of questions about the privacy of information and the potential for abuse. He wondered whether children's prints would automatically be deleted from the server when a family moved. He questioned whether eliminating cash would really affect bullying in the school. Furthermore, he suspected that altogether too much was being claimed in the name of progress, but no one seemed to be willing to challenge the claims that were being made. After all, technology was just a tool—a means to an end—rather than an end in itself.

Ricardo could see that several teachers, particularly the younger ones, were using their interactive whiteboards to great effect. They used the interactive media to foster rich discussions with their students, and the students seemed to be highly engaged in their learning. Others, like him, were less familiar with the technology and merely used their interactive whiteboards as the latest way to project PowerPoint presentations. In time, he knew, he would have to make the effort to integrate technology more effectively into his teaching, but for now his priority was to implement the provincial curricula in his Grade 5 class.

He was very impressed with the school's successful pursuit of funding for technology, but he wondered whether there had been any formal evaluation built into the process. How would they even know whether the technology actually made a difference? Although Ricardo really wanted to have a discussion with his colleagues and administrators about the questions he had regarding their implementation of technology, he knew that, as a new staff member, he would do so at his own risk. These days, no one seemed to be interested in hearing doubts about technology, and he didn't want to jeopardize his chances of securing a more permanent position in the district. In any event, he was fairly sure that the frenzy would have to die down soon, because Greenbriar, like every other school, couldn't sustain the current momentum indefinitely. Technology in schools would always lag behind what was possible.

In the meantime, Ricardo couldn't help thinking that the promise of technology was blinding his colleagues to the greater need for the so-called digital natives to learn important life skills, like critical thinking, social responsibility, and interacting positively with others. After all, wasn't education supposed to be about broadening students' minds rather than narrowing their experiences?

Questions

The Case

What were the issues in this case that Ricardo was trying to resolve?

History

For over 50 years, schools have seen a series of technological bandwagons roll through. Which of these do you think have been the most significant and why?

Philosophy

Do you think that critical thinking, social responsibility, and interpersonal skills are necessarily compromised when an educational system embraces technology? Justify your position.

Sociology

In this case, Ricardo seems to be experiencing what sociologists call "sociological ambivalence." On one hand, he wants to be a team player, but on the other hand, his professional judgment keeps him from joining his colleagues in embracing technology uncritically. How might teachers manage the tensions associated with these kinds of conflicting role expectations?

Implications for Practice

In adopting new technologies, how will you ensure that you keep both student learning and student safety at the forefront?

Blurred Reflections

Faculty members were gathering up their papers, closing their laptops, and beginning to break into conversation as the Monday morning Curriculum and Pedagogy Department meeting finally wrapped up. Millie, a veteran faculty member in the two-year After-Degree Bachelor of Education program, struck up a conversation with Ben, the bright-eyed new colleague sitting next to her. Offhandedly, she asked Ben how his courses were going.

"Thanks, I'm really enjoying teaching and getting to know the students. Actually, I've had some wonderful conversations with the second-year students in my Philosophy and Practice class," Ben responded, smiling as he closed his laptop and collected his office keys, proud of how well his first university teaching assignment was going.

"Oh, those second-year students," Millie sneered disgustedly as she shook her head. "They think they know it all by this time in the program. They've already set their sights on teaching next fall. Their minds are barely here at all. They're not thinking about teaching. They're just thinking about how to get a job!"

"Well, I've been having some good experiences with them so far," Ben replied hesitantly. He had no wish to argue with Millie, a tenured professor who deservedly commanded much respect from her colleagues, but he decided to gently press on. "Many of the students have written some very compelling journal entries. You know, they're struggling with ideas, posing difficult questions—I've found their responses quite insightful, and often useful when I'm planning my classes."

The two stood up and started to make their way through the other faculty members and walk towards the door.

"Arghh! Journals!" Millie snapped. "I've been marking students' journals all weekend. What a disappointment! The students were supposed to respond to the readings—they just don't get it. They rattle on about the content of the articles but don't connect critically with them! I know what the articles say. I don't want to read a summary, a quick response about how it made them *feel*, and then a recap of what they liked and didn't like. I want critical engagement! I've actually had to fail a few of them on this assignment," Millie scowled and shook her head, clearly frustrated.

Ben's eyes widened as he wondered how students could be failed on reflective journal entries. He wondered, too, why he seemed to be getting such rich responses from the students when Millie apparently was not. Perhaps he misunderstood what Millie's purpose was for the assignment, or worse, maybe his standards were too low. The conversation ended abruptly as Millie turned to talk with another colleague. As Ben returned to his office, he continued to think about the value of having students respond in reflective journal assignments. He knew what the research said about the importance of reflection and the ways it can inform teachers' practice. In addition, Ben valued the opportunities to read the students' reflections and often spent much time responding to their journals with comments and questions. He thought the exercise was valuable and worthwhile both for the students and for him as a teacher.

Later that week between meetings, Ben scurried to the food court to grab a coffee. He had been up late marking papers and craved some caffeine before he had to endure another hour-long meeting, discussing issues for which he had little context and even less understanding. As he waited in line, he counted out the coins in his palm, hoping he had enough for a dark roast. Having secured his payment, his eyes and mind wandered and he began listening in on the conversation between the two young men in front of him.

"I am exhausted," the tall, brown-haired student yawned.

Ben was pretty sure it was Prabjot, one of his top students. Ben thought about greeting the students, but didn't recognize the shorter student and besides, he felt uncomfortable interrupting.

"I hear you," responded the shorter of the two, adjusting the tuque that he had pulled down low on his head. "I can't wait until the term is done and we can get into the schools. That's when we'll finally learn how to teach!"

"You've got that right. Most of my classes are such a joke—group work and incessant talking," Prabjot continued, "Yak, yak, yak! Let's get on with it already!"

The line shuffled forward. Ben was starting to feel a bit uncomfortable. He thought about dropping out of the line and just slipping off to the meeting, but his yearning for a morning coffee—and his curiosity—kept him rooted to the spot. He looked down at the tiled floor, pushed his hands into his pockets, and tried to look casual and inconspicuous.

"What assignments have you got left?" the shorter student asked Prabjot indifferently, pulling his wallet out of his back pocket and thumbing through a few cards.

"Um, a couple. I've got a group project, an integrated unit plan, and an annotated bibliography for my literature course. Plus, I've got to finish up my reflective journal. I tell you, if I have to do one more reflection, I'm going to scream! Honestly, it's like in every class! How much reflecting can one person do?" Prabjot threw his head back, exasperated, and stuffed his hands into his pockets. "Man, I feel like they're reflecting us to death!"

Ben froze. He waited a few seconds, then turned quietly to his right and made a stealthy beeline to the other end of the food court, hoping the students wouldn't see him. He was trying to process what he had just heard. How could the reflective journal assignments be so painful for students? He had thought that writing a journal was meaningful and worthwhile—not just for him, but for his students as well. Were there too many assignments requiring reflection, or did the students think of journal writing as just another hoop to jump through so they could get on with their practicum? Maybe the reflections were written just to please *him* and were not really a reflective engagement at all. How was he supposed to know what was a legitimate reflection and what was just a boiler-plate response? Maybe he needed a rubric, he thought desperately.

Ben arrived in the dreary board room as the other committee members were filing in. He moved quickly to the back of the room and found a spot at the far end of the table, plopped down into a chair, and dropped his head into his hands. He had felt so confident about the reflective-journal assignment, but now he was rattled. He was starting to doubt his ability as a professor and wondered whether keeping a reflective journal necessarily translated into becoming a reflective practitioner. Does keeping a journal *really* engage students in critical reflection, or is it simply just one more meaningless task? Can teachers at any level really force students to reflect on command? Ben had a lot of questions but few answers. He felt he needed some time to think about his certainties and to sort out what he had just heard. Just then, the Dean stood up at the front of the room and called the meeting to order.

Questions

The Case

When Ben tries to judge the value of journal writing for his students, which specific points from his conversation with Millie and the conversation he overheard between the two students should he consider?

History

In the past, teacher candidates were expected primarily to demonstrate what they had learned through rote questions on examinations. In recent years, teacher educators have increasingly gauged students' understanding through entries in reflective journals and project work. What do you think has accounted for this change?

Philosophy

What does it mean to be a "reflective practitioner"?

Sociology

Why do you think reflective journaling has become a cornerstone in the socialization of teachers into the teaching profession?

Implications for Practice

How might you maximize the benefits and minimize the limitations of journal writing for your students?

DEAR Me!

It was a cold day in mid-February, during what it commonly known as I Love to Read Month in the province. At a different time every day in February, students at Fairmont School were summoned to drop everything and read (DEAR). Today, the call came just after lunch recess, allowing the kids enough time to get out of their winter clothes and settle down to work on their Heritage Fair projects. The sound of the tinkling bell erupted over the intercom, and the familiar "It's time for DEAR!" was proclaimed excitedly by two students chosen for the honour from one of the Kindergarten to Grade 8 classes in the school. As the students scrambled to get their books out of their desks or backpacks, their teacher, Morgan McAllister, reached into her own oversized leather bag to pull out her latest indulgence, an eReader, recently loaded with a best-selling book she had just bought with a Christmas gift card.

Morgan looked forward to this time of day, and so did her students. Out of the corner of her eye, she could see her students' shoulders visibly relax as they leaned, with their heads down and eyes bright, over their cherished books. She had to admit that the instant calm was almost eerie as the students settled into suspended animation for 15 minutes. However, it had not always been easy to get all of her class to enjoy reading. When she first heard about her principal Karl Wiebe's idea to adopt DEAR for I Love to Read Month, in September, Morgan wondered whether he had given any thought to her class.

At the beginning of the school year, Morgan recalled, it was like pulling teeth to get some of her Grade 4 students to pick up a book for pleasure. She had decided that she would need to get students ready for February by instituting a period of Uninterrupted sustained silent reading (USSR) once a week. However, for the longest time, these were neither uninterrupted nor silent and very little "reading" was accomplished. Morgan was an avid reader herself, and she felt strongly that schools had an important role to play in opening up the world of literature to young minds. She considered the classics to be part of the cultural heritage that schools were responsible for transmitting, and she was firmly committed to providing time for students to read in school. Although she knew that her Grade 4s were a boisterous and highly active group, she trusted that they would settle down eventually and was certain they would come to enjoy the opportunity to curl up with a good book as much as she did. She was pleased with the book collection in her class, which included some of the finest books ever written for children, courtesy of several successful Parent Council fundraising campaigns.

However, the months had gone by and Morgan was still finding USSR to be a chore for her and a struggle for many of her students. Not all, of course. There was a dedicated group of girls who loved reading the *Ramona*, *Anne of Green Gables*, and *Little House on the Prairie* series in the classroom collection. When Morgan announced that it was time for USSR, they would rush to the back of the room, where they had appropriated the bean bags and the couch, sprawling happily and obliviously, turning pages to their own internal rhythm. Along the window ledge, another less interested group of boys and girls would congregate with their backs against their lumpy reading pillows, reading half-heartedly and keeping their peripheral vision fixed on what the rest of the students were doing. This group practised the art of *appearing* to be engrossed in their books, but Morgan could see that it was becoming harder and harder for them to pretend to be engaged. Frankly, Morgan had thought to herself, too many of her students were still adrift. Some of her boys had perfected a task-avoidance routine that bordered on defiance. They would pick up a book, quickly leaf through it to appear to be checking it out but then would quickly discard it and reach for another, repeating the process until finally they had managed to waste the entire USSR period without ever having read anything.

Morgan was almost ready to abandon the idea of USSR completely but decided to approach some of the veteran teachers for their advice. There had been considerable buzz in the staff room lately about the "**boy crisis**" in education, and Morgan wondered whether this was underlying the problem in her class. Molly Travers quoted some statistics about how more boys were dropping out of schools and that boys were being overtaken by girls in scholarships and admissions to university programs. David Warkentin suggested that boys typically struggle with reading, and he offered to share some of his high-interest low-vocabulary books with her. Brenda Goodbrandson reminded her that this was the "wired generation" and that maybe she should buy a set of Play Me devices so the boys could listen to books instead of reading them. Morgan wasn't sure that this was a boy problem, because there were a number of boys in the class who *were* happy to read and none of her students were struggling readers. However, by December, when Morgan was no further ahead, she decided to call a class meeting. It was this meeting that was replaying in her mind.

"Well, Miss McAllister, like, the books we have, are like—you know—lame," said Allie nervously.

"Yeah, lame," echoed Ethan and Connor.

"Okay, that's a start. Let's talk a little about what you mean by 'lame,'" probed Morgan, as she picked up her marker and pulled the chart stand closer.

At the top of the chart paper, she wrote, "WHAT MAKES A GOOD BOOK?" At first the less vocal students squirmed in their seats as if they were afraid to say something that might upset their teacher.

"It's okay," she reminded them, "remember that in our class meetings, all answers are acceptable unless they are hurtful or untrue. Try to say something that no one else has said. Let's go around the room and give one or two words each, starting with Greg," prompted Morgan.

"Scary."

"Crazy!"

"Funny!"

"Real stories and real facts."

"Yeah, real, not stupid!"

"Crashes and fights!"

"Happy endings."

"Superheroes and bad guys."

"Lots of pictures."

"Real kids helping real people."

"Long ago and far away."

About halfway through the class meeting, Morgan began to see what her students were talking about. As she thought about her class library, she began to wonder whether she had been too rigid in what she thought was appropriate reading for Grade 4 students. The truth was that most of the so-called classics were actually of little interest or relevance to most of her students. As she thought about the titles on her shelves, she realized that few of them reflected the experience of those born outside of North America or portrayed the kind of action and drama that her students enjoyed.

That evening, Morgan called her friend, Renate Martinez, who worked in the public library a few blocks away and asked her what Grade 4 students were reading. The next day, Morgan shared the contents of the bucket of reading materials she had gathered from the library. The graphic novels, magazines, *Captain Underpants* books, books on social justice and global themes, and the fact-filled *Guinness Book of World Records* were snapped up excitedly. Students who had never sat still to read for more than five minutes were instantly absorbed and actually groaned when USSR was over.

As she switched on her eReader to dive into her "whodunit," she asked herself why it had taken her so long to realize that not all students would be captivated by the same sorts of reading materials. As she looked around the room, she wondered whether she had succeeded because she had addressed the so-called boy crisis or whether she was just being more responsive to her students' interests. As she settled down to read, her thoughts turned to the other subjects she taught, and she wondered how what she had learned might be transferable to other aspects of her teaching.

Questions

The Case

In this case, Morgan realizes that the way she was implementing DEAR wasn't working for many of her students. What steps did Morgan take to improve the experience of sustained silent reading in her classroom?

History

Research shows that reading for pleasure among school-aged children has been declining continually. What do you think has contributed to this decline, and what might we do to reverse it?

Philosophy

When are school-wide initiatives beneficial, and when are they a waste of precious instructional time? Explain your position.

Sociology

Some might point to activities like DEAR as an example of how teachers are relinquishing their authority to their students and giving them too many choices. How would you respond to such a claim? Justify your response.

Implications for Practice

If you had serious misgivings about the value of a school-wide initiative like DEAR, what would you do?

A Test of Wills

Trish McDonnell could feel her anxiety mounting. As the teacher of a Grade 9 class at Lansdowne Middle School, filled with new Canadians, she—and they—were starting to see progress, but the question of whether it was enough to meet the district's mandatory outcomes for Grade 9 Social Studies hung over all of them. She would soon know—the first quarterly test was scheduled for later in the day.

Trish was known by her colleagues as having the "strength of will" that was needed to work with challenging classes, particularly ones where the students were still learning English. She had learned to be patient and responsive to her students' interests, expanding their vocabulary through discussions and using relevant examples to sustain their attention. Since her students were neither completely fluent nor completely socialized into Canadian ways of life, Trish assured them right from the beginning that they would do better if they relaxed a little and took their time to figure out what was expected of them. She had never rushed them but, instead, had paced her lessons and set expectations that took her students' language abilities into account. More than once she decided that it was more important to spend time on topics of interest than to stick rigidly to the district's tight timelines for each unit of study.

Trish was also well aware of high parental expectations. At the first parent–teacher meeting of the year, a line quickly formed at her table with mothers and fathers who were anxious to know if their son or daughter was working hard enough to become a doctor or a lawyer. It was abundantly clear that anything less than top marks from their offspring would be embarrassing and viewed as a family crisis. She sympathized with the parents but tried to explain that learning, especially in a brand new country in a different language, took time. She repeated this again and again at the first meeting.

But, now, as the first test was closing in, Trish began to feel increasingly anxious for her students and for herself. She knew how strictly the district office viewed teachers whose students had lower-than-normal test scores. If her students didn't do well, it could come back to haunt *her*, as well as her students. And maybe the parents would come down even harder on their children or even demand her resignation.

After lunch, her students were sitting up straight at their desks, nervously ready to receive their tests. Not everyone had settled yet; there was the usual re-arranging of pens, books, iPods, and desks. Some of the students talked in undertones in their first language, while others were tense and silent. As they opened their booklets and scanned the questions she could read disbelief, frustration, and anger in their facial expressions and body language. Whispering became a chorus of low moans:

"I don't understand!"

"I wasn't here last year!"

"How much does this count?"

"Did we even take *this*?"

"Why didn't we know this could be on the test?"

"What will my mother and father say?"

Chatter finally gave way to silence as the students settled down to work their way through the questions. The test certainly wasn't easy, and as Trish perused it, she realized she had taught only about two-thirds of the material on which the questions were based. Knowing how poorly her students would fare, she wasn't sure who to blame. Silently, she began to fret, "Why, oh why do students have to suffer through questions some faceless test-writer decides are important *and* according to a schedule that doesn't even take into account that English is a foreign language for them? Why aren't my own professional standards sufficient for judging my students' progress? Maybe it's my fault. Why do I allow myself to go off on tangents with my students, instead of teaching strictly to the tests?"

Before long the test ended, and the students, sad-faced and dejected, quietly left the class.

Later, as Trish prepared to begin the next unit, "Canada at War," she was determined that there would be no surprises for her students on the next district test. She had carefully outlined the topics they would need to cover and planned ways to make the content relevant and engaging for her students. She was going to focus on the effects of the two world wars on families and youth at home and abroad. Trish was certain that by drawing on her students' experiences and their ability to empathize with victims their own ages she would help them not only learn the historical facts but also get a sense of the tragedy and human costs of war.

At least, that was her plan. As Trish neared her classroom and reached for the doorknob, someone slunk past her. It was Hassan, and he was clearly not his usual bouncy self. The students were sitting in their circle groups, most with their heads down and their books closed. There was a tense undercurrent full of sighs and whispers. There was something eerie about the scene. As she entered the classroom, the room fell completely silent.

"Sorry, I'm a bit late," she said, scanning the room as an attendance check as she chattered. "But *you're* here, aren't you? You make me very proud. Hey, what's with everyone? Up too late studying? Where is Mustapha . . . and Gurpreet? Has anyone seen them?"

The silence stretched on and no one dared to make eye contact.

"Well, what is it, Hassan? What has happened?" Trish demanded. When she still received no reply, she added more gently, "Tell me, please."

Gathering the courage to speak, Hassan finally blurted out, "You are right, Ms McDonnell. Mustapha and Gurpreet aren't here. They can't be. My mother said they tried to . . . make themselves . . . you know . . . stop . . . *living* . . . last night . . . something about an agreement, a 'pact' or something . . ."

Hassan's breath was short and tears started to roll down his cheeks as some of the other students began to sob, too. Trish was caught completely off guard and didn't know immediately what to say.

"They didn't do it. I mean, whatever they tried to do didn't work—they're still alive, Ms McDonnell. They are both in the hospital," continued Hassan haltingly. "All the families . . . my mother . . . father . . . they're so sad. Mustapha and Gurpreet live in the houses behind us. It's been a *terrible* night. We didn't sleep much. Their parents asked me to tell you that the boys apologize for how they did on the test. They say they must have failed . . . you know . . . that Social Studies exam we had last month."

Trish felt as if all the air had suddenly been sucked out of the room. "No, no, not the test! What a terrible waste!" Pulling herself together, she calmed down a little, saying, "But we can all be grateful that both boys are . . . as you say . . . alive . . . that's *good* news."

Trish knew she would have to inform her principal immediately, and she was anxious to reach out to the boys and their families, but her first order of business was to bring the school counsellor into her class. Jane Marks was far more experienced and skilled in handling this type of crisis than Trish.

"Oh my . . ." gulped Trish, as tears welled up in her eyes. "Sit tight, guys. I'll be back right away, I promise."

As she scurried along to Jane's office, she realized that she was still gripping the envelope with the Social Studies test results in her hands. Trish quickly skimmed the letter and the words "disappointing," "curriculum," "**criterion-referenced tests, standards**," and "improvement needed" leapt out at her. She gasped as she glanced down the list of names and scores. Not good. Mustapha and Gurpreet: *bare passes!* Three others had failed outright. How was she going to break the news to her students and their parents? More importantly, how much longer could she continue to teach in a system that didn't acknowledge that the high-stakes testing of ESL students simply didn't make sense?

Questions

The Case

What has led to the students' poor performances on the district-mandated test?

History

Immigrants are generally held to the same standards as native-born Canadians in spite of the struggles they may have in learning a new language. In what ways do you think we have moved forward in this regard, and in what ways are we still stuck in the past?

Philosophy

Is it morally defensible to hold students who are struggling with English accountable to the same standards as native speakers of English? Why or why not?

Sociology

How might non-native speakers of English navigate and succeed in educational systems that do not provide sufficient ongoing support?

Implications for Practice

In your teaching, what will you do to adjust your instructional practices and testing procedures for students who are non-native speakers of English?

Teaching for Dummies

Don, Pete, and Aaron, three teachers at MacDonald High School, were sitting together in the staff room during a common afternoon prep time discussing the amount of marking they had left to do before report cards. Don was teaching a full roster of Math courses, Pete was teaching three options—German, Psychology, and Sociology—and Aaron was teaching three sections of Grade 12 English.

"You're lucky Pete. You don't even have to give exams, let alone mark them," said Aaron.

"What exactly is it that you do all day, anyway, Pete?" Don joked.

"We all make our choices, guys," replied Pete, "I wouldn't want to teach core subjects for that very reason. I subscribe to the idea that the students should be the ones doing the hard work, not me. How does it really help the kids if I lose sleep just to give one of them a 90 per cent and the other a 92 per cent when the difference in the marks is completely arbitrary?"

"English is the same," agreed Aaron. "You can give me a stack of rubrics as tall as I am, but when I mark the standards exams, I have to admit that I can't be completely objective."

"Well that's why *I* wouldn't want either of your jobs," said Don. "Give a kid a math test and tell 'em to show me their steps. When you mark it, it means something—the difference between the 90 per cent and the 92 per cent is real. It's easy to set standards and it just makes sense."

"Well, it may not be easy to set standards in English, but that doesn't mean that we shouldn't try," replied Aaron. "Of course, it would be a lot easier if all I had to do was teach and mark grammar, but in high school, students should be way beyond the basics. Math just happens to be a subject where students are still doing the basics in high school—most never see really advanced, high level math."

"You see, Pete, even the young pup agrees that standards and testing are necessary" said Don triumphantly.

"Oh, he's young, alright," said Pete. "He'll soon see how everything that goes around comes around. Right now we may be all about standards, but just wait, it won't take long before everyone's loosey-goosey like me again."

"I don't know about that," said Don. "It sure seems like *everything* is more standardized compared to 20 years ago. I remember teaching when curriculum documents were just outlines that were completely open to interpretation. Back then, teachers actually had to figure out for themselves what they were going to teach and how they were going to teach it."

"That still happens," said Aaron. "I do lots of my own lessons—I don't depend just on the Blackline masters from the curriculum documents."

"Oh, were we actually supposed to take the curriculum documents out of the shrink wrap?" laughed Pete. "Don, you are probably right that there is more standardization, but unlike you, I don't welcome it. I don't see it as necessarily a good thing. All of the foreign language curricula are starting to look uncannily the same."

"How so?" asked Aaron.

"Well, for starters," said Pete, "all the language curricula go through the topics in a similar order. We don't have a standards exam, thank goodness, but I can see that the curricula are written with testing in mind in case the Ministry ever decides to go that route. That would be such a terrible mistake! When you teach a language you have to take the particular learners into account. What works for one group of students doesn't necessarily work for another. Curriculum documents and standardized tests just don't capture that reality."

"Okay," said Don, "so how do you know whether your students are prepared for further study? Without provincial curriculum and tests, I have no way to judge whether my pre-calculus students are ready for university-level math."

"With most of our students on track for some kind of post-secondary education, we have to make preparation for university a priority," Aaron agreed. "But, speaking of common standards, before I came here, I was teaching Grade 8 Social Studies and I was sure glad I had a curriculum guide then!"

"Why is that?" asked Pete.

"The outcomes were clear, and I could see when a student was meeting them. It was good to have a guide so I knew what was important. I'm no expert on ancient peoples, so having the outcomes and activities all right there was like having a *Teaching for Dummies* book—I could just go through it day by day and not have to worry about what to teach or how to teach it."

"I can't believe what you just said," exclaimed Pete. "That's why I pick on you young guys—when I started out it was 'sink or swim.' If you couldn't teach a subject, you were sunk."

"Sure, but that only hurts the students," replied Aaron.

"But too much standardization hurts students even more," argued Pete.

"How do you figure that?" said Don skeptically.

"I think it runs the risk of degrading the whole profession. We didn't have to follow some bureaucrat's notion of what should be taught in the 'good old days.' Good teachers were expected to be knowledgeable, authentic, and creative," Pete declared.

"Are you saying that teachers can't be those things any more?" asked Aaron.

"No, it's not that black and white," Pete insisted. "It's just that the more directive and standardized the system gets, the less input we have as professionals and the less we are going to care about the quality of our teaching because it won't feel like *ours* anymore. Look guys, I feel lucky to teach electives because, unlike you, with your outcomes and exactly how you are supposed to reach them all laid out in front of you, I can still make professional decisions. I can't imagine how anyone in your shoes can find teaching rewarding and intellectually stimulating under those circumstances."

"Gee Pete, tell us what you *really* think," said Don sarcastically.

"I'm just saying that teachers ought to be able to do their own thing in spite of what's written in the Ministry documents. We're professionals, after all. We've earned our autonomy, right? The Ministry's job is to set guidelines, my job is to teach. Let me teach—if you want to tell me how it is supposed to be taught, come and teach my class for me!" said Pete.

A bell chimed over the intercom, indicating that that the last period of the day was beginning. "To be continued," said Don.

As the three teachers left the staff room, Aaron and Pete headed for the stairs to the second floor. "What you were just saying is really interesting, Pete," said Aaron. "I've never really thought of standards that way before."

"Well maybe that's a good thing," replied Pete. "At this stage of your career, you don't need to become jaded and cynical like me—I am probably just feeling my age."

"I don't think so. I mean, I love teaching English, but if I didn't have the standards exams to teach towards, I don't know what I would plan or how I would measure the students' success in a meaningful way," admitted Aaron.

"Give it some time—you'll just know intuitively," reassured Pete. "And if you don't, you can always teach Math," he added jokingly.

As Aaron walked the rest of the way to his classroom he thought about what his students were doing in his class in a new light. They were writing a literary essay and were expected to find an example of subtext in a short story. As usual, some students would already be finished and others would be lucky to hand the assignment in at all. Yet he knew that he would have to translate the students' work into a percentage mark that was as fair and meaningful as possible. Now, as he replayed the conversation with Pete, he had to admit that the only reason he was having his students do *this* assignment was so that they would be better prepared to write the standards test. As he entered his classroom, he wondered if that exam had become his own copy of *Teaching for Dummies*.

Questions

The Case

In this case, there is a heated debate on standardization in the teaching profession. What arguments are made for and against standardization?

History

As this case suggests, we are now living in an era of increased standardization at all levels in education. What do you think has contributed to this trend?

Philosophy

What does it mean to be an "authentic" teacher?

Sociology

Sometimes, experienced teachers, like Don, become cynical and may even become alienated from the teaching profession. What are some likely causes of alienation? What can teachers do to avoid becoming cynical?

Implications for Practice

How will you balance your personal approach to teaching with the requirement to follow mandated curriculum and standardized assessment practices?

Corporate Takeover

"And . . .," said George Papadopoulos, holding the word for emphasis, "here is your new Physical Education Centre."

As he opened the door with a flourish to show the recently refurbished gymnasium, dotted with shiny new equipment on the floor, George flashed a toothy grin as the crowd tentatively entered the room. The renovations to the gym were all the more amazing because just two years earlier, when he arrived as the new principal of East End Collegiate, all that EEC was known for was poor test performances and run-down facilities. In that short time, the newcomer had managed to keep funds pouring in. Now, to showcase the innovations he had spearheaded,

George led the Parent Council and interested teachers on a tour of the renovations. No stranger to public relations, he had also invited a local television crew.

"I wonder where all the money is coming from?" whispered Arden to a small group of her colleagues, out of earshot.

"Maybe he's knocking over banks," chuckled Jacques. "I've worked on enough of our fundraisers to know that we shouldn't be able to afford a set of dumbbells, let alone equipment of that quality."

"Looks like a scam," mused Janice as she folded her arms skeptically.

"Jaundiced Janice. That's you," chimed in Coach Menard, repeating a well-worn nickname. "You've been nitpicking about every change he's made." He leaned towards her. "Remember what things used to be like? Other schools were always getting the cream while EEC waited for the leftovers . . ."

"I know what you are saying, Andy," said Janice, cutting him off, "but something's just not sitting right with me."

"Well, there's nothing wrong from where I sit. You know where that is? On a big pile of new sports equipment! Hey, I know Papadopoulos isn't the straightest arrow, but he wasn't hired to be a Boy Scout. I'm sure you'll get your share of the goodies, too. Just give him some time."

"I teach Social Studies, remember?" replied Janice. "Let's just say that I won't hold my breath."

The principal's voice boomed from the microphone. "And now, Coach Menard, would you kindly step up and give our guests a tour of the miracle before us?"

Andy wondered why he was now in the spotlight, but he quickly understood when he saw George hang back to give an interview to the local news channel. The coach dutifully led the crowd around the refurbished gym floor, pausing to describe the various pieces of new equipment along the way. However, because they had been rushed in overnight, an itemized list was all he had for guidance. As they reached the end of the excursion, Andy smiled when he spotted the large box marked "FOOTBALL EQUIPMENT." He eagerly reached in to pull out one of the new team outfits. Expecting to see the team name and traditional crimson and grey colours, the coach dropped the yellow and pink jersey he had drawn out as if it were on fire. Emblazoned on the shirt lying in front of him were garish capital letters: JRKN ADDIKTZ.

"What on earth is this?" he yelped.

George, who heard the shout from across the room, dashed up beside Andy and without missing a beat, held the fallen jersey up to the crowd.

"Isn't this a hoot? It's the latest craze called 'Jerkin.' It's hip. And Jerkin' style is here and happenin'—It sure beats those dark saggy, baggy pants that all the kids are currently wearing. Won't it be great to get rid of that 'gangsta' and 'clothes pegs through the nose' look?" This brought a chuckle from the group as he continued, "And the new edge is bright coloured clothing, novelty graphic tees, and those Chuck Taylor All-Star shoes that we all remember." He pulled one from another box.

"Hey, I had a pair of those when I went to school!" shouted a parent.

"I think what we're seeing here is a return to traditional fashion—and values. I just want us to be on the cutting edge, and that's why 'Jerkin' is such a good fit for EEC."

"What about the Cougars? What happened to our team name?" blurted out Andy.

"Let's just say that we've *evolved* the name to one that's more relevant to students."

"But I've got to send my players out on the field with these things," spluttered Coach Menard. "They'll be known as Jerking Addicts for God's sake! In pink and yellow! They'll be laughed off the field!"

"No they won't, now they'll dominate the field as the cool kids. They got 'da killa swag,' now."

"The what?"

"Get with the program, Andy."

As they argued, Janice quietly searched the recesses of her mind. Something was very familiar. Then it struck her—the colours, the name, the jargon.

"Uh, excuse me, Mr Papadopoulos . . . isn't JRKN that big multinational clothing line? Don't they have a store down at the mall?"

"Thanks for giving me the proper segue, Janice." George turned to the parents and signalled the cameras in his direction. "Ladies and gentlemen, I am proud to announce the rebirth of your gymnasium as the new JRKN Centre." Surprisingly, the parents seemed impressed, but the teachers became very silent. "Next week," he continued, "the entire gymnasium is getting a new paint job. It will get a total make-over . . ."

Janice clicked her tongue and finished his sentence, ". . . in JRKN colours, of course—pink and yellow, right?"

"What a great idea, Janice," George smiled sweetly, "That would be a fitting gesture of thanks for the largest donor EEC has ever seen—the company that made all of these wonderful changes possible. And now, please follow me into the media room. I have a great video outlining the help that our sponsors are giving and what they stand for."

Gone for what seemed like a mere second, George grimaced as he turned back to face the belligerent teachers. "Hey, what did you want me to do? These guys guarantee a steady flow of money—and what do we sacrifice, really, for a little company visibility? What's the difference between that and Apple computers, or even Papermate pens? And we don't even have to pay for *this*."

Janice folded her arms, "But don't you think people will have a problem with this 'deal' when they find out that there's a new JRKN store in the mall?"

"Listen," George said, dropping his smile, "look around—we aren't exactly in the richest neighbourhood. This sponsorship is considered a blessing by most of these parents—see how they ate it up? The kids'll be the same. The new facilities will keep them off the street, and in case you haven't noticed, the streets aren't as friendly as you might remember them."

"But, you really know why JRKN is giving us money—it's the thin end edge of the wedge. I can't believe you got this scam past the school board."

"That's because you don't pay attention," George hissed. "Who do you think is pushing me to do this? According to new fundraising policies, private donors who want to 'invest in education' are now being encouraged to fund capital projects."

"Which are ...?"

"Just about anything that isn't nailed down. And with that comes certain incentives."

"Ah, like naming rights and paint colours?" Jacques smiled grimly.

"And, no doubt, coming soon—logos in the classrooms!" Janice finished the statement. The famous Papadopoulos grin returned. "Not yet, but I'm working on it. Hey, we can't do fundraisers like rich schools. Those things are just hidden user fees, anyway! I think advertising is the great equalizer."

"That way everyone gets brainwashed at the same rate, right?" Janice sneered.

"Man, you are a cynic, aren't you, Janice. Your nickname is certainly well-deserved. You'll be surprised how quickly you will stop noticing the changes."

"Kind of like subliminal advertising." Janice tilted her head in mock coyness. "Teaching kids to be good consumers rather than good citizens. I get it."

"Hey, I'm just doing my best to keep the public education system afloat. Heaven knows the funding formula and chocolate bar sales aren't helping, so I'll just hitch my wagon to this star for as long as I can. In the meantime, just everyone take a pause for the cause—you're branded now." On this note he strode back to the parents and cameras with a smile plastered on his face.

Janice looked around the room and plaintively murmured to herself, "And it only cost us our souls."

Questions

The Case

How does George Papadopoulos justify the actions he took to keep his school well-resourced?

History

Over time, there has been an increase in commercialization in education. Why do you think corporations are increasingly targeting schools to sell their products?

Philosophy

In this case, who is more open-minded, George or Janice? Why do you think so?

Sociology

East End Collegiate is located in an impoverished neighbourhood where traditional fundraising has yielded disappointing results. Is corporate sponsorship more justifiable where other sources of funding are not available? Explain.

Implications for Practice

What would you do if you were a teacher at a school like EEC and you were expected to embrace the kind of corporate sponsorship depicted in this case?

Over the Rainbow

"Do you have a minute, Miss Dykstra?" asked her colleague Jeff Penner as they nearly collided in the busy hall of Camstock Elementary School.

"Sure, come into my classroom. My kids are in the gym this period," replied Mona.

As they entered the classroom, Jeff glanced around the room and saw that Mona's students had finally completed their unit on Egypt; he was looking forward to bringing his Grade 5 class to tour the Grade 4 museum later in the week. He knew his Grade 5 class would enjoy looking at all of the artifacts the students had created, but none of this was on Jeff's mind as the colleagues sat down to talk.

"Mona, it looks as if we are both on the hot seat!" Jeff began.

"What did we do this time?" laughed Mona.

"You won't be laughing when you hear what happened at the school board meeting last night! Principal Morgenstern was at the meeting, too, and it turns out that Mrs Toews and her friends took over the entire meeting. They were complaining about those training certificates we got at the provincial institute on diversity that we attended a few weeks ago. They were upset that we posted those Rainbow Cards with the Ally Pledge in our classrooms. It turns out that Artie Toews went home Monday and repeated the conversation I had with him when he asked about the card. He wanted to know what 'bisexual' and 'transgender' meant, and I told him. Mrs Toews argued that the cards are too sensitive to be put up in elementary classrooms and she demanded that the cards be removed immediately. Then John Wilder got up and said that the pledge gives students the wrong message and that as teachers, we have stepped over the line."

"But all the pledge says is that our classrooms are safe for LGBTTQ youth. How can that be such a problem?" wondered Mona, shaking her head in disbelief.

"Well, apparently the superintendent took a lot of heat from parents who think that terms like lesbian, gay, bisexual, and transgender aren't age-appropriate. They said that these words raise questions and these kids are not mature enough to handle the answers. They argued that provincial guidelines state that the primary responsibility for sex education rests with parents and not the schools. Mostly, they felt that the pledge goes way too far, especially the part that says, 'As an ally, I envision a society that embraces, values, and celebrates diverse sexual orientations, gender identities, and gender expressions.'"

"It seems that it's the word 'celebrates' that really sticks in their craws. It's interesting because Morgenstern said that although they didn't bring religion into it, all of these parents happen to belong to the same religious group. You know the one, the group that has been lobbying to infuse Bible studies into the curriculum? They have been complaining that if we don't agree to their demands, we'll lose even more parents to the private Christian schools in the area."

Mona and Jeff were among the majority of teachers who commuted to the farming town of Camstock from a nearby urban centre. Neither was involved with the town's religious institutions, nor were they much influenced by the religious leaders, who could be very outspoken at times about the 'godlessness' of the Camstock public schools. Mona suddenly thought about what the card would look like to the local church pastors.

She admitted regretfully, "I really didn't think about that group of parents when I posted my card, did you?"

"To be honest, not really," sighed Jeff. "But then, we know that parents can choose to have their children opt out of sensitive issues in the Family Life curriculum, and since Artie's parents weren't among the families that had opted out, I didn't give it much thought until he started to ask me about the card."

"So, what did the superintendent have to say?" asked Mona.

"In the end," Jeff went on, "he said that teachers would be told to remove the pledge from the cards and just leave the icon of the rainbow and the word Ally on the top."

"So, parents now get to decide what we put up in our classrooms, do they?" asked Mona self-righteously. "What's next, bulletin board police?"

"Well, you're probably not that far off. The parents are pressuring the superintendent and the board to let them form an advisory committee to review sensitive material before it is presented to students. So far, they haven't agreed, but just stay tuned."

"You're right, this is far from over," agreed Mona. "I guess I'd better get out my scissors."

Jeff left, feeling perplexed about this latest turn of events. At the workshop he and Mona had attended, they had been so moved by the heart-rending student presentations that they really hadn't thought about possible repercussions if they posted their training certificates and pledges in their classrooms. The presenters had asked all of the participants to make their classrooms safer for students with diverse sexual orientations.

Mona and Jeff felt that by posting the pledges they were doing their part to show their support to these often marginalized and misunderstood students. Neither teacher had gone any further than that. They didn't explain what the cards meant to the whole class, and they didn't make a point of explaining what each word on the card meant. They thought that if a student read the card and wanted to talk about what it said, they would take the opportunity at that time to engage in a one-to-one conversation and that is precisely what had happened. Artie had asked Jeff about the words, and now, rather than making their classrooms safer for students, it seemed that it was less safe for the teachers. It didn't take long for the issue to capture the imagination of the media, which alternately portrayed the issue as a tug of war between the rights of parents and schools or further proof that society was intolerant of diverse sexual orientations. It seemed as though everyone had a different opinion.

A week after the school board meeting, the superintendent met with all of the school principals in the district. He told them that the board had decided that no parent advisory committee would be struck. Instead, the district's Inclusive Education Priority Committee, made up of administrators, would be asked to develop a procedures manual on child safety, teacher training, the posting of certificates, and protocols for children who came forward to talk about their sexual orientation or gender identity. Teachers across the district were relieved to hear that they would not have to ask a parent committee for permission for everything that went up on their walls. In the meantime, the superintendent sent out a memo stating that all training certificates were to be removed and that the Rainbow Card was to be replaced with a card, which was to be displayed in all of the Kindergarten to Grade 6 classrooms, saying, "As your teacher, I am your ally. I accept and support you in every way."

Mona doubted whether the new card would mean very much at all to students or would encourage them to come forward to talk to their teachers if they had questions or concerns about sexual orientation. However, she was confident that she would find other ways to be an ally of LGBTTQ children without displaying a card about it. As she took down the card, she wondered whether she and Jeff had responded too impulsively to what was obviously a serious concern for parents in this tight rural community.

Questions

The Case

How did the controversy over the Ally Pledges come to light, and how was it handled by the board and the media?

History

Over the past few decades, school districts have become more inclusive in acknowledging and supporting students from diverse gender orientations. What has happened in society that has contributed to this change?

Philosophy

In your judgment, were the parents of this community legitimately involved in the affairs of the school? Justify your answer.

Sociology

LGBTTQ students are often marginalized in schools. How might teachers better meet the needs of such students?

Implications for Practice

What would *you* do if you were asked to remove the Rainbow Card and Ally Pledge from *your* classroom? Why would you choose to do that?

CHAPTER FOUR

Moral Panics

Introduction

In the previous two chapters, we focused on myths and bandwagons and their effects on education. In this chapter, we shift our attention to the most volatile barrier to critical thinking—moral panics. We discuss what moral panics are, which moral panics pervade education, and how the foundations disciplines can help us to recognize moral panics and deal with the sense of urgency and alarm evoked by them. The moral panics highlighted in this chapter are illustrated by 10 cases that were either reported in the media or inspired by personal experiences. Each is followed by five questions: one asks the reader to answer a question about the facts, three consider historical, philosophical, and sociological perspectives, and finally, one asks how the case can be applied to the reader's own teaching.

What are moral panics?

Moral panics refer to the exaggerated fears and outrage aroused by apparent threats to the moral fabric or stability of society. These fears are given credibility by the claims of moral crusaders or moral entrepreneurs whose assertions are amplified by the media through repetition and sensationalist reporting. Moral panics may be promoted by groups with vested interests or even orchestrated by governments or elite groups (Goode & Ben-Yehuda, 1994). Often, public opinion is inflamed to such a degree that those in power are roused to make moral pronouncements or enact legal or social policies to contain or limit the alleged damage. The institutions, regulations, or laws created to solve the problem may persist long after the moral panic has slipped from public consciousness. In many cases, "the moral campaign leaves the real causes . . . unaddressed" (K. Thompson, 1998, p. 3).

The term "moral panic" gained currency early in the 1970s with Jock Young's (1971) study of the interaction of media, public opinion, interest groups, and authorities on the prevalence of drug abuse and with Stanley Cohen's (1972) highly influential book *Folk Devils and Moral Panics*. These two publications provided a theoretical framework for the study of media and furthered our understanding of the nature and dynamics of moral panics. Specifically, Cohen investigated the intense overreaction that ensued as a result of seaside clashes between British teen groups—the Mods and the Rockers. Most notably, he explained how moral crusaders fuel moral panics and how groups or ideas become stigmatized as folk devils that personify evil and are therefore safe to "demonize and despise" (Lukianoff, 2013).

Folk devils, who reside at the centre of moral panics, may be constructed as either deviant groups of people or immoral ideas. However, the scope of what we consider to be folk devils has changed. Earlier moral panics targeted single groups or ideas, such as witches in nineteenth-century New England, teenagers who frequented coffee bars in the 1950s, bra-burning feminists in the 1960s, Black muggers in the 1970s, missing children in the 1980s, pedophiles in the 1990s, and video games in the 2000s. More recent campaigns focus on whole populations, such as youth, males, or females; entire institutions, such as the family or the CIA (K. Thompson, 1998); or conditions that threaten human extinction, such as global terrorism, superbugs, or global warming (Furedi, 2011).

Since the 1970s, the term "moral panic" has been widely used (some would say, overused) in discourses about a number of contentious issues, particularly those that involve power, sexuality, morality, youth culture, technology, media, and politics. Kenneth Thompson (1998) argues, "It is widely acknowledged that this is the age of the moral panic. Newspaper headlines continually warn of some new danger resulting from moral laxity, and television programmes echo the theme with sensational documentaries" (p. 2). Indeed, just as Chicken Little's hysterical warnings that the "Sky is falling!" or the little boy's repeated cries of "Wolf!" were eventually ignored, the increasing tendency to label worrisome issues as moral panics means that even genuine concerns may eventually be regarded as irrational or not genuine (K. Thompson, 1998, p. 10). The fact that knee-jerk responses to moral panics often miss the mark and result in legislation and long-lasting changes to social arrangements suggests that "moral panics are therefore neither marginal nor trivial in their effects" (Ben-Yehuda, 2009, p. 3). Herdt (2009) goes even further: "Moral panics in their awful sweep do material damage, undermine careers, incite riots, and kill people" (p. 17).

Caught up as we are in one moral panic after another, we may have difficulty distinguishing between those issues or phenomena that merit legitimate attention and those that have been blown out of proportion and should not be taken as seriously. Unfortunately, we may not always realize what is fuelling a moral panic, as Cohen (2002) points out:

> Moral panics are condensed political struggles to control the means of cultural reproduction. Studying them . . . allows us to identify and conceptualize the lines of power in any society, the ways we are manipulated into taking some things too seriously and other things not seriously enough. (p. xxxv)

One way to distinguish moral panics from other urgent concerns is to use the five characteristics identified by Goode and Ben-Yehuda (1994) as criteria—concern, hostility, consensus, disproportionality, and volatility.

First, moral panics are grounded in existing widespread and heightened concerns about specific groups or ideas that are characterized as fundamental threats to society (i.e., folk devils). Such concerns are manifested concretely in such forms as proposed legislation, opinion polls, media attention, action groups, and social movements. Second, as hostility increases, distinctions between folk devils on the one hand and folk heroes on the other become very clear (Cohen, 1972). Third, a minimum consensus about the seriousness and genuineness of threats is necessary to launch moral panics although this does not necessarily mean that the majority of people are gripped by them or that the public definition of these concerns is uncontested (Goode & Ben-Yehuda, 1994). Fourth, disproportionality is evident through the exaggerated or even fabricated statistics that tend to accompany moral panics, the singling out of social problems as being exceptionally threatening when they are no worse than others, and the decrying of conditions as being severe threats when they are no worse at this time than at other times (Goode & Ben-Yehuda, 2009). Finally, volatility is evident because "the fever pitch that characterizes a society or segments of it during the course of the moral panic is not sustainable over a long stretch of time" (Goode & Ben-Yehuda, 1994, p. 158), thus ensuring that moral panics are destined to be temporary phenomena.

Although the term "panic" suggests "being out of control," Herdt (2009, p. 5) reminds us that "panics have a social shape" and that some are even orchestrated. Like bandwagons, moral panics appear, disappear, and reappear in different guises, but they nevertheless follow a predictable path. We think that the "**issue attention cycle**" developed by Downs (1972) captures the volatility of moral panics very well. This cycle, which illustrates how public interest fluctuates in successive social crises, consists of the following five stages: 1) pre-problem stage, 2) alarmed discovery and euphoric enthusiasm, 3) realization of the cost of significant progress, 4) gradual decline in intense public interest, and 5) post-problem stage (Downs, 1972).

In the pre-problem stage, moral crusaders and experts are alarmed, but the public is either unaware or not expressly concerned about the issue or situation. It is important to note that the moral panic may not target the apparent threat directly but may focus attention on a symbol of it. For example, heightened anxieties about levels of literacy may be a proxy for fears about competition for employment from immigrants and those willing to do the same work in their own country for lower wages. Similarly, Green and Hodgens (1996) argue that the overheated concern about grammar in the history of English teaching is actually a code for "a tight nexus of 'literacy, grammar and power' that sets up discourse in literacy debates of 'us' in relation to 'them,' of 'our proficiency' in relation to 'their deficiency'" (p. 211).

In the second stage, the public becomes suddenly aware of a worrisome problem or situation and although this causes alarm, there is a sense, at least among some, that an easy solution is readily available if only legislation is passed or appropriate action is taken. The media, experts, opinion makers, and moral entrepreneurs weigh in, influencing public opinion, organizations, and politicians and, often, they escalate the rhetoric by casting the particular event or crisis as only the "tip of the iceberg" of an even greater social menace. While the moral panic is being amplified, the public is often treated to a barrage of emotional images and frightening statistics which depict folk devils as representing everything that is wrong with modern society. The public is exhorted to return to the past when people conformed to a common morality. As Gannon and Sawyer (2007) point out, however, a simpler, more moral past society does not need to have actually existed for people to be swayed by this nostalgic narrative.

Once the threat has been constructed and the folk devils have been identified, attention turns to action, including fundraising, volunteering, enacting laws, and making promises directed at correcting the errors of the folk devils. It is at this point that certain groups begin to question the financial and human costs of dealing with the moral panic effectively and some may even begin to realize that a universally acceptable solution does not actually exist. It becomes clearer which specific groups are most likely to benefit from the proposed solution and why power brokers resist any changes and try to maintain the status quo.

In the fourth stage, the sense of urgency subsides because while some may become discouraged, many others simply become bored. Often, attention is shifted away from the issue at hand by the emergence of yet another moral panic. Finally, in the post-problem stage, moral panics move into a prolonged limbo in which little attention is paid to them unless random events or deliberate efforts by moral entrepreneurs revive them.

Legitimate concerns and moral panics may appear to be the same when a serious or tragic event, such as a school shooting, occurs. However, as issues expand and become overheated, it may become evident that the whole story is not being told, that there may be a particular agenda driving media and community outrage, or that suggested solutions or reforms may not really address the underlying issues. Since youth are perceived as a vulnerable sector of society, schools are often fertile grounds for moral panics and must try to deal with the consequences of hasty and far-reaching legislation and policies that may ultimately make matters worse.

What moral panics pervade education?

Moral panics may emanate from inside or outside of schools. Beyond the school walls, existing concerns about economic and global stability can devolve into moral panics about what happens in schools. For example, yearly reports of the results of international tests (such as the Programme for International Student Assessment) and, in some parts of Canada, province-wide tests often fan the flames of existing fears that our graduates are not sufficiently prepared to compete for jobs with skilled workers from other parts of the world. Within schools, the kinds of educational bandwagons which were discussed in the previous chapter may trigger moral panics. For example, attempts to create a more even academic playing field for girls have resulted in the current "boy crisis" in education. Similarly, the push to integrate technology into all aspects of school life has spawned moral panics both when progress seems too slow and when it appears to be too fast. The introduction of each new technology, such as filmstrips, calculators, television, interactive whiteboards, or cell phones, is viewed with suspicion, and often excessive concern is expressed that students' morals will be compromised if they have too ready access to such learning aids.

Like myths and bandwagons, moral panics permeate the four commonplaces of education—students, teachers, content, and context—but as in the previous chapters, we will focus only on those which are illustrated in the cases in this chapter, that is, students, teachers, and context. As in the previous two chapters, each case is followed by five questions that are organized to help you consider the facts of the case; its historical, philosophical, and sociological implications; and how the case may apply to your own practice.

Students

Diversity

Classrooms increasingly include a wide range of students who differ in race, ethnicity, socio-economic status, sexual orientation, physical maturity, and many other ways. As we discussed in Chapter 2, myths of normalcy and multiculturalism represent pervasive beliefs about what these differences mean and how schools should best address them. In Chapter 3, we examined the kinds of educational bandwagons that result from beliefs about student differences, such as mandated inclusion and single-sex classrooms. Occasionally, students' differences become the locus of moral panics because certain groups or ideas are seen as challenges to society's fundamental beliefs or preconceptions of what is, in fact, *normal*.

Historically, marginalized groups, such as recent immigrants, have been the targets of moral panics. Latent suspicion and anxiety about strangers and outsiders, never far below the surface, may be easily aroused by the media and moral crusaders when new groups arrive and begin to assert their independence (Kostogriz, 2006). In the late nineteenth century, all Asian immigrants were pejoratively labelled the "yellow peril." This racial slur became a rallying cry for those who feared that a wave of immigration from the East would threaten White wages and living standards and would eventually take over and destroy the way of life and values of Western civilization. Successive groups, most recently Blacks and Muslims, have suffered from similar negative profiling.

The fear of strangers, which is fundamental to forging national identity, involves two strategies—assimilation and exclusion. According to Kostogritz (2006), "Both strategies are central to the process of nation-building described by Anderson (1991) as 'imagining' sameness by homogenizing differences and expelling strangers beyond the borders of managed and manageable territory" (pp. 3–4).

A recent example of how a provincial government positioned itself between the strategies of assimilation and exclusion was the tabling of the controversial Charter of Quebec Values. This charter would have, among other things, prohibited public employees, including teachers, daycare workers, and university professors, from wearing religious headwear. Although this did not come to pass owing to a change of government, the mere suggestion of such legislation sent a strong message to ethnic and racial minorities that boundaries were being drawn between what is considered to be acceptable or unacceptable within the public sphere.

Schools also use the strategies of assimilation and exclusion to homogenize differences. Assimilation takes the form of policies and codes of behaviour that limit expressions of cultural diversity and, in the upper grades at least, exclusion occurs in the form of tracking or ability grouping that is designed to weed out low-performing students. Critics argue that tracking conflates ethnicity and race with academic ability and condemns low-performing students to low expectations and impoverished learning experiences that focus on remediation rather than substance. Despite the chorus of demands from professionals and parents that tracking or ability grouping should be reduced or abolished, researchers have consistently found that homogeneous ability grouping increases as students move through school (McEwin, 2003; Valentine, 2002).

In "A Place to Belong?" Black students in an ethnically diverse public school threaten to move en masse to a separate school to avoid the effects of assimilation and exclusion. As you read this case, consider how public schools can better accommodate the needs of *all* students and whether separate schools are more likely to resolve or exacerbate feelings of isolation among ethnic and racial minority groups from Canadian society.

Bullying

There has likely never been a time when peer aggression was *not* a part of human interaction, but until relatively recently, bullying was simply discounted as a natural part of growing up. However, after 30 years of research about the long-term harmful effects of bullying and after such shocking events as high-profile school shootings, teenage suicides, and the murder of Reena Virk in Victoria, bullying is no longer being summarily dismissed. On the contrary, media attention and the alarms set off by moral crusaders about the dangers of bullying have created a moral panic. Blumen (2010), for example, who claims that bullying is an "epidemic," argues that it is symptomatic of a wider societal problem of incivility and increased immorality.

Contrary to popular beliefs, studies by Pellegrini (2002), Porter (2013), and Smith (2004) show that bullying is not actually increasing; in fact, as Bazelon (2013) suggests, our impression that bullying has become an epidemic is related to how we define bullying in the first place: "The word is being overused—expanding, accordion-like, to encompass both appalling violence and harassment and a few mean words" (para. 3).

Part of the difficulty in determining the prevalence of bullying is the failure to distinguish between the circumstances that surround bullying from those that occur during rough and tumble play or when the high emotions aroused by sports and games spin out of control. Olweus (1993) makes a clear distinction between bullying and conflict between two students of approximately the same physical or psychological strength. He stresses that in order to use the term "bullying," there should be an asymmetric power relationship in which one has difficulty defending oneself and is somewhat helpless against the harassment.

In an effort to clarify what bullying is and what it is not, variations of the following definition by Nansel et al. (2001) have been widely adopted:

> Bullying is a specific type of aggression in which (1) the behavior is intended to harm or disturb, (2) the behavior occurs repeatedly over time, and (3) there is an imbalance of power, with a more powerful person or group attacking a less powerful one. This asymmetry of power may be physical or psychological, and the aggressive behavior may be ver-

> bal (e.g., name-calling, threats), physical (e.g., hitting), or psychological (e.g., rumors, shunning/exclusion). (p. 2094)

Nevertheless, as Smith (2004) points out, "All definitions are fuzzy" (p. 98). He questions whether "intended" adequately distinguishes between those who set out to hurt and those who are aggressive without understanding the consequences. He wonders whether "repeatedly" captures the number of times or the duration over time and whether it is the victim's subjective perception of harm and imbalance of power or some objective assessment of the strength and number of the bullies involved that should count. **Cyberbullying**, the latest incarnation of ongoing peer aggression, further challenges our ability to define bullying, since perpetrators can remain anonymous and may never be identified. Furthermore, the criteria of "repeatedly over time" takes on new meaning when an on-line message remains visible, is almost impossible to remove or ignore, and has the potential to be broadcast and re-broadcast.

The problem of defining bullying is further complicated by the language teenagers use to describe interpersonal conflict and how they perceive power relationships. Teitel (2011) argues that

> In classic teenager style, ironically and maybe even more insidiously, they call it "drama." Why drama? "The emic use of 'drama,'" wrote Boyd [sic] and Marwick, "allows teens to distance themselves from practices which adults may conceptualize as bullying. As such, they can retain agency—and save face—rather than positioning themselves in a victim narrative." (para. 3)

In other words, if teenagers themselves do not frame situations as examples of bullying, it is even more difficult for adults to intervene when necessary.

In the case "A Stitch in Time," a parent who is upset when his child is hurt considers that his son is the victim of bullying. As you read this case, however, think about whether this is an accurate assessment and consider how peer aggression takes place differently in face-to-face and on-line interactions among males, females, adults, teenagers, and students with special needs.

Teachers

Technology: Social media, cell phones, and violent video games

The myth of digital natives and digital immigrants discussed in Chapter 2 is constructed as a moral panic when the assumption of an unbridgeable **digital divide** between teachers and students is accepted as real and is amplified by worrisome examples of criminal activities (Bennett, Maton, & Kervin, 2008). The notion that young people have greater technological expertise than adults challenges accepted norms of authority and upends traditional values (Bennett & Maton, 2011). However, according to Thurlow (2007, p. 219), at the same time as youth are being cast as folk devils, they are also being portrayed as "arch-consumers or tragic victims of technology" in need of protection. To capture the prevalence of moral panics involving technology and youth, Marwick (2008, p. 5) coined the word "**technopanics**." She characterizes these as efforts to pathologize young people's use of computer-mediated technologies by over-emphasizing the prevalence of hacking, indiscriminate file-sharing, and obsessive playing of violent video games. Technopanics are attempts to modify or regulate young people's behaviour, either by controlling their access to certain technologies or restricting the freedom of the creators or producers of media products.

Wartella and Jennings (2000) point out that exaggerated concerns about the effect of technology on youth are not new. In the 1920s the fear was about movies, in the 1930s about radio, in the 1940s about comic books, and in the 1950s about rock 'n' roll and television:

> With the introduction of each new wave of innovation in mass media throughout the twentieth century—film, radio, television—debates on the effects of new technology have recurred, especially with regard to the effect on young people. Each new media technology brought with it great promise for social and educational benefits, and great concern for children's exposure to inappropriate and harmful content. (p. 31)

Lynn (2010) argues that these fears have led to "a perpetual state of moral panic regarding the impact of technologies on the development of youths since the early twentieth century" (p. 4).

Technopanics may have far-reaching consequences, including legislation and local policies aimed at restricting access to a broad range of available technologies (Marwick, 2008). Losh and Jenkins (2012) argue that, paradoxically, erecting barriers to limit children's access to technology at school simply means that students are left to navigate uncharted waters at home without a knowledgeable guide. Consequently, they miss the opportunity to learn responsible use, develop social capital with like-minded people, and acquire valuable skills for future employment.

Three of the cases in this chapter illustrate different technopanics. "Brave New World?" explores moral panics around **social media**. "On-line or Off-base?" considers fears about whether cell phones should be allowed in the classroom, and "Bang! Bang! You're Dead!" addresses the moral panic about violence in the media. As you read these cases, think about whether concerns about new media are justified and whether legal restrictions and school policies are necessary or counterproductive.

Professional identity

The **professional identities** of teachers are informed by a long and complex history, rooted in the gender and normalcy myths we discussed in Chapter 2. As a highly gendered profession, teaching is the site of recurrent moral panics because of the widespread belief that children must be shielded from all evidence of sexuality. Cavanagh (2005) points out that this fear of sexuality was a factor in the professional identities of teachers from the earliest days of public schools:

> Women teachers commonly faced marriage bans in North America before the 1950s. The influence of organized religion, the belief that husbands adequately supported married women, and widespread agreement that women *only* worked in the short-term—all these help explain why the female teacher was expected to remain single and chaste. (p. 247)

Women who wanted a life-long career in teaching or who did not marry were widely viewed as unfeminine "spinsters." Such women were financially independent and better educated than other women (and many men) and often lived with other women. Concerns about the "queerness" of such living arrangements flared up into a "sex panic," which irrevocably cast the "lifelong, single female teacher as latent homosexual, as 'mannish' woman, as emotionally maladjusted and as social deviant in a period inhospitable to variegated gender and sexual identifications" (Cavanagh, 2005, p. 273). By the 1950s, changing ideas about what role models were suitable for children, acceptance of female employment in the public sphere, and post-war efforts to support family life meant that communities no longer demanded that female teachers be celibate and unmarried. It would be decades later, however, before women were allowed to remain in the classroom while pregnant.

Professional identity is most visibly inscribed in the clothes that teachers wear. As Abbott and Sapsford (2001) point out, "The ways in which bodies are fashioned through clothes, make-up and demeanour constitute identity, sexuality and social position" (p. 28). Atkinson (2008) takes up this theme and identifies various styles of dress, including "teacher gear" (for example, denim jumpers, sweaters, socks, or ties with school symbols like buses and ABCs or seasonal decorations), shapeless track suits, and bland, tailored "uniforms" which serve as markers of teacher identity while managing to neutralize sexuality:

> The teacher's physical body, especially if it is female, must be "erased" to privilege the body of knowledge she is supposed to transmit (hooks, 1994), because the sexual knowledge ascribed to the feminine body is distracting to the male gaze dominating social institutions. For women teachers particularly, "the erotic potential" (Richardson 1985, 15–16) of their sexualized bodies distracts from the academic and assumed moral purposes of schooling, and so must not be present in the classroom. (p. 112)

Although what is considered sexualized clothing differs by local normative expectations, there is broad consensus that it is unprofessional for male or female teachers to show themselves as sexual beings. Beyond concerns about their professionalism, Cavanagh (2004) argues that sexualized teachers, especially females, face the additional risk of being cast as predators:

> Although male teachers in the Canadian context are far more likely to have committed acts of gross indecency involving minors, it is female teachers who are more likely to be subject to highly sensational and personally invasive media coverage. The mechanisms through which female sexual predators are constructed as femme fatale-like figures [are] of paramount significance to the female school sex scandal cases. (p. 316)

It is perhaps not surprising that the prevalence of sexual abuse by female teachers has been highly exaggerated considering that sex panics have "an entertainment value . . . and voyeur or curiosity capital that 'sells' or markets products, whether newspapers or books, television products, souvenirs, and kitsch memorabilia" (Herdt, 2009, p. 15). Unfortunately, this type of sensationalism disregards the needs of victims and fails to take into account the role of the media in devastating the lives of those who are falsely accused (Bradley, 2011).

In this chapter, two cases, "A Lapse of Judgment" and "A Cougar in the Schoolhouse," illustrate the tensions that arise when the professional identities of female teachers are perceived to be sexualized. As you read these two cases, think about how social norms and expectations shape teachers' professional identities and how they behave in the public sphere.

Context

Youth and youth culture

Moral panics about youth and **youth culture** have continued to erupt with regularity since Cohen (1972) wrote about the Mods and Rockers in England over

50 years ago and Willis (1977) wrote *Learning to Labour*, which was based on his study of the relationship between schools and working-class youth in industrial regions of England. Exaggerated fears about youth and youth cultures are rooted in the kinds of unexamined assumptions that we explored as myths in Chapter 2, and they find expression in the bandwagons we examined in Chapter 3. Our responses to youth and youth culture reveal both our fears for the safety of this highly vulnerable group and our concerns about the safety of others *from* this group (Krinsky, 2008; Lynn, 2010; Wartella & Jennings, 2000). Furthermore, as Lynn (2010) points out, these ambivalent feelings are all too often compounded with racism:

> Moral panic literature has demonstrated that moral panics of youth reflect the dual constructions of youths as potential victims and potential perpetrators: Panics involving white, middle-class youths are likely to be framed as nefarious external threats corrupting impressionable youths, while panics involving youths belonging to subordinate racial, ethnic, or socioeconomic statuses are more likely to portray the youths as perpetrators. (p. 4)

Childhood was not separated from adulthood as a distinct stage until the mid-1800s, when the term "juvenile delinquent" was coined to describe groups of disaffected youth. Youth and youth cultures continue to be regarded with suspicion, if not outright fear, by adults. The media often exacerbate existing concerns about youth, particularly youth crime, and according to Mallea (1999)

> Media hysteria has fuelled a fear of violence out of all proportion to its presence in the community. Racism, sexism, and ageism have played their part. Politicians have seized on these to promote tough legislation and the effective demonization of our children. (p. 16)

Cohen (2002) argues that such characterizations occur because

> adult society actively uses the whole idea of adolescence[,] and the youth culture in particular, to neutralize any real generational conflict. The young are consigned to a self-contained world with their own preoccupations, their entrance into adult status is frustrated and they are rewarded for dependency. The teenage culture makes them into ineffectual outsiders. (p. 151)

The alienation of adolescents from public life negatively affects public perceptions of them. According to Schissel (2008), there is a growing antipathy to youth, who are viewed as being less respectful and more dangerous than in previous generations. He points to a recent Canadian poll in which 63 per cent of adults favoured stiffer penalties for young offenders even though Canada already incarcerates more of its young offenders than any other country in the industrialized world and in proportionally higher numbers than adults, who commit more crimes, most of which are of a more serious nature.

Moral panics about youth and youth culture also affect the way schools operate. Inner-city schools with large populations of ethnically identifiable students and low-income families are becoming increasingly criminalized, looking more like fortresses and prisons, where reactive disciplinary policies, pervasive surveillance, metal detectors, lock-downs, and unwarranted searches may even feed the so-called school-to-prison pipeline (Farmer, 2010; Wotherspoon, 2009). Furthermore, many school jurisdictions have established elaborate dress codes to restrict displays of youth culture. This is often done to prevent clashes between rival subcultures that might be triggered by the wearing of certain colours or items of clothing. Concerns about female sexuality, male aggression, and gang presence in schools have led to bans against girls exposing their midriffs, wearing shorts, short skirts, or certain types of jewellery, and penalties for boys who wear baggy pants, long hair, t-shirts with inappropriate messages, hats, and "do-rags."

Two cases in this chapter explore some of the tensions around youth and the outward trappings of youth culture. In "No Beeping Song!" the suggestive lyrics of a popular song come under scrutiny. In "Gangster Fashion," the choice of material being used in the sewing class becomes contentious. As you read these cases, consider the reasons for censorship and school dress codes, and think about whether it is ever possible to bridge the so-called generation gap.

Moral education

Although moral development has always been central to the educational enterprise, the sense of crisis about the decline of morals in society has placed morality, once again, at the top of the educational agenda (Helwig, Turiel, & Nucci, 1997; Sojourner, 2012). As we noted in Chapter 2, public schools may be officially secular, but they are still expected to play a pivotal role in shaping morality (Purpel, 1999). Over the years, moral-education bandwagons have appeared and reappeared in a variety of guises, including "character education," "values clarification," "zero tolerance," "life skills education," "violence prevention," "ethical reasoning," "conflict resolution and mediation," and "citizenship education." Although there is little consistency, clarity, or coherence across Canada about the definition of moral education or how best to teach it, five provinces (Saskatchewan, Ontario, Quebec, British Columbia, and Alberta) have policies which mandate or make provision for optional moral-education programs (Leinweber, Donlevy, Gereluk, Patterson, & Brar, 2012, p. 26).

The most widespread formal programs are those described as "**character education**," of which Character Counts is an example. Character education focuses on the inculcation of specific virtues, such as trustworthiness, respect, responsibility, caring, and citizenship, in the belief that such efforts will "cure the moral problems of society (street crime, violence in the schools, drug use, teen pregnancy, decline in civility, etc.) by molding the character of the next generation" (Davis, 2003, p. 32).

Fears about moral decline may be justified, but there is little evidence that formally teaching virtues through character education is an effective way to reverse the trend (Davis, 2003; K. Ryan, 2002; Sojourner, 2012; Yu, 2004). A number of critics (Davis, 2003; Helwig, Turiel, & Nucci, 1997; Kohn, 1996) reject the notion that character can be broken down into constituent traits or that it can be trained through practice. Even if educators could agree that character can be developed in a behavioural fashion, there is no consensus on which virtues are universal across cultures or even within communities and certainly not for all students in all situations. Furthermore, Holt (1982) points out that

> Teachers and schools tend to mistake good behavior for good character. What they prize is docility, suggestibility; the child who will do what he is told; or even better, the child who will do what is wanted without even having to be told. They value most in children what children least value in themselves. Small wonder that their effort to build character is such a failure; they don't know it when they see it. (p. 234)

Moral education may be taught explicitly or integrated into core curricula as outcomes, but perhaps even more importantly, it is conveyed implicitly through the hidden curriculum, or what Davies and Guppy (2010) describe as "the school rules, procedures, structures, and covert norms that can shape students" (p. 289). When we examine the hidden curriculum closely as a vehicle for moral education, we can appreciate how schools communicate tacitly what is right and what is wrong, what is deemed acceptable and unacceptable, and whose voice is privileged and whose is ignored. The compulsory and hierarchical nature of schools, as well as the styles of teaching adopted and the modes of discipline employed, clearly mark the boundaries of authority and the place of various subjects, such as arts, languages, or sports as core or elective courses. Even the types of extracurricular activities available demonstrate what kind of learning society values most, just as the responsibilities of the student government reveal how committed the school is to developing active citizenship among its students. In these and countless other ways, the hidden curriculum reinforces dominant norms and societal values without the students (and often the teachers themselves) being aware of the moral lessons that are being taught.

In the case "Character Counts," gang violence prompts different responses by school administrators and the community. As you read this case, consider the role of moral entrepreneurs, and think about whether moral education is a viable solution to conflict between groups of students.

Conclusion

Moral panics evoke strong emotions which often serve to exaggerate the importance of minor concerns and distort our understanding of society's major problems. As we discussed earlier, it is not always easy to distinguish a moral panic from a legitimate concern. Furthermore, McRobbie and Thornton (1995) point out that both society and the media have become more fragmented and contradictory since the concept of moral panics was first made popular in the 1970s. It is increasingly difficult to see moral panics as discrete events with definite beginnings and ends. However, by asking the kinds of essential questions posed by the foundations of education (see Chapter 1) we are more likely to recognize when issues are being overblown and which groups (or ideas) are being constructed as folk devils. The answers we uncover will prevent us from being swayed by exaggerated claims or misguided efforts to stereotype and stigmatize groups of people or ideas.

The history of education shows us that youth have regularly been the targets of moral panics. It is not surprising perhaps that heightened concerns about youth coincide with times of uncertainty, high youth population, and weak economies (Nieftagodien, 2011, p. 2). Historians of education argue that if we ask questions about the sources of our information and the credibility of the evidence being presented, we can determine whether we are being deliberately distracted from deeply rooted social problems by orchestrated panics and whether moral entrepreneurs have a vested interest in amplifying public fears. For example, since the data show that youth crime and violence are down, we should challenge claims that youth are out of control and we should ask in whose interest it might be to assert otherwise. Taking a historical perspective, Cohen (1972) explains how moral panics have operated over time:

> Sometimes the object of the panic is quite novel and at other times it is something which has been in existence long enough, but suddenly appears in the limelight. Sometimes the panic passes over and is forgotten, except in folk-lore and collective memory; at other times it has more serious and long-lasting repercussions and might produce such changes as those in legal and social policy or even in the way the society conceives itself. (p. 9)

The philosophy of education encourages us to examine our assumptions about what is normal and to consider our beliefs about what is morally permissible. Interestingly, as Goode and Ben-Yehuda (2009, p. 29) explain, moral panics can actually help us in this reflective process because they clarify the "normative contours" and "moral boundaries" of society and demonstrate the limits of society's tolerance for diversity. When we use tests of logic on the arguments and counter-arguments made by moral entrepreneurs, we can decide whether the threats to society they have identified are valid. We can draw relevant conclusions about youth, for example, not only by paying attention to random acts and tragic events perpetrated by individuals, but also to the large numbers of youth who are engaged in worthy pursuits on behalf of social justice, environmental stewardship, and responsible citizenship. As Nieftagodien (2011) suggests, "There is nothing automatic about youth being visionary, progressive, and the standard bearers of a brighter future. But neither can they be dismissed as the pall-bearers of a grim future" (p. 10).

The sociology of education reminds us that moral panics are actually examples of what sociologists (Critcher, 2008, p. 1138) describe as an "**ideal type**"—a sociological tool for beginning an analysis rather than being a perfect fit with social reality. In spite of this limitation, moral panics nevertheless explain how and why "issues have been selected for public and policy attention, who are consulted as claims makers and experts, what kinds of discourses are generated, and which remedial measures are advocated" (Critcher, 2008, p. 1141). Applying sociological questions to moral panics helps us to understand how and why various groups are labelled, how societal norms change, and how various forms of capital are affected by moral crusaders with a vested interest in passing laws or enacting regulations. Goode and Ben-Yehuda (1994) observe, "Even those panics that seem to end without institutional impact often leave normative or informal traces that prepare us for later panics or other events" (p. 169).

In this chapter, as in the previous chapters, we present 10 illustrative cases, which are each followed by five questions that will help you to examine the details of each case; further develop your skill in asking historically, philosophically, and sociologically minded questions; and apply the particulars of the case to your own practice. Becoming accustomed to asking essential questions posed by the foundations disciplines will enable you to confront the fears, exaggerated claims, and stereotypical blaming of groups or ideas characteristic of moral panics with a healthy amount of skepticism.

A Place to Belong?

It was the beginning of another school year, and Claire Silverman, a Grade 10 Social Studies teacher at Rosemount High School, had offered to be the faculty adviser for the school's Diversity Club. Claire's former colleague, Len Durand had worked with the group for the past few years and had watched the club grow from a gay–straight alliance to a club that now encompassed a broader cross-section of students. Increasingly, students from ethnic minorities were turning to the Diversity Club in hopes of reducing tensions in the school.

The Diversity Club president, Charlie Demers, was a friendly, outgoing Grade 12 student with a positive attitude and charismatic leadership style. Charlie had been involved with the club since its inception and was best known for saying "Let's just do it!" He had played a significant role in planning and promoting last year's anti-bullying workshop, which had attracted students from across the district. As a result of Charlie's efforts and the success of last year's program, the club was starting this year with an increased membership and a wider representation of the student body.

For her part, Claire was particularly pleased to note that there were more Asian and Aboriginal students signed up for the club this year than ever before. Although the students still segregated themselves along ethnic lines, a growing number of students who were interested in connecting with students from other groups were showing up at the Diversity Club's Tuesday afternoon meetings. As today's meeting was about to begin, the students engaged in small talk as they made their way to Claire's room.

"Great game last night," Aadi said to Coreen as he tossed his backpack on a desk.

"Thanks," said Coreen. She was a quiet student, but Claire had seen her come alive on the soccer field; she was a real asset to the senior girls' team.

Aadi played soccer too, but was only playing on a community team this year. He had dropped school sports to spend more time on schoolwork in hopes of getting a scholarship to attend university.

As the chairs filled and the meeting began, Claire welcomed them all and reminded them of the guidelines of the club—to provide opportunities for students to connect, to develop leadership skills, and to raise awareness about diversity. She then turned the meeting over to Charlie. The main agenda item for the meeting was the planning of a multicultural event.

"I think we should organize a Multicultural Day," Charlie said. "We could have all sorts of ethnic food and entertainment."

As the other students considered Charlie's idea, Claire deliberately kept silent. Although she wanted the students to lead the meetings themselves, she couldn't help thinking that they could do something more substantive than organizing a Multicultural Day to raise awareness about diversity. While many of the recent immigrant families worked hard, they still lived below the poverty line and their circumstances often prevented their children from taking full advantage of the opportunities available in the school. For such students, band and sports trips and excursions abroad were simply beyond their means. Although Claire would have preferred the students in the club to address issues like unequal access to extra-curricular activities, she re-focused her attention on the students' conversation, realizing that such initiatives needed to come from the students themselves.

"I like the idea," said Aadi. "Maybe we'd learn more about each other." His own family still followed many of the old Korean traditions. His grandparents lived with them and didn't speak English, so the family spoke both languages at home.

"Maybe we would learn something more about ourselves," Coreen added. "Not all of us know that much about our own heritage."

Coreen had recently become more interested in her Aboriginal heritage and was exploring art and dance at the local Native Friendship Centre.

"I know enough about my heritage," Aadi argued. "I just want students from different cultures to mix more at school instead of always sticking with their own kind."

Allicia, whose family came from Jamaica, had been listening quietly to the conversation, so Claire asked her what she thought of the idea of a Multicultural Day.

Unexpectedly, Allicia replied, "Yeah, well, I think we're kidding ourselves if we think a Multicultural Day will make any difference. I still get picked on a lot in class. People think it doesn't happen here but believe me—racism is alive and well at Rosemount. I hear a lot of nasty jokes and my friends do, too. That's why a lot of them have already left and more are thinking of moving to Chilton, the Blacks-only school."

Claire hoped Allicia's disturbing comments would spark a deeper conversation, but to her disappointment, no one in the room took up the issue.

Claire looked out the window as she listened to the students resume talking about the proposed event. In the courtyard below, she could see the Asian students sitting in their own sections, the Black students in theirs, and the Aboriginal students in their space close to the fence. As she looked at the students outside, Claire suspected that Allicia was right about the school kidding itself about how well students from different cultures were getting along. She had to admit that Rosemount didn't have a particularly good record in responding to ethnic differences. Perhaps, like other public schools, they still tended to look at the world through Eurocentric eyes. She wondered what it would be like for Allicia and her friends to attend an Afro-Canadian school. Claire had heard that such schools had lower drop-out rates and that their students tended to be more motivated. She wondered whether students would have greater opportunities in separate school programs or would become even more isolated from society.

Later that day, Claire overheard Allicia talking to her friend, Keisha, in the hallway. She was trying to persuade her friend that they would all be better off if they moved to Chilton. She also told Keisha that her parents were going to meet with the school's administrators and the district superintendent the following Monday afternoon to make the case that Rosemount was short-changing Black students, who made up at least half of the Rosemount's population.

Early Tuesday morning, Dave Bagley, the principal, appeared at Claire's doorway in obvious distress. He recounted the difficult meeting he and the superintendent had had with Allicia's parents the day before. He described how seriously the superintendent took their concerns, given that Allicia's parents were well-educated, well-connected, and very influential in the local Black community.

"Claire, you've got to do something with the Diversity Club. Allicia's parents are convinced that we are doing nothing significant to address the cultural divides in the school. They believe that their daughter and students like her feel that they don't have a place here at Rosemount. They've threatened to call a meeting of the parents of other Black students and encourage them all to transfer out if we can't get our act together."

Claire was taken aback and replied, "I hear what you are saying, Dave, and I can understand why you and the superintendent are concerned, but I'm not at all sure what I can do as the supervising teacher for the club. You have always stressed that clubs should be run by the students themselves and that as teachers, we should 'guide from the side.' Remember?"

"Yes, of course, I remember, but I need you to move from guiding to outright directing or we could have a mass exodus on our hands! Don't you have a meeting this afternoon? Get in there and let those kids know that Rosemount is the place to be and that no students should feel like they have to move to another school. We've got to do something drastic before our school population is cut in half!"

Claire was speechless at the directive she had just been given. What could she do in short order that would make a difference, and was it even her place to do so? She wondered if it was ever possible for schools like Rosemount to make *all* students feel that they had a place to belong.

Questions

The Case

Why did Dave Bagley ask Claire to "do something" with the Diversity Club? What else might he have done to deal with the problem?

History

How might *separate* ethnic schools balance their own historical perspectives with those mandated by the provincial curriculum?

Philosophy

How do segregated schools further or diminish Canada's commitment to multiculturalism? Justify your response.

Sociology

Students from similar backgrounds tend to seek each other out. Why do you think this happens, and should this be a cause for concern? Explain.

Implications for Practice

What do you think your role should be as a school club adviser?

A Stitch in Time

It was lunchtime and the students at Prairie View Elementary School were eating in small groups in the hallways as well as in their classrooms because of overcrowding in the school. Teaching assistants were poking into the rooms, monitoring the hall, and talking with the children. Most of the Grade 3 students in Room 5 were engaged in conversations, and those who had already eaten were anxious for the bell to signal the start of their outdoor recess.

There were about 10 minutes left in the lunch period when Jayce strolled into the classroom from the hallway. With his black hoodie pulled up over his head, he wandered over to the coat area, shoved his Stone Cold Steve Austin wrestling lunch bag into his cubby, and lifted his winter jacket off the hook. He backed away from the coat area, head down, as he struggled to do up his jacket zipper. Kyle, who was on his way to the garbage can to throw away his orange peel, was laughing with a friend and had his head turned back to his table. As Kyle continued to advance to the garbage can looking back over his shoulder, he bumped into Jayce, who was still moving backwards as he tugged on his zipper. The boys were momentarily startled by their inadvertent collision, and when their eyes met, there was a second of stillness as they both calculated the next move in their long-standing contest of wills.

"You idiot! Watch out!" snapped Kyle, drawing his classmates' attention.

"You watch out!" Jayce retorted, dropping his hands from his jacket and taking a step forward.

"You're such a jerk," sneered Kyle dismissively, moving back to his table.

Stinging from the remark, Jayce lunged forward to grab Kyle's shoulder and force him to turn around. Instead, Kyle was caught off guard and flew into a table and hit his chin on the table's edge, splitting the skin open. Blood gushed from the wound while Jayce stood frozen, eyes wide. He tried to run from the classroom but collided with Doug Speers, his teaching assistant, who was walking in at that very moment.

Doug immediately took control of the situation, checking Kyle's injuries and calling Ted Redekopp, the teaching assistant on hall duty, to come and get Jayce. Taking Kyle to the office for first aid, Doug called the boy's home since Kyle would undoubtedly require stitches from his collision with the table. Within a half hour, Kyle's father, Mark Loewen, arrived at the school, flushed and angry. He quickly checked to see that his son was in no immediate danger and then stormed into the principal's office.

"Mr Halderson, I have had it with this Jayce kid! He is constantly bullying Kyle, and it is so bad that now my son needs to go to the hospital because of that jerk! It is obvious that bullying is out of control in this school, and it is high time you did something about it!" he ranted.

Although the door to Jack Halderson's office was closed, the tirade was clearly audible in the outer office, where Janis Cooper, the school secretary, was helping Kyle zip up his jacket while he held a bloodied compress to his chin.

Moments later, Kyle's dad came out of the principal's office and grabbing his son's backpack from the floor, motioned for Kyle to get up, saying thickly, "Come on, buddy, we'd better get you to the hospital."

Jack emerged from his office, sighed deeply, and walked over to see Fran Desrocher, his vice-principal. In addition to valuing Fran's advice as a member of his administrative team, Jack needed her insight as a former resource teacher and Jayce's case manager for the past two years. He sat down at Fran's table and got right to the point.

"Fran, we might have to suspend Jayce. I'm not sure how many more of these outbursts we can tolerate." Jack continued, "He really hurt Kyle, and his dad is not going to let this one go. He's claiming it's an issue of bullying, but I sincerely doubt that. These two boys have been like caged lions ever since the first time they met, but neither of them is what I would call a bully. Sometimes I think Mark Loewen uses the 'B' word just a little too loosely! As far as he is concerned, his kids are always in the right and everyone else is picking on *them*."

Fran considered the situation and began to rub her forehead in frustration. Jayce was a boy with special needs who had been identified as being emotionally and behaviourally disturbed. Because of his impulsive behaviour and cognitive deficits, he had an individualized education plan and a behavioural intervention plan that included having a full-time teaching assistant. His classroom teacher, Audrey Astaire, had been working closely with the school's support team and Jayce's mother to accommodate Jayce as fully as possible within the daily life of the classroom. The plan was reviewed and revised regularly by the support team in consultation with the district psychologist.

In addition to providing details of how to prevent more of such incidents, the plan called for school staff to try to disrupt Jayce's notions that he was "bad" and to make him feel valued by school personnel and classmates. In the event that Jayce had a violent outburst, however, various alternative consequences were outlined for consideration since his mother was a single parent employed in shift work who was unable to supervise him at home if he was suspended.

Jack told Fran what he knew about the incident and asked her to talk to Audrey and the teaching assistants to get more details. As Fran investigated further, she began to see gaps in the support afforded to Jayce, particularly at lunchtime. Previously, it had been arranged for him to eat his lunch at one of the many hallway tables with a teaching assistant and a friend of his choice. Fran soon discovered, however, that his teaching assistant had been called to the phone and the colleague who had been asked to supervise in his absence had turned away momentarily to check on one of the older students who seemed to be having an allergic reaction. It was at this moment that Jayce, who had long finished eating and was anxious to get outside for recess, went into the classroom to get his jacket.

Jayce was supposed to be within an arm's length of an adult at all times but especially when he found himself in tight spaces like the cloakroom, where students might accidentally bump one another. Jayce had also been coached to take his jacket on his way *to* lunch so he wouldn't need to return to the classroom at all. However, on this particular day, he had forgotten his jacket, so he simply returned to the classroom to get it.

After Jack and Fran discussed the incident, they met with Audrey at the end of the school day and once again reviewed the behaviour plan. Audrey, who was opposed to any talk of suspending Jayce, reminded them that Gerald, a non-verbal autistic student in her class, regularly pinched, bit, and pulled the hair of his classmates but was never suspended. "We don't suspend Gerald when he hurts other students," insisted Audrey. "Why would we punish Jayce for *our* failures to support him?"

Indeed, the school had failed not only Jayce but also Kyle, who would end up needing several stitches. It was highly unlikely that Mark Loewen, who was known to have a short fuse, particularly on the subject of bullying, would be satisfied with the consequences outlined in Jayce's plan. He had already been in contact with the superintendent and the school trustees on several previous occasions to complain about minor incidents concerning his older boys that he had characterized as "flagrant and unchecked bullying in the school."

For his part, Jack knew how easily the bullying rhetoric could spin out of control, especially when an outraged parent, supported by trustees and district personnel, felt that the school had not responded adequately to his or her complaints. He could easily imagine how this incident could even become fodder for the media. Jack and Fran knew they would have to weigh their options carefully, considering not only their actions, but also what the political, social, and moral implications would be.

Questions

The Case

What viable options do Jack and Fran have for managing this dilemma?

History

Given that anti-bullying laws are now in place, have we gone too far or not far enough in making schools safe places for all students? Justify your answer.

Philosophy

How should schools balance the rights of behaviourally disordered students with the rights of their classmates to be safe? Explain why you think so.

Sociology

What forms of power and powerlessness can you identify in this case?

Implications for Practice

How will you create a classroom culture in which parents and students feel that they can talk to you about their safety concerns?

Brave New World?

It was Monday morning in the staff room at Jeanne Sauvé School. Over a steaming cup of coffee in the middle of a discussion of a controversial blog posting, Tom Di Giuseppe turned to a few of his colleagues and asked, "By the way, what do Tom Brady, Prince Charles, Barack Obama, Christina Aguilera, Paul McCartney, and I all have in common?"

His colleagues looked puzzled.

"The answer," he said, "is that all of us have had our privacy invaded. We are all victims of hacking. You name it—Facebook, cell phones, email—even Twitter. Early this morning, I found out that all my personal email contacts had been deleted and a message had been sent to everyone on my contact list. The message says that I'm in Swansea, Wales, and that my bag was stolen with my passport and credit cards in it. Let me read the rest of the message to you:

> "The Canadian Embassy is willing to help by letting me fly without my passport, I just have to pay for a ticket and settle the hotel bills later. Unfortunately, I can't have access to funds without my credit card. I've made contact with my bank but they need more time to come up with a new card number, so I am pleading with you to lend me some money that I will give back as soon as I return. I really need to be on the next available flight. Western Union transfer is the best option to send the money to me. You can reach me via email or the hotel's desk phone. The numbers are +447031804805 or +447031804806. I await your response."

"Sounds pretty realistic, doesn't it?"

"Except for the part that says 'I await your response'," joked Celia LaFrance. "Since when did you ever say something like that?"

Laughter rippled around the room and heads nodded in agreement.

"But, seriously, it's easy to see how someone getting that email could be taken in," Celia admitted. "You know, social media has a lot to answer for. Look at how often we hear about cyberbullying on social media sites! That's why the board is so concerned about on-line security when students and staff use computers. But I guess we'll have to accept the fact that social media is here to stay and, if you listen to our students, it is often the only way that they communicate with their friends."

"You're right," agreed Mike O'Leary. "But that means we need to be very careful. We should never forget that instantaneous and global contact with others can be used by terrorists to commit violent acts. Think about the many disturbing examples we have had when social media was used to create havoc on the global stage. Remember the London bombings of July 2005, the 'BlackBerry riots' of 2011, and the revolts in Egypt and Libya in 2011? Add to that, social media is a perfect vehicle for spreading false information. Did you hear what happened in Mexico, where two people were charged with 'Twitter terrorism' for wrongly reporting an attack on an elementary school?"

"No. What happened?" asked Celia.

"People were frantic! Parents rushed to the school, causing a number of car accidents and emergency phone lines were jammed as parents tried to get information about their kids," explained Mike.

"Hold on, social media isn't all bad," said Tina Verbeck. "It helped spread the news about the devastation in Haiti. As a matter of fact, last year, I responded to a tweet asking for a donation of $10. I texted the word 'Haiti' to a number used by the Red Cross and their Twitter account ended up raising over $32 million for the victims."

With Tina's comment, the staff room fell silent for a few moments.

"Celia, I want to go back to what you said earlier about our students and how they communicate with their friends via social media," said Diana Portofino. "Some of you seem to think that social media is the best thing since sliced bread, but others seem to believe we should ban it altogether." Looking around the room for a response, she asked, "So where do we go from here?"

"Well," said Renate Wexler, "I've said this before, but I want our students to learn about the impact of social media on their lives and how to use it responsibly. They should be able to create web content that they can post, use photo sharing sites like Instagram, be adept at on-line publishing, and contribute to discussions. Even more importantly, they need to become aware of how social networking can affect relationships, both positively and negatively."

"I agree," said Jim Rogers eagerly. "Social media has so much potential for all of us. I have a Facebook account, I update it regularly for my family and friends, I text regularly, and I have a blog on schooner building in Newfoundland. I started it several years ago, and now some of my students who are interested in boats follow it regularly, and believe it or not, we have discussions about schooners outside of class."

"Well, after my account got hacked, I support our district's policy on social media more than ever! I think it's good that students are prohibited from accessing social networking sites at school except for educational or instructional purposes and then only with prior approval from the school administration," said Tom ruefully. "I know some of you think that students should be banned from accessing all social networks, but I think the policy goes just far enough—allowing it but keeping some controls."

"Apparently, other school districts are grappling with the same issues," added Ibrahim Dali. "The superintendent of Lakeshore School District told the trustees there that the 'horse is out of the barn' as far as cell phones and social media go. His trustees have been asked to figure out how teachers can integrate social media into their classes most effectively and safely."

"Well, I hope it isn't catching!" said Sharam. "I actually cheered when the board banned the use of cell phones at school and posting photos on-line that were taken on school property. I would go even further and ask our board to adopt an extra strong filtering program, similar to Net Nanny, to block objectionable sites. But what would make me happier still would be a decision to prohibit *all* social media contact between teachers and students. In this way, no student, or teacher, for that matter, would ever be victimized in any way."

As the bell rang, Jim seized the opportunity to have the last word. "Thanks Tom for sharing your experience. It looks to me like there is some difference of opinion about social media here, but there is just one more point I want to make before you go. This is not just a school issue. We need to keep in mind that employers are asking us to prepare our students to function in the modern workplace. They want employees who can collaborate, think creatively and critically, and use technology responsibly and ethically. Social media can really play a role there. In fact, we need to remove constraints and not add them if our students are going to be able to navigate this brave new world of ours."

As the staff filed out, most remained unconvinced that there was any place for social media in their teaching. Tom's experience just reminded some of them that technology was the source of more problems than it solved. Jim and Renate stayed behind for a moment and agreed that they were obviously still alone in wanting greater freedom to integrate social media in their teaching. They reminded each other that it was early days, but they couldn't help wondering what it would take for their colleagues to see the potential of social media, and not just the drawbacks.

Questions

The Case

In this case, convincing arguments are made for both sides of the debate on whether or not social media should be used in the classroom. What are the arguments? Which did you find most persuasive, and why?

History

How do you think social media will affect students' understanding of historical events? Explain.

Philosophy

How can teachers act responsibly and still be open-minded about the use of social media in the classroom?

Sociology

How might social media both enhance and disrupt relationships inside and outside the classroom?

Implications for Practice

Given the increasing prevalence of social media in our lives and in our schools, how will you manage it in your classroom?

On-Line or Off-Base?

It was an early fall day and a few of the teachers in the staff room at Georges Vanier Secondary were hotly debating the value of allowing cell phones in class. Although the conversation had just started, Kostas Leo, a new teacher in the

English department, was already becoming frustrated with some of his more experienced colleagues.

In response to their reservations, he protested, "We should be bringing the world into our classrooms so that our students understand that what they learn in school actually applies to the real world. Like it or not, the on-line world *is* the real world to our students."

Julian Penner quickly retorted, "But don't you see that bringing cell phones into class comes at a steep price? Just think about how many more students will be off task and how hard it will be to get their attention! It's a slippery slope, my friend. Do we really want to go there?"

The principal, Tom Ewatski, agreed. He took up Julian's argument with relish. "I don't think that cell phones have a place in schools. They just undermine teaching and interfere with student learning. I actually support the district's proposal to ban cell phones in class, and I think Vanier should be among the first to adopt this recommendation."

Tom paused to gauge the reaction to this announcement and seeing general approval, continued more confidently, "In fact, the board has just published a press release outlining the problems associated with cell phone use in the class. Let me summarize the main points for you," said Tom. "One—students can use cell phones to cheat on tests. Two—students are being conditioned to be 'on call,' feeling pressured to answer every text the moment they receive it no matter how inappropriate the timing. Three—students can use cell phones to take improper pictures and upload them to YouTube and Facebook. Four—students can use their phones to bully other students and five—students are distracted from learning by texts from friends and even parents who are becoming accustomed to having instant access to their children. All in all, pretty compelling arguments for getting them out of the classroom, don't you think?"

Kostas thought this speech was somewhat ironic given that Tom had hired Jayne Phillips and him for their expertise in integrating technology into their English and Math classes. Tom had even called the two of them to a meeting before school started to discuss how technology could be used for educational purposes to connect with students in more meaningful ways. However, judging by the principal's announcement, they were not exactly in agreement about what that meant.

Jayne and Kostas asked to be put on the agenda for the next staff meeting. They hoped that sharing their positive experiences would persuade Tom and some of the teachers to reconsider their support for the proposed ban at Vanier. They began their presentation to the staff by addressing the issue of assessment. They pointed out that although cell phones could be used for multiple-choice questions, these types of questions were least effective for assessment and the answers could indeed be easily copied by students just as they were when such tests were administered on paper. Kostas and Jayne showed how, in their respective specialities, they had devised test questions that required critical thinking and inquiry. In addition to making it more difficult for students to share their answers with their friends, such questions had the added advantage of forcing students to move beyond content learning and to go deeper into a topic.

Next, they tackled the argument that too many students are "on call" when cell phones are permitted. Jayne and Kostas talked about the strategies they used for managing students' attention. Both young teachers had taken class time to teach students texting etiquette and how to manage their attention and resist the compulsion to text. Both Jayne and Kostas felt that this time had been well spent since students who had been exposed to this training did less inappropriate texting during class.

Kostas also pointed out that today's phones were, in fact, minicomputers, and as such, provided students with low-cost digital searching tools. Kostas described how he had posted questions to the Wiffiti, an interactive message board, and at times, had even used text lingo such as: "w@ wz d most impt part?"

Appalled, Stan Willis, a veteran English teacher, spluttered, "Are you kidding? Kostas, you teach English and you encourage that form of communication? That's not modelling proper English! And besides, how do you know that they're doing what they're supposed to be doing and not texting their friends?"

Kostas laughed. "Before I handle those hot potatoes, Stan, let me remind you that texting meets the same outcomes in the English curriculum as we might teach through more conventional methods. In order to create an effective text, a writer must be able to synthesize his or her thoughts and express them succinctly. I use an activity called "25 words" for this purpose, and it would work in any subject and any topic. The students, working in pairs, may use no more than 25 words to pitch their favourite song and then, using their cell phones, they record their promotion on the class Voki account. Students use a persuasive speech rubric as a guide to prepare their pitch and use peer feedback to make improvements before they record their final version."

Sama, one of the Science teachers, seemed intrigued and asked, "Why did you use Voki?"

"I like the fact that students can upload their work to the Voki any time in a password-protected environment and that parents can also use it to track their children's progress. As you are all aware, many of our students are second-language learners, and having the option to re-record their assignments is extremely helpful. When the assignment is completed, I ask the students to comment on their effort and achievement using a self-assessment rubric from a Canadian-based web site, askitonline.com. This allows me to access the pitches and the peer reviews at the same time and to see the tabulated results immediately for both individuals and groups. No paperwork for me!"

"I also use askitonline.com," interjected Jayne, "but I use it to review the students' knowledge of the previous day's work. They have to answer the questions with their cell phones, and their answers give me instant feedback on whether they have any misconceptions or gaps in their learning. I really like being able to check for understanding when I'm dealing with math concepts that need to be scaffolded."

Before Jayne could provide any more examples, the room erupted with questions and comments coming from every direction.

"What about students who don't have smart phones?"

"What do you do to ensure equity of access?"

"How did you decide when the students could use cell phones and when they couldn't?"

"Wasn't that confusing for them?"

Jayne and Kostas tried to answer all the questions, but they could tell from the general tone that the naysayers were in the majority. As their allotted time drew to a close, they concluded the presentation with their most controversial idea.

"In each class," Jayne reported, "we build in a short break in the middle for students to check for their personal text messages and answer them."

"Are you guys crazy?" blurted out Martha Mays, from the History department. "Why would you give up valuable instructional time in an already overcrowded curriculum to allow your students to text? Don't you realize that you are just pandering to the students? This whole presentation has been for nothing. When the cell phone ban is enforced, you will have to use textbooks to get through your courses just like the rest of us. And by the way, as new hires, you would do well to avoid rocking the boat!"

This last point stopped Kostas and Jayne in their tracks, and as they left the staff room, they looked at each other and wondered if, in fact, they needed to prepare for the inevitable ban no matter how wrong-headed they believed it to be. They agreed to think about it overnight and discuss the matter in the morning, but at this point, neither of them was prepared to jeopardize their new jobs.

Questions

The Case

The district has identified five major problems related to students' use of cell phones in schools. Which of these do you think is most contentious and why?

History

Until recently, the idea of teachers using cell phones as teaching tools was unthinkable. What has happened to account for the greater acceptance of cell phones in the classroom?

Philosophy

Were Kostas and Jayne courageous or foolhardy in making their presentation to the rest of the staff? Explain.

Sociology

How might the use of cell phones affect the ability of teachers to exercise authority and manage their classrooms? Why do you think so?

Implications for Practice

In this case, Jayne and Kostas are reminded that as new hires, they should be more circumspect about what they say and do. As a new teacher, what strategies will you use to teach authentically while not violating school norms or jeopardizing your future?

Bang! Bang! You're Dead!

Jackie Warner, a Kindergarten teacher at Willow Park Elementary School was talking to Walter, an educational assistant, and Terri, a Grade 3 teacher, as they gathered their materials before the monthly staff meeting.

"Well, I couldn't believe it—it just seems that that kid is always in trouble," Jackie said of Ben, a student in her class. "He walked right up to Martin while they were getting ready to go home and swung his lunch box right into his head! Can you believe it?"

"On purpose?" asked Terri.

"It certainly seemed that way to me," replied Jackie.

Ryan, one of the Grade 6 teachers, who was sitting at the next table, turned his head and started to listen in on the conversation.

"Yes—the little brat," Jackie continued, "I was standing right there, and for no apparent reason he turned around and took a swing. He did it right in front of me!"

"Martin is Bradley's little brother, right?" asked Ryan.

"Yes, do you have Brad in your class this year?" asked Terri.

"Yes, I do—so was Martin hurt?" continued Ryan.

"Well, his head was certainly red—I wouldn't be surprised if he ended up with a nasty bruise," replied Jackie.

"You know how their parents are—you should call his Mom right now to tell her about the incident or you'll hear from her by tomorrow morning. I would bet on it! That woman never misses a chance to criticize what we do," Ryan advised.

"I already did," sighed Jackie.

"Did you call Ben's parents, too?" asked Terri.

"I'm letting the office do that, not that it will help at all," replied Jackie bluntly.

"His parents are the problem," added Walter adamantly. "He's allowed to do whatever he wants at home. You know, just yesterday he was talking about playing *Art of War* with his dad. Think about what he does when he goes home—he plays violent video games!"

"That's so inappropriate," Terri chimed in. "What are his parents thinking of?"

Just then, an announcement came over the intercom directing all staff to make their way to the library for the staff meeting that was about to begin.

"You know, I agree that he may be too young for it—I mean, *my* students are probably still too young for it, but they all play it. Anyway, I doubt that it is the video game that is really the problem. I mean, at least his dad is spending time with him when he goes home, right?" argued Ryan.

"I don't know," replied Terri, "there are boys in my class who play it, too. After recess one day last week, I overheard them talking about how realistic it was when you shoot someone in the head. Isn't that disgusting?"

"Yeah, maybe it is," replied Ryan, "but were they *being* violent or just talking about it?"

"That's not the point!" said Walter. "We didn't have any games like that when I was a kid. They are teaching kids that it's okay to be violent!"

"Look, I agree that what Ben did was wrong. I just think it's too simplistic to say that exposure to video games contributes to violence in young children," Ryan continued. "And besides, we all *did* have games like that when we were kids. Remember? We played cops and robbers and other games where it was expected that at least one child would go home crying."

"Yes, but that was different," said Walter.

"Not the same at all," agreed Terri.

"Sure it was—you made sides and ran around pretending to shoot each other. When you got hit, you acted out the most realistic death you could. When I was a kid we didn't have any video games that were that violent or realistic either, but I had a pretty big collection of toy guns. Was that any better?"

"I can see both sides," acknowledged Jackie, "but you have to admit that playing violent video games at Ben's age is not going to help matters."

"Precisely," agreed Walter. "His parents might as well tell him that what he did was okay!"

"Come on Walter, when we were allowed to play with toy guns we knew that it was just playing. Kids today know the difference between video games and real life," said Ryan. "If you pointed your fingers or a toy gun at someone and said, "Bang, bang! You're dead!" no one batted an eyelash. Today, teachers see that kind of behaviour and feel pressured to report it as a potential threat—it's just the time in which we're living. If you ask me, we've gone way overboard. No wonder some experts are talking about a whole generation of 'bubble-wrapped kids'!"

"Well, regardless of that, aren't you against violent video games as a matter of principle?" asked Jackie. "After all, you *are* a teacher!"

"I'm not sure how I feel exactly. I just think it's too simplistic to blame video games without more evidence," replied Ryan.

The staff meeting was starting, so Ryan turned his attention back to the agenda. He felt awkward about the exchange that had just occurred and wished that he hadn't got involved. He spent the rest of the staff meeting preoccupied with his colleagues' remarks. He thought about showing them some of the inquiry projects that students in his class had done on their favourite video games so they could see how much educational value they could actually have. He considered sending them the articles he had read on the potential for game-based learning in the classroom. He even thought about telling them that video games were used in a training capacity by the military, but he knew *that* argument would dig him even deeper than he already found himself. His arguments were valid, but with each one he also felt a sense of futility about trying to convince them of his point of view. He knew they weren't really interested in the argument at all—they were just looking for a convenient way to explain behaviour that made everyone uncomfortable.

The next day during a discussion time, Ryan asked his class what they thought about violent video games.

"I had an interesting conversation recently and I was wondering what you think of this topic: Do violent video games make people more violent?"

"Oh—is this going to be like a debate?" blurted out Dylan.

"Maybe," replied Ryan, "I guess it will depend on where the discussion goes."

Terrence raised his hand, "I have a lot of video games that you could say are violent, but I've never been in a fight."

"Thanks, Terrence," replied Ryan. "So if Terrence is right, what might that tell us?"

Another hand went up, "Do you mean that not everyone who plays video games goes out and kills people?"

"Yes, I would say that's obvious, but is that the whole picture? I mean, think about it—might the opposite be true as well?"

Dylan looked confused and asked, "What do you mean by the opposite?"

"What I mean is that not everyone who plays video games acts violently, but do a lot of violent people also play violent video games?" Ryan asked.

Ryan could sense his students mulling over his questions in their minds and trying hard to look at the many sides of the issue, and he was quite encouraged by what he saw. He thought it was ironic that his Grade 6 students were more willing to suspend judgment and to look at various sides of the issue than his colleagues were, and he wondered how that could be the case given the differences in age, experience, and education. This exchange with his students had definitely piqued his curiosity, and he asked himself if he should pursue this topic with his colleagues when he saw them again or if it was safer in the long run to drop the whole issue. After all, he had to work with these people, and he wanted to maintain good working relations with them.

Questions

The Case

Do you agree that playing violent video games at a young age can lead to violent behaviour? Why or why not?

History

Do you think we, as a society, have become more tolerant of violence as depicted on television and in video games? What evidence would you use to support your position?

Philosophy

In this case, Ryan assumes that his Grade 6 students are more open-minded than his colleagues. In your opinion, is it truly open-mindedness that his students are exhibiting? Why or why not?

Sociology

What is it about modern cultural phenomena such as video games that people find so threatening?

Implications for Practice

As a new teacher, how will you decide when to challenge your colleagues' certainties and when to refrain from doing so?

A Lapse of Judgment

It was a snowy and overcast Friday morning in March, and all of Pearson High School was abuzz with "Spirit Week" activities, in which students were pitted against the teachers in a series of good-natured competitions, from floor-hockey matches to hot-dog-eating contests. Everyone looked forward to this week each year because it provided such a welcome relief from the seemingly endless winter semester. Many of the events included a fundraising component so that students could help those who were less fortunate.

Today, on the last day of Spirit Week, excitement was mounting for the finals of the dance competition at noon. All week, the students had been outperforming their teachers on most of the contests, so the students knew that the teachers would be pulling out all of the stops to win. If the teachers came up with the most innovative and crowd-pleasing dance they might even be able to compensate for some of their weaker performances and boost their overall standings for the week. Not only was the dance competition fun, but the winners were allowed to donate the monies that were raised during the week to the charity of their choice. As the time ticked by and noon hour approached, no one could have predicted just how "innovative" a few of the younger teachers would be.

By all accounts, the two youngest teachers, Stephanie Grierson, a Physical Education teacher with two years' experience teaching at the school, and Andrew Pike, a recent graduate hired to teach Physics and Chemistry on a term contract, were well-liked by their students and respected by the rest of the staff. The two had been thrown together as dance partners since all of the other volunteers had already paired up. After students and teachers doing everything from the chicken dance to the hustle and the infamous bump from the 1970s for half an hour, it was Stephanie and Andrew's turn to perform. Much to the surprise of over a hundred students and at least a dozen staff members assembled in the gym, the two teachers began to assume provocative poses and to simulate a lap dance, with Stephanie seated on a chair and Andrew grinding his hips into hers. Keeping in time to the pulsating rhythm of the bass, their dance moves became more and more sexually charged. At one point, Andrew pretended to engage in oral sex and in return, Stephanie pretended to tuck money inside his belt. Giggles quickly tuned to disbelief and then to outright embarrassment and even shock as the two teachers became so completely engrossed in the dance that they were oblivious to the stir they were causing in the gym. Little did they know that the complete dance, almost three and a half minutes' worth, was being caught on a student's cell phone camera. Thanks to YouTube, the entire incident travelled almost instantaneously from the Pearson gym to the Internet and into the homes of millions of viewers on their television screens by suppertime. The two young teachers didn't realize that having a little fun during Spirit Week would provoke a media feeding frenzy that would have serious consequences for the school and their careers.

Almost as soon as Sandy Thatcher, principal of Pearson School, arrived back from a budget meeting at the board office, Vince Boychuk, the vice-principal, intercepted her at the school door. From the look on Vince's ashen face, Sandy knew that something serious had happened in her absence. Out of breath from running to meet her, Vince quickly recounted the events that had happened over the lunch hour while he had been busy trying to get the school's ancient boiler fixed.

Sandy's thoughts immediately shifted to the other teachers in the gym. Why had none of them stepped in before things really got out of hand? Were her teachers reluctant to sanction the unprofessional behaviour of their colleagues or had they simply been too stunned to act as things began to escalate? She wondered what the two teachers had been thinking and why they thought their behaviour could possibly be appropriate. She tried to remember if they hàd attended the staff meeting early in the year when she had talked about professional distance and had reminded her teachers that they were role models for their students both inside and outside of class. Beyond that, Sandy wasn't at all sure that the newly revised teacher education program with its curriculum and methodology focus still covered ethical issues, professional behaviour, or sexuality, for that matter. Did they think that their graduates would simply pick it all up on the job?

Sandy also wondered whether the dance had been scripted ahead of time or had been conjured up in the heat of the moment and whether that should even be a consideration. What they did was obviously totally unacceptable, and maybe that's all that really mattered. Sandy believed that, as relatively new teachers, they should they be forgiven for making the odd mistake, but she suspected that this "lapse of judgment" went so far beyond the norm that she might not have any choice but to dismiss them both immediately.

Sandy made her way grimly through the knots of keyed-up students in the hall, and as she was closing the door to her office, she told her secretary not to interrupt her for anything or anybody except for the superintendent. As she sank into her chair, she could hear the incessant pinging of emails piling up on her computer and watched call after call flashing on its way to her voice mail. She tried unsuccessfully to ignore her own rising agitation as she fretted about what the parents would think of her teachers and the school, in general. She had worked very hard in the past few years to earn their trust and to turn Pearson's reputation around. What could she possibly say to them now?

Her thoughts reluctantly turned to Carmen, the student who had caught the whole sorry scene on his cell phone and then posted it on YouTube. Was Carmen, at 15 years of age, just as guilty as the teachers of acting irresponsibly? Shouldn't he be held accountable? After all, he had flouted the school rules on cell phone use and had caused the video to go viral. A knock on the door interrupted her thoughts about the student's role in this affair. As Sandy picked up the phone to talk to the superintendent, she knew that her teachers' lapse of judgment would take days, perhaps even weeks, to resolve and she was certain that this would be the ultimate test of her 10-year administrative career.

Questions

The Case

In what ways do you think Sandy's relations with parents and the community at large will be affected by the incident in the gym? What kinds of things do you think she will need to do to restore the community's trust?

History

Over time, informal events like Spirit Weeks have become common as schools attempt to engage students in less formal ways. Does the situation depicted in this case signal that this trend has gone too far? Why or why not?

Philosophy

As the title suggests, this case is about judgment or more specifically, a lack of judgment. In your opinion, can judgment be developed over time, or is it a quality that you either possess or do not possess? Justify your answer.

Sociology

What is missing from the professional socialization of all the teachers in this case, and who is responsible? Explain your response.

Implications for Practice

What will you need to keep in mind when working with student groups and planning events like pep rallies and Spirit Weeks?

A Cougar in the Schoolhouse

Roberta Townsend, a 23-year-old teacher candidate, anticipated her first practicum experience eagerly. She was excited to have been placed at suburban Deerfoot High School with its solid reputation for high academic standards. Although there were no signs early in her teacher education program that there would be any problems, Roberta confided months later to the Dean of her Faculty of Education that she had been previously cautioned about being overly flirtatious, dressing inappropriately, and misunderstanding boundaries. It turned out that these same issues would surface as early as the first week in her practicum and would have far-reaching consequences.

It started within days of her arrival at Deerfoot. Roberta initially raised eyebrows in the staff room by making what appeared to be seductive overtures to male staff members. Perhaps it was Roberta's low-cut blouse and alarmingly short skirt that made these gestures seem improper, but as Roberta made her way from one male teacher to the next asking personal questions and giggling at their jokes, her friendly banter definitely created an unwelcome stir. Although most of the male teachers seemed to be unaware that there was anything questionable about her behaviour, the majority of the women in the staff room became visibly uncomfortable. After she made a passing reference to being at a party with some of the Grade 12 students the previous weekend, there were some barely suppressed gasps, a few pained expressions, and a sudden silence broken only by the ringing of the bell as staff considered the implications of this revelation. Anyone else would have immediately picked up on these social cues, but oblivious to the reactions around her, Roberta carried on in the same manner at the afternoon break, not realizing that in her first week at Deerfoot, she had already earned a reputation for all the wrong reasons.

A few days later, when Roberta was picking up some photocopying for her co-operating teacher in the main office, she managed to make things even worse. While she was leaning provocatively against the counter waiting for her materials, Brad Hoskins, one of the graduating students, came along and stood beside her. He asked the school secretary, Margery Williams, if he would be able to have a few words with the principal. Margery checked Tannis Glavin's schedule and said she would be free in about five minutes and suggested that Brad take a seat on the bench.

Before Brad could even turn around, he found himself face to face with Roberta, who had placed herself in front of him. It was clear to Margery that they had met before and, from the way Roberta was tossing her hair and fluttering her eyelashes that she found the young man very attractive. After making a little small talk, Roberta asked Brad if he and his friends were getting together again this weekend. Brad glanced at Margery out of the corner of his eye to see if she was listening and was mumbling something distractedly about having to talk to the rest of the group when Tannis appeared in the doorway and beckoned him inside. Apparently relieved by the rescue, Brad grinned widely and moved quickly around Roberta to shake Tannis's outstretched hand. He accepted her congratulations on the football team's performance in the last game as he went inside and closed the door. As the captain of the team, it was his job to get the principal's permission to hold a fundraiser at the weekend football game, and once the preliminaries were out of the way, he would do just that.

Margery was still digesting what she had seen and heard when Roberta surprised her by leaning toward her and whispering that she had noticed Brad looking suggestively at her every time she walked down the hall. Margery couldn't believe what she was hearing and managed to ease Roberta out of the office as she sorted out her own thoughts about who was trying to seduce whom.

As Tannis walked Brad out of her office, she ended their brief conversation with a smile and a pat on the shoulder. As she turned to go back inside Margery was not far behind.

"You won't believe what just happened out there!" Margery blurted out as she stood facing Tannis.

"Whoa. Slow down. What happened—where?" Tannis replied.

"In the office! That teacher candidate—that Roberta—she just asked Brad what he and his friends were doing on the weekend. She was also very suggestive in her body language, and to top it all off, she accused Brad of looking at *her* inappropriately! What is with this girl?" spluttered Margery.

Tannis reassured her that she would take care of it and had a message sent to Roberta asking her to come to the office before she left for the day.

Later, when the last of the students had made their way onto the school bus, Tannis found Roberta waiting for her outside her office. By this time, she had also heard what had happened in the staff room earlier in the week, so she was not looking forward to what would no doubt be a difficult conversation.

Tannis began by stating that it had come to her attention that Roberta had been overly attentive toward the male teachers in the school. At first, Roberta didn't seem to know what Tannis was talking about. Judging by her responses, it was clear that Roberta thought that she was simply being friendly and showing an interest in the teachers' lives, starting with the male teachers since the female teachers appeared to be somewhat standoffish. Disposing quickly of that topic, Tannis broached the even more serious issue of her interactions with Brad. She sensed that Roberta neither appreciated the legal and moral implications of her behaviour nor understood why her behaviour was so problematic. Finally, Tannis had to carefully spell out to Roberta that her actions had at least been perceived as being sexually motivated. By the end of the conversation, Roberta seemed to understand and assured Tannis that she would be much more circumspect and more conservatively dressed in the future. A little while later, Tannis made her way to the parking lot and as she did so, she wasn't convinced that Roberta could actually live up to her promises.

As the days wore on, Tannis became more and more preoccupied with the questions that her interaction with Roberta had raised. She wondered how an individual with so little self-awareness and such weak professional judgment could have ever been admitted to a teacher education program. Later that week, she found herself informally sharing her concerns with other principals at the district administrative meeting. Many of them were outraged when they heard about what had happened and soon began to share their own stories about other unsuitable candidates. Before long, one of her colleagues, Stan Roznowski, brought forward a motion recommending that the district discontinue the practice of accepting teacher candidates from that Faculty of Education altogether until, in his words, "they got their act together."

Caught off guard, Tannis argued that such an extreme response wasn't really justified, but unfortunately, the tide had already turned and the motion was approved. To make matters worse, Tannis was designated by her colleagues to break the news to the Dean of the Faculty of Education. Tannis was shocked by this turn of events. Sure, she was disappointed and surprised that Roberta hadn't understood the implications of her actions, but did she really want to break off the long-standing and productive relationship between her school district and their university partner? What was she going to say? The immature behaviour of one teacher candidate had suddenly turned into a vendetta against the entire faculty of education.

As Tannis left the meeting wondering what she was going to say to the Dean the next day, she hoped that this story would not get leaked to the media because if it did, it was quite likely that it would be seized upon and blown completely out of proportion. She now regretted saying anything to anyone and wished that she had just managed the matter herself, but this story had now taken on a life of its own and time would only tell where it would go.

Questions

The Case

In this case, Roberta creates quite a stir when she acts unprofessionally in the staff room and in the school office. Although the teachers are surprised at her behaviour, none of them actually steps in and intervenes. What do you think they could have done to help her?

History

Do you think the expectations of how teachers should behave have changed over time? What evidence would you use to support your position?

Philosophy

In your opinion, did the school district act responsibly when it decided to sever relationships with the faculty of education? Why or why not?

Sociology

Becoming a teacher is a process that involves learning and enacting the norms of the profession. Which professional norms are either present or absent in this case?

Implications for Practice

You will likely encounter situations where one of your colleagues or a teacher candidate placed at your school acts, in your judgment, inappropriately. What questions will go through your mind before intervening and doing something about it?

No Beeping Song!

Don noticed the students' elaborate footwork and was immediately impressed; it was obvious that this small group at Arcadia Middle School had been practising a lot. When the group attended the school's "Dance Off" information session a few months earlier, Don had been doubtful that they would come up with anything since the seven students in the group usually spent their time hidden away in corners of the school or behind the local convenience store, smoking. Although many found the group intimidating, Don hadn't heard any reports that the group had ever been aggressive to other students; however, their edgy behaviour and outlandish dress conveyed animosity and unpredictability. Generally, the other students gave them a wide berth.

Don was surprised and pleased when the group asked to perform in the school's "Dance Off." However, he was even more delighted to see they had become so engaged in perfecting their routines that they hadn't missed a single rehearsal. At times, they even mingled with other students to discuss choreography and the choice of music.

Unfortunately, their music selection was problematic because the group, now known as Head-on Collision, had planned to dance to music about a tragic school shooting. Don asked them to find a different song, explaining that, although it was moving, he thought it would be too upsetting for members of the audience. The group reacted angrily and threatened to boycott the school performance, but nevertheless, approached him a few days later with an alternative: a popular love song that students often sang and hummed in the hallways. The group spent the next few days working hard to choreograph and practise their new selection, but before long Don began to realize that their second song might prove to be even more contentious than the first. Although technically there were no offensive lyrics in the song, the sound "beep" had been inserted strategically throughout for maximum effect. For example, when the lyrics recounted how a boy "put his *beep* on her *beep*," there was really no question about what was intended.

Don became increasingly nervous when he started to pay attention to what the other students were substituting for the "beep" sounds when they thought no one was listening. The inappropriate lyrics made the song questionable, but rejecting the group's second choice would surely mean that the group would drop out permanently, retreating back into the shadows of the school. However, it didn't take much imagination to see that their choice of music could be seen as deliberately provocative by some of the staff and many of the parents.

Realizing that he had better brief his principal, Sandra Bolton, on these latest developments, Don took care to start by sharing his excitement about Head-On Collision's willingness to compromise on their initial music selection before expressing his reservations about the second song they had chosen. He tried to make an articulate argument for including the song in the school event, but he could see that Sandra was growing visibly agitated and tenser as he spoke.

Sandra, who was well acquainted with the song and its lyrics, pointed out that students were incessantly inserting inappropriate words in place of the "beeps" or using "beeps" in place of offensive words in the halls as they moved around the school.

"Don, remember that we are inviting students' families to watch the performance. Some school trustees might even come. They will be incredibly uncomfortable with the song's lyrics, and they will certainly question our professional judgment in letting this get as far as a public performance. We just can't be seen to condone offensive language."

Don nodded reluctantly, but countered, "Technically, Sandra, there is no offensive language in the song. It's the students who *make* the song offensive. Maybe the real issue that we need to be dealing with is how music can objectify males and females."

"Give me a break, Don," Sandra responded. "The issue that we have to deal with is offensive music. I want Head-On Collision to perform in this event just as much as you do and I fully agree that we need to engage them as much as possible in the life of the school. However, you need to tell them immediately that they will have to replace their song selection if they are going to be included in the 'Dance Off.' This is simply not negotiable. I wish we had more time to talk about this, but I am already late for a meeting at the district office. We'll talk some other time about how we might better engage this group of students."

Disappointed, Don wondered why he and his colleagues couldn't use this issue as a learning opportunity for the students. Since, as Sandra suggested, the song was already being transformed into an offensive message across the entire school, how could they ban it? Wouldn't it be better if they took the opportunity to have a critical discussion about the general use of offensive words in lyrics and explore what makes people uncomfortable with them? Maybe he, or some of the other performers, could rewrite the song so that it remained appealing but not offensive. Surely, Don thought to himself, once we explained how we worked together to address the issue, the audience would understand why we included the song.

Discouraged, Don entered the practice hall and noticed Head-On Collision rehearsing. As soon as the students saw him, they greeted him excitedly and asked him to watch their newest steps. Almost immediately, as the music filled the room, the rest of the students joined in and were either dancing or singing along. Don couldn't help but be pleased with the enthusiasm and the growing sense of community he was seeing among the performers.

However, those thoughts just made him feel worse as he began to feel the weight of what he was going to have to do next. Did he have any choice? Sandra had been adamant that the group had to make yet another selection and had been crystal clear about her position on using the offending music. Don knew that banning the song would alienate the group from the school and might anger many others. The administration would be cast in a negative light, and as the "Dance Off" coordinator he would not escape the students' ire. As the music faded and the students enthusiastically began to crowd around Don for instructions, he took a deep breath and reluctantly began to explain why things couldn't proceed as planned.

Questions

The Case

In retrospect, should Don have acted differently during the "Dance Off" practice when Head-On Collision presented their second music selection? Justify your answer.

History

In this case, Don is concerned that alienated students like those in Head-On Collision were at risk of dropping out of school. How have our views about high school drop-outs changed over time?

Philosophy

Should Sandra Bolton have been more open-minded given the history of the students involved or do you think she acted appropriately as a principal? Explain.

Sociology

This case addresses how challenging it can be to try to integrate students from marginalized subcultures. In trying to integrate such students, what kinds of things should teachers keep in mind?

Implications for Practice

What will *you* do when faced with a choice between acknowledging the role of youth culture in the lives of students and upholding the expectations of the local community? Can teachers do both? Explain.

Gangster Fashion

The student population at Sun Valley High School included a large number of students who were first- and second-generation immigrants to Canada from the Caribbean and South-East Asia. Many of these students were interested and immersed in hip-hop culture. During breaks, they could often be seen rapping and beat-boxing while they worked on their schoolwork or waited for classes to change. Hip-hop slang could be heard throughout the school, and some of the students were avid "taggers" whose authorship of artistic graffiti was well known in the tightly knit community. However, it was the gangster-style hip-hop fashion, including baggy pants worn low without a belt, baseball caps, sweatshirts with hoods worn over hats, bandanas, do-rags, and camouflage fabrics that set this group apart, with both males and females adopting the "look."

Community members and many of the teachers were outraged by hip-hop culture. They saw it as wholly negative, worrying that it condemned their youth to a future life of crime. Parents couldn't understand why their children would adopt militaristic fashion and reject beautiful clothes, but most of all, they feared that gangster fashion was more than just a passing fad. For many parents, hip-hop culture represented a rejection of their core values and beliefs and a slap in the face for the citizenship they had worked so hard to get.

In response to mounting pressure from the community and concerns expressed by many of the teachers at Sun Valley, the administration developed a dress code with two policies that were aimed directly at suppressing the outward trappings of hip-hop culture. One provision was a "no headgear" policy, which had already been adopted in many of the schools in the district to reduce tensions between rival gangs. "No headgear" meant that no baseball caps, hooded sweatshirts, or "do-rags" were allowed in the school. Another provision banned baggy pants, exposed underwear, flashy jewellery, and most importantly, any clothing made of camouflage fabric.

Needless to say, the clothing policies were extremely unpopular. Some students openly resisted the dress code every day, especially the provision that restricted camouflage clothing. These students also wore baseball caps, hoodies, and "do-rags" whenever they could get away with it. Over time, they had come to learn that in spite of the formal school policies, a number of teachers chose to look the other way rather than try to enforce the rules that some of them, at least, didn't believe were very important.

However, the administration remained committed to the dress code and regularly reminded teachers to enforce it. Teachers were expected to stop students if they entered the school or their classrooms wearing headgear. Any student who refused to comply with school policies was sent to the office, where administrators confiscated the "contraband." The rows of baseball caps on display in the principal's office served as a visual reminder to students to follow the policy. A large supply of clean, slightly fashionable oversized clothing was also available for students to change into if they had made the mistake of trying to wear camouflage pants, shirts, or jackets to school.

When Julie Martin, an energetic 24-year-old, was hired halfway through September to replace a veteran teacher who had unexpectedly needed to go on medical leave, her late start meant that she missed the new teacher orientation sessions, which were held in August. Had the administration stopped to think about what Julie had missed, they might have avoided the inevitable collision that occurred.

As a young Home Economics teacher, Julie was intrigued by popular culture and saw it as an excellent way to connect with her students. Upon her arrival at Sun Valley, she quickly realized that hip-hop culture was extremely popular, and she was excited by the idea of capitalizing on her students' interests to teach the principles of design and the mechanics of sewing. Shortly after she began teaching, Julie found a good source of inexpensive camouflage-patterned fabric and bought a large quantity, not knowing the dynamics of the community or that there was a school policy against wearing this pattern. Delighted with her purchase, Julie explained to her senior class that they would be expected to design and sew a project that drew from hip-hop culture for their major term assignment. When she announced the intent of the project, the students couldn't believe their ears but locking eyes, they instantly and silently made a tacit pact not to warn Julie about the problems that this particular assignment would likely cause.

A few days later, Julie came to class with the bundle of camouflage material under her arm, and her students were eager to begin. However, just as they settled down to work, the class was interrupted by an announcement over the public address system that the school assembly was about to begin. Julie walked with her class to the gym and sat down with them to listen to the principal, Bev Speers, discuss a variety of things, including some of the school's policies and expectations regarding student behaviour and appropriate dress. Bev reminded the students to observe the school's rules on wearing headgear and the ban on all forms of camouflage clothing.

As one, her class turned to Julie to see her reaction. Some of them felt guilty that they hadn't mentioned anything earlier, but others were clearly satisfied that they had been able to subvert the school's authority in a small way. Julie was shocked to discover she had violated the school's policy on student clothing and realized that both her assignment and credibility were in jeopardy. She motioned to her students not to worry and whispered that she would speak to the principal as soon as possible after the assembly.

At the end of the day, Julie asked to see Bev to discuss her dilemma. She described her lesson plans and the camouflage fabric that she had bought for her class. She explained that the students were excited and that she believed the use of this material made the project particularly engaging for students who might otherwise be disengaged. Although Bev clearly wasn't keen on the idea, she blamed herself for not making sure that Julie, as a late hire, had been made aware of the school's policies before she got started. Since her new teacher had obviously invested a great deal of time and effort in planning, Bev felt she had to give her permission to follow through on the assignment. However, she made it clear that this did not mean that the students would be allowed to wear the finished products in school.

As the days wore on, Julie's students found creative ways to express hip-hop culture, using the camouflage fabric to make shirts, pants, pillows, and even quilts. Their original designs were photographed and displayed in the school's annual fashion and photography show. On the day of the show, as some had predicted, the students proudly wore their creations in open defiance of the school's clothing policies. As Bev stormed down the hallway, Julie wondered if she should have taken some kind of action to prevent this obvious act of defiance, although privately she was very proud of their creations. As she left the show that day, she wondered if breaking the rules was ever justified and whether she had just been taken for a ride.

Questions

The Case

Hip-hop culture has often been demonized in educational settings and viewed only in relationship to gangs and violence. How does Julie view hip-hop culture differently?

History

Successive waves of immigration to Canada from various parts of the world have challenged the ability of school systems to integrate students effectively. In what ways is the attempt to integrate students in this case both similar to and different from the integration of other immigrant students in the past?

Philosophy

At the end of the case, Julie wonders if breaking school rules is ever justified. What factors ought she to consider and why?

Sociology

The youth subculture of hip-hop music and fashion is often perceived to be a threat to the well-being of society. Why do you think this might be so? Explain.

Implications for Practice

Think about the school's policies in this case or another policy with which you disagree. What can you do when faced with policies that challenge your deeply held beliefs?

Character Counts

Jessica Grégoire began her job as principal of West Hills High School with cautious optimism. West Hills was a large urban high school that had its share of challenges. It served a largely working-class and immigrant neighbourhood in one of Canada's largest cities. The previous year, before Jessica's arrival, the community had been rocked by several eruptions of gang violence, but efforts to divert the animosity and build a positive school culture seemed to have been fairly effective. To date, there had been no major incidents, but Jessica could sense that tensions were building and she couldn't help worrying that these would soon find an outlet.

As she feared, in early October, well before the school day was about to begin, anger between two rival groups flared up into a brawl in one of the school's parking lots, leaving one boy, Roy Herman, with severe enough injuries to require a trip to hospital. Fortunately, despite a broken arm and sore ribs, Roy was well enough to be released the same day. Rumours about the fight spread throughout the school like wildfire. By the time reports of the early morning fight reached Jessica's office, the magnitude and ferocity of the conflict had already been exaggerated beyond recognition. Over the course of the day, the brawl was being recounted as an epic melee involving dozens of combatants from four competing gangs with the victim hanging onto his life by a thread.

Over the next few days, Jessica and the local police constable consulted with the two vice-principals at West Hills, as well as with several veteran teachers. Together, they developed a plan for addressing the incident. The elements of the plan involved meeting with students and parents to discuss the findings of the investigation, suspending all students involved for a period of time, and requiring them to take part in a restorative justice program as a condition of returning to school. The meeting with parents went as well as could be expected, and all seemed willing to go along with the plan the school had developed.

Roy Herman's parents, however, weren't satisfied. They felt that justice was not being adequately served, and they decided to go public with their grievances. They contacted a local newspaper, claiming that their son was an innocent victim. Not only had the school failed to protect him from gang violence, but it had also punished him with a suspension equal to that of those students who his parents believed were responsible for his injuries. The paper ran the story with a photograph of the cast on Roy's arm on the front page under the headline "Victim of Gang Violence Treated like a Criminal."

The story caused a sensation across the city, particularly in the neighbourhood served by West Hills. Much to Jessica's dismay, the local media were suggesting that she had mishandled the whole situation. The reporter cast her in the role of a new and inexperienced principal who had blown her first tough assignment and, as a consequence, violence at the school was in danger of spinning out of control.

Bert Tulliver, the local Member of the Legislative Assembly (MLA) met with the Herman family and promised his support. At a hastily arranged press conference, he argued that what had happened to Roy was reflective of a broader social and moral decline among today's young people. He pointed to the violence at West Hills High School as yet another example of irresponsible youth being allowed to run amok in the local community. Bert went on to blame the school and its staff for failing to address student morals in their teaching. He wound up his press conference by calling for a public meeting to hear a presentation from Character Counts, an American character-education program that tackled the issue of violence by teaching students the core values of trustworthiness, respect, responsibility, fairness, caring, and citizenship in a systematic way.

The meeting, which was well attended by a number of parents from West Hills High School, also drew a wider audience of parents and community members from other neighbourhoods across the city. At the conclusion of the Character Counts presentation, Bert led a question-and-answer period. A litany of complaints aimed at the school and its administrators quickly surfaced. Jessica listened with alarm as angry audience members described a school that bore no resemblance to the West Hills High School that she had come to know.

Jessica seized the opportunity to set the record straight, reminding the audience that this was a single incident that had been dealt with promptly and that the conflict had resulted from a broader territorial dispute that had been brewing *outside* of the school throughout the summer. She acknowledged that the fight had occurred on school grounds, but she argued that it was not indicative of ongoing school violence at West Hills.

Bert dismissed the principal's report, countering that it was obvious that she and her staff were more interested in saving face than in solving a long-term and vexing problem, which had plagued their community for years and continued to tear at its moral fabric. The answer was clear in Bert's opinion. The school needed to adopt the comprehensive Character Counts program or suffer the consequences of escalating violence. Finally, Bert promised to do everything in his power to ensure that the Character Counts program was implemented without delay. The sustained applause that greeted this pronouncement showed that the room was almost unanimous in its support.

The meeting received a great deal of media coverage, locally and nationally. The most sensational comments decrying gang violence in the schools and demanding a mandatory character education program received the most media coverage. Although the superintendent, Dr Maude Calhoun, had supported the plan that Jessica and her school team had devised, she was so concerned about the negative attention being drawn to the school that the day after the town hall meeting, she came to the school to talk to Jessica and her administrative team. She wanted something done quickly and publicly to counter the impression that behaviour in the school was uncontrollable.

The administrative team was prepared for Dr Calhoun's visit and had data ready to demonstrate that violence at West Hills had not increased and that the number of violent incidents had actually decreased. Jessica reminded the superintendent that the school's carefully planned responses had been effective and that an American program, developed without the local context in mind, was unlikely to be as successful. Dr Calhoun shook her head sympathetically, but countered that the situation had moved well beyond local sensibilities and that the district had no choice but to demonstrate that it was taking public concerns seriously. Although she didn't insist on the adoption of Character Counts, she ended the conversation by directing the administrators to review all available character-education programs and select one within a week. As the superintendent left, Jessica wondered whether this was going to be case of the cure being worse than the disease.

Questions

The Case

How do Jessica Grégoire, Bert Tulliver, and Maude Calhoun interpret the incident at West Hills High School differently? What perspectives does each bring to the situation?

History

From a historical perspective, what factors do you think have contributed to the increasing popularity of moral education programs in Canada?

Philosophy

In your opinion, should the new principal, Jessica Grégoire, show more courage in countering the directives of her superintendent? Explain.

Sociology

Since her arrival at West Hills, Jessica had been working hard to build a sense of community in the school. In your opinion, what are the characteristics of a positive school culture?

Implications for Practice

Imagine you are teaching at a school that is at the centre of a media storm. What might *you* do to counter the attack on your school's reputation?

CHAPTER FIVE
Conclusion

In this book, we have explored the notion of certainties and uncertainties and specifically highlighted the ways that myths, bandwagons, and moral panics affect teachers and teaching. We have defined myths as unexamined assumptions about teaching and learning; bandwagons as untested ideas, causes, or theories that we follow because they are popular; and moral panics as unsupported fears about threats to the well-being of society. Even though each of these unwarranted certainties is unique, we have made the case that they do have a number of things in common: they are rooted in beliefs, they are context-specific, they are responses to real or perceived needs, they affect educational policies and practices, and they tend to be resistant to disconfirming evidence. We have also made the point that the boundaries between these unwarranted certainties can sometimes be blurred because they are so closely related to one another.

To show how myths, bandwagons, and moral panics play out in real classrooms, we presented 30 cases, 10 for each type of unwarranted certainty, and then we posed a number of questions that each case raised. We included these cases because we know from experience that case studies can be effective tools for analyzing critical incidents and dilemmas in teaching, and for developing the critical thinking skills and flexibility of mind that are so important in teaching (Mandzuk & Hasinoff, 2010). As a backdrop or organizational scheme, we also introduced Schwab's (1977) four commonplaces of education—students, teachers, subject matter, and context (or milieu). Although we have focused most of our discussion in the book on the first three of the commonplaces, we think that, taken together, all four provide beginning and experienced teachers alike with a simple but useful framework for examining educational issues of any kind.

With the four commonplaces in mind and in spite of how tricky predicting the future can be (Davies & Guppy, 2010), we focus the remaining part of this chapter on four illustrative trends that we think will influence the course of education: increasing student diversity, changing roles of teachers, blurring boundaries between disciplines, and widening disparities in society. We also acknowledge the significance of the trend to "infinite connection" identified by the Organisation for Economic Co-operation and Development in *Trends Shaping Education 2013* as a powerful influence on anything related to schools (OECD, 2013, p. 91). In keeping with our attention to unwarranted certainties throughout the book, we discuss these trends by examining the relevant myths, bandwagons, and moral panics that are associated with each one.

Trends

Students: Increasing diversity

The myth that all children belong in the regular classroom and that all outcomes can be taught to all children is challenged by the increasing diversity of students in schools. Teachers have long been expected to accommodate a range of student abilities, but these days, teachers are expected to differentiate their instruction for all learners, including non-native speakers of English, severely physically handicapped children, and students with special learning needs, such as autism and fetal alcohol syndrome. Parents increasingly expect children with special needs to be accommodated appropriately in the regular classroom and to meet the same expectations as their classmates. However, teachers may become disillusioned and may blame themselves when they realize that their experience, skills, and commitment to their students are outstripped by the diversity they face every day.

In response to the increased diversity of classrooms, educators will continue to be exposed to bandwagons designed to address the diversity of learners. Just as we have seen in the business world, we think that in the future, educators will jump on the "**gamification**" bandwagon and try to apply the strategies and principles developed in popular gaming software to re-design learning activities for different kinds of learners. These strategies may include the use of ready-made applications for future technological devices or the adaptation of existing teaching materials to include more meaningful choices, built-in rewards and challenges, scaffolded instruction, and more opportunities for students to gain mastery by learning from their own mistakes. Just as teachers used to complain that they couldn't expect to compete with television shows like *Sesame Street*, the expectation that schools should make learning more like video games or other forms of "edutainment" is likely to overwhelm some teachers.

We also think that diversity will continue to be a source of moral panics. As immigration expands and legal, moral, and pedagogical imperatives require that all children, regardless of their special needs, be accommodated in the regular classroom, pressure will continue to mount on teachers and schools. Increased diversity in the regular classroom can also arouse exaggerated fears in parents that the curriculum is being "dumbed down" or that too much diversity means that their so-called average children are being ignored.

Teachers: Changing roles

The myth that teaching can be done anywhere, any time, and by anybody is well entrenched. This assumption is fuelled by the belief that, given the vast storehouse of information and teaching materials now available on-line, anyone with an Internet connection can teach. The widespread belief that teaching is simply a matter of learning a set of techniques means that teaching is mistakenly considered to be easy whereas, in fact, it is even more complex and demanding than ever (Darling-Hammond, Hammerness, Grossman, Rust, & Shulman, 2005). Moreover, as universal Internet access continues to untether learning from institutions, questions about the purpose of "bricks and mortar" schools and the role of the teacher arise more frequently. In the meantime, teachers can expect to continue to face competing demands to be, on the one hand, more accountable for curricular outcomes and, on the other hand, to provide more engaging and creative work for their students.

Bandwagons like "**distributed learning**," "blended learning," and other non-traditional teaching methods are already being adopted. Some schools are requiring high school and even middle years students to take some of their courses by distance learning to prepare them for post-secondary options that are offered only on-line. Home schooling will likely continue to grow as an option, as more parents conclude that they can just as easily teach their own children at home, promote their own values, and avoid what they may consider the negative influences of public schools. Many schools are also experimenting with "flipped classrooms," in which students read and research on-line at home and do their homework with the help of a teacher at school.

The changing role of teachers can be expected to lead to moral panics about the cohesion of society and the adequate preparation of students. It will inevitably become more difficult, as more learning takes place beyond school walls, for students to develop shared values and learn social norms through common academic experiences. Moral panics about youth and youth culture are never far from the surface. Consequently, if socialization becomes unmoored from schools, and teachers are no longer involved in face-to-face teaching relationships with students, concerns about the future of democracy and the development of informed and engaged citizens are likely to rise.

Subject matter: Blurring boundaries

Although the assumption that authentic learning cannot take place under the constraints of traditional subject teaching is continually promoted by education reformers, the power of the credit system as the gatekeeper to post-secondary education has not yet been seriously challenged. However, a number of factors suggest that subject-matter boundaries will continue to break down. For example, we think that there will be upward pressures from the highly integrated teaching practices of early and middle years educators to teach in a more interdisciplinary fashion, as well as downward pressures from the business community to focus more on developing fundamental skills, including critical thinking and problem solving, personal management skills, and teamwork skills (Conference Board of Canada, 2013). These trends, coupled with the increased acceptance of alternative entry paths to post-secondary institutions, such as the work portfolios produced by home-schooled students, suggest that in the future, educators will be more likely to look for connections across the disciplines rather than teach them as though they were discrete and unrelated entities.

We have seen the bandwagon to integrate curriculum come and go, and once again, it appears to be gaining momentum. This time around, curriculum integration appears to be driven by pressures to integrate technology and to infuse social values, such as social justice and environmental sustainability, as a means of engaging students in purposeful inquiry. The widespread adoption of interdisciplinary programs like Reggio Emilia and International Baccalaureate, and the increasing number of interdisciplinary courses, such as Topics in Science, suggests that subject-matter boundaries are already blurring. Furthermore, ministries of education are under increasing pressure to reduce the enormous number of disconnected outcomes that students are expected to meet and to consolidate the curriculum through essential questions and themes. The challenge embedded in this trend is that it is extremely difficult to integrate curricula and ensure that students acquire fundamental skills at the same time. This may be why Ravitch (2003) found that many of the 20 educational reform movements she reviewed were eventually replaced by "what was called 'back-to-basics' or 'essentialism,' or something else that suggested the death of a wave of failed innovation" (para. 14).

Moral panics about subject matter often accompany weak results on international or provincial tests. Critics point to these results as confirmation that educators are straying too far from the basics. Movements to integrate content and to concentrate more heavily on so-called soft skills like collegiality can lead to moral panics if it is feared that students don't really know about anything in depth and will not be prepared to contribute productively to the national economy or to compete in the global marketplace.

Context: Widening disparities

There is a pervasive myth that public schools would be more successful if they operated as if they were businesses or private schools. The practice of offering parents more choices within public school systems has already taken hold in many jurisdictions, whether it means allowing students to attend any public school inside or outside their catchment area (as long as space is available) or to attend publicly funded programs that are structured around special interests or needs. Proponents of the business model of education argue that free choice serves as quality control since parents, as consumers, will quickly sort out good schools from bad and will thereby weed out the underperforming schools.

Even now, parents in some jurisdictions are faced with a bewildering choice of schools in both the public and private sectors. These wide-ranging choices reflect educational bandwagons that continue to excite people and influence educational decisions. Students can enrol in schools that immerse them in one of many languages, including Mandarin, French, and Ukrainian; enable them to earn international accreditation through the International Baccalaureate or Advanced Placement programs; follow an educational philosophy, such as Reggio Emilia, Montessori, and Waldorf; focus on a specific art, science, or sport; take classes through distance or blended learning; or learn with others who have the same religion, gender, ethnicity, or race. Such choices, however, may be illusory for those who either cannot afford to take advantage of them or who live in areas of the country where such variety is unavailable.

Moral panics about equity are likely to gain momentum as a result of the demand for more individual choice. Although such fears may be more rooted in economic worries about declining neighbourhoods and falling property values, the trend to privatization and individual choice may have serious educational consequences for students who are already disadvantaged. Paradoxically, instead of raising academic levels, increased school choice can result in greater marginalization and less access to support for students whose families are unaware of the range of educational opportunities, are physically or financially unable to transport their children to schools of interest, or who do not understand how to navigate the educational system. In other words, in providing more options, school boards may in fact be subverting the mandate of the public school system to ensure equity for youth by widening rather than narrowing the gap between their privileged and less privileged students.

Summary

In this book, we have argued that while some uncertainties in education are inevitable and even warranted, our aim as educators is to reduce these by becoming better informed, more thoughtful, and more willing to disrupt our certainties about what constitutes effective teaching and learning. We encourage you to use the four commonplaces as reference points, to keep an eye on educational trends, to ask the questions that often go unasked about myths, bandwagons, and moral panics, and to consider what influence they are likely to have on you and your practice. Finally, we would like to take one last opportunity to advocate for the foundations of education, which help us to pose the right kinds of essential questions so that we can recognize and manage both the unwarranted certainties and inevitable uncertainties that characterize teaching.

GLOSSARY

accountability Requirement that schools and teachers be responsible for students' performance through frequent and systematic use of achievement tests.

alienation Feelings of estrangement from social structures, from other people, or even from oneself.

apprenticeship of observation Informal and often unconscious acquisition of skills, dispositions, and beliefs by observing our teachers when we are students.

authority Legitimate power exercised by teachers who have earned the trust, respect, and willing compliance of students.

back-stage Term used to describe a setting in which our actions are hidden from view and which is presumed to be the site of our more authentic selves. *See also* **front-stage**.

bandwagon Idea, cause, or theory that people support because it is fashionable or seems likely to succeed; fad.

bonding Close inward-looking relations between like-minded individuals with similar interests and goals; a dimension of social capital.

boy crisis Moral panic caused by the belief that boys are systematically disadvantaged in school and at risk of being surpassed by girls in all areas of human endeavour.

brain-based teaching Teaching approaches that are based on recent research about the structure and functioning of the brain.

bridging Broad outward-looking relations between people with different interests and goals; a dimension of social capital.

character education Conscious inculcating of a defined set of core virtues (for example, trustworthiness, respect, and a sense of responsibility) as a means of counteracting moral problems of society.

commonplaces of education Common reference points for understanding education; includes students, teachers, subject matter, and context or milieu.

confirmation bias Tendency to look for information that confirms our beliefs or theories and that discounts anything that contradicts them.

constructivism Belief that students learn best by constructing their own knowledge with others.

criterion-referenced test Test that is designed to measure how well a person has learned a specific body of knowledge and skills, in contrast to standards-referenced tests, which are designed to measure what students should know and are able to do in different subjects at various grades.

cyberbullying Anonymous use of social media to send harassing, intimidating, or threatening messages.

digital divide Gap that some people believe exists between those who grow up with technology ("digital natives") and those who come to technology later in their lives ("digital immigrants").

distributed (blended) learning Use of a variety of delivery formats (print and digital) and media (on-line and face-to-face) allowing instructors, students, and course content to be located in different, non-centralized locations.

encyclopedia of knowledge Body of knowledge accumulated through research and scholarship.

encyclopedia of mythology Body of knowledge acquired through personal stories and anecdotes.

entity theory Belief that intelligence is a fixed and unchangeable trait.

ethnicity Person's cultural inheritance, including language, values, customs, beliefs, and cultural identity.

extrinsic motivation Willingness to do something because it may lead to a desirable outcome or a reward.

folk devil Targeted group of people or ideas that are perceived as threats to society.

foundations of education History, philosophy, and sociology of education.

full inclusion Practice of including *all* children in the regular, or "mainstream" classrooms.

front-stage Term used to describe a setting in which our actions are visible. *See also* **back-stage**.

gamification Application of strategies and principles developed in popular gaming software to re-design learning activities for various kinds of learners.

gender expectations Social norms that shape our beliefs about what behaviour is appropriate for each gender.

groupthink Tendency of individual members of groups to think alike, regardless of available evidence, as a way of preserving social dynamics and promoting group harmony.

habits of mind Set of problem-solving and critical thinking skills and dispositions that are used to confront a problem whose resolution is not immediately apparent.

hidden curriculum Socializing processes implicitly transmitted through school rules, procedures, structures, and covert norms rather than taught formally or explicitly as part of the academic curriculum.

historical-mindedness Interpretation and understanding of current events through familiarity with the past.

ideal type Sociological tool that aids understanding by purposefully exaggerating a certain aspect of reality.

identity A person's conception and expression of individuality or group affiliation. *See also* **professional identity**.

implementation dip Point at which an innovation is often abandoned after the initial enthusiasm for the innovation has worn off and there are no immediate or visible signs of progress as a result of its implementation.

impression management Self-presentation techniques used to influence others to view us favourably.

incremental theory Belief that intelligence is a malleable and boundless trait.

intrinsic motivation Desire to do something because it is inherently interesting or enjoyable.

issue attention cycle Model that illustrates the volatility of public interest and attention over time.

learned helplessness Sense of powerlessness often associated with the belief that success is a matter of chance or luck rather than personal effort.

loose coupling Characteristic of systems that are composed of separate, idiosyncratic, and weakly related components, which therefore make them resistant to standardization and relatively unchanged by external influences.

marginalization Voluntary or involuntary exclusion from one or more spheres of life in which one is expected to participate.

meaninglessness Sense that the unintelligibility of complex affairs makes predictions about future results of one's actions extremely difficult or even impossible.

moral entrepreneur Individual, group, or formal organization that launches a campaign promoting laws or policies that are consistent with strongly held moral beliefs.

moral panic Socially constructed, widespread, and unsupported fear about perceived threats to the safety and well-being of society.

multiculturalism Belief that all cultures are equally valuable and have the same right to be encouraged and accepted in society.

myth Unexamined assumption that underlies one's actions.

neuroplasticity Ability of the human brain to change throughout life in response to changes in its environment.

normal child Term referring to those children who are believed to share common desirable traits and against whom all others can be judged as deviant or undesirable.

normlessness Inability to identify with the dominant values of society, leading individuals to rely more often on their own judgment than conform to social norms.

open classroom Architectural and pedagogical arrangement that was popular in the 1970s which grouped students of varying grades in a single, large classroom with several teachers.

power Using coercion, threats, and sanctions to force students to comply with the rules of the school or classroom.

powerlessness Sense that one does not have the means to achieve one's goals.

presentism Error of interpreting past accounts of events as if they had happened today.

professional identity Internalizing of the values, beliefs, and attitudes of one's profession.

secularism Belief that religion should have no place in laws, government policies, or public institutions.

self-estrangement Feeling of having become a stranger to oneself or to some parts of oneself.

self-fulfilling prophecy An expectation about something or someone that comes true because we believe or have acted as if it is true.

single-sex education Organization of education based on the belief that boys and girls learn best when they are placed in boys-only or girls-only settings.

social capital Benefits that accrue to individuals by virtue of their relationships and networks in the communities of which they are a part. *See also* **bonding** and **bridging**.

social inclusion Social arrangements by which all socio-economic, racial, and ethnic groups are equally valued.

social isolation Feeling of being segregated from and disaffected with one's community.

social media Synchronous and asynchronous technologies (such as cell phones, web sites, and applications) that are used by individuals and groups to communicate with one another.

socio-economic status Sociological term for the social standing of an individual or group as measured by a variety of indicators, such as level of parents' education and family income.

sociological ambivalence State of uncertainty that results from conflicting role expectations associated with different social structures to which one belongs.

standard Benchmark used to measure achievement.

standardization Process of requiring schools to adopt a common set of benchmarks in the belief that this will improve achievement and raise the quality of education.

technopanic Emotional response that pathologizes young people's use of computer-mediated technologies.

tracking (streaming) Practice of channelling students into certain courses on the basis of measures of intelligence or achievement in order to create homogeneous groups for teaching and learning.

unwarranted certainty Socially constructed and usually unconscious belief that is immune to reasoned arguments or disconfirming research; examples are myths, bandwagons, and moral panics.

virtues of teaching Ideal attributes and dispositions of teachers, such as empathy, humility, judgment, and courage.

whole language Holistic method of reading instruction, popularized in the 1970s, that emphasizes meaning and the integration of all language skills (reading, writing, speaking, and listening) and context and that de-emphasizes decoding and spelling.

youth culture Values, beliefs, styles of self-presentation, and tastes in entertainment shared by adolescents that often evoke suspicion, if not outright fear, in adults.

REFERENCES

Abbott, P., & Sapsford, F. (2001). Young women and their wardrobes. In A. Guy, E. Green, & M. Banim (Eds.), *Through the wardrobe: Women's relationships with their clothes* (pp. 21–38). Oxford: Berg.

Abdal-Haqq, I. (1998). Constructivism in teacher education: Considerations for those who would link practice to theory. *ERIC Digest: ERIC Clearinghouse on Teaching and Teacher Education.*

Achterman, D. (2010). Literacy leadership and the school library. In S. Coatney (Ed.), *The many faces of school library leadership* (pp. 67–84). Santa Barbara, CA: Libraries Unlimited.

Allan, B., & Fryer, R. (2011). *The power and pitfalls of education incentives.* Washington, DC: Brookings Institution.

Anyon, J. (1981). Social class and the hidden curriculum of work. In H. Giroux, A. Penna, & W. Pinar (Eds.), *Curriculum and instruction* (pp. 317–341). Berkeley, CA: McCutcheon.

Atkinson, B. (2008). Apple jumper, teacher babe, and bland uniformer teachers: Fashioning feminine teacher bodies. *Education Studies, 44*, 98–121.

Bamburg, J. (1994). *Raising expectations to improve student learning.* Oak Brook, IL: North Central Regional Educational Laboratory.

Bandwagon effect [Electronic (2013). Version]. *Wikipedia.* Retrieved November 18, 2013, from http://en.wikipedia.org/w/index.php?title=Bandwagon_effect&oldid=577657061.

Barakett, J., & Cleghorn, A. (2008). *Sociology of education: An introductory view from Canada* (2nd ed.). Toronto, ON: Pearson Prentice Hall.

Bayne, S., & Ross, J. (2007, December). The "digital native" and "digital immigrant": A dangerous opposition. *Annual Conference of the Society of Research into Higher Education.*

Bazelon, E. (2013, March 12). Defining bullying down. *New York Times*, p. A23.

Beadie, N. (1996). From teacher as decision maker to teacher as participant in shared decision making: Reframing the purpose of social foundations in teacher education *Teachers College Record, 98*(1), 77–103.

Becker, H.S. (1963). *Outsiders: Studies in the sociology of deviance.* New York: Free Press.

Ben-Yehuda, N. (2009). Moral panics—36 years on. *British Journal of Criminology, 49*(1), 1–3.

Bennett, S., & Maton, K. (2011). Intellectual field or faith-based religion: Moving on from the idea of digital natives. In M. Thomas (Ed.), *Deconstructing digital natives: Young people, technology, and the new literacies* (pp. 169–185). New York: Routledge.

Bennett, S., Maton, K., & Kervin, L. (2008). The "digital natives" debate: A critical review of the evidence. *British Journal of Educational Technology, 39*(5), 775–786.

Berger, P. (1963). *Invitation to sociology.* Garden City, NY: Doubleday-Anchor.

Bigler, R., & Eliot, L. (2011). The feminist case against single-sex schools [Electronic Version]. Slate. Retrieved May 1, 2013 from http://www.slate.com/articles/double_x/doublex/2011/10/the_single_sex_school_myth_an_overwhelming_body_of_research_show.html.

Blumen, L. (2010). *Bullying epidemic: Not just child's play.* Toronto, ON: Camberley Press.

Blumenfeld, W.J. (2006). Christian privilege and the promotion of "secular" and not-so "secular" mainline Christianity on public schooling and the larger society. *Equity and Excellence in Education, 39*(3), 195–210.

Boyd, M. (2002). Educational attainment of immigrant offspring: Success or segmented assimilation? *International Migration Review, 36*(4), 1037–1060.

Boyd, M. (2008). Variations in socioeconomic outcomes of second generation young adults. *Canadian Diversity, 6*(2), 20–24.

Bradley, J. (2011). False accusations: A growing fear in the classroom [Electronic Version]. *Education Canada*, 51. Retrieved September 8, 2013, from www.cea-ace.ca/education-canada/article/false-accusations-growing-fear-classroom.

Buchart, R.E. (2011). What's Foucault got to do with it? History, theory, and becoming subjected. *History of Education Quarterly, 51*(2), 239–246.

Bullock, S.M., & Christou, T. (2009). Exploring the radical middle between theory and practice: A collaborative self-study of beginning teacher educators. *Studying Teacher Education, 5*(1), 75–88.

Butin, D. (2004). The foundations of preparing teachers: Are education schools really "intellectually barren" and ideological? [Electronic Version]. *Teachers College Record.* Retrieved July 15, 2012, from www.tcrecord.org/Content.asp?ContentId=11349.

Cahill, W. (2005). On teachers access to the discourse of education [Electronic Version]. *Teachers College Record.* Retrieved February 26, 2013, from www.tcrecord.org.

Cavanagh, S.L. (2004). Upsetting desires in the classroom: School sex scandals and the pedagogy of the femme fatale. *Journal for the Psychoanalysis of Culture & Society 9*(3), 315–332.

Cavanagh, S.L. (2005). Female-teacher gender and sexuality in twentieth-century Ontario, Canada. *History of Education Quarterly, 45*(2), 247–273.

Christou, T., & Bullock, S. (2013). Foundations of teacher education: A Canadian perspective. Retrieved February 10, 2014, from https://docs.google.com/file/d/0B2i27L6z1IlUTHl5OTFZN2lFdkU/edit

Clandinin, D.J., & Connelly, F.M. (2000). *Narrative inquiry: Experience and story in qualitative research.* San Francisco, CA: Jossey-Bass.

Clarke, P. (2005). Religion, public education and the charter: Where do we go now? *McGill Journal of Education 40*(3), 351–381.

Clifton, R.A. (1989). Knowledge and mythology in teacher education. *McGill Journal of Education, 24*(3), 267–279.

Cohen, S. (1972). *Folk devils and moral panics.* London: MacGibbon & Kee.

Cohen, S. (2002). *Folk devils and moral panics* (3rd ed.). London: Routledge.

Coish, D. (2005). Who works in Canadian libraries? *Focus on Culture, 15*(2), 8–10.

Conference Board of Canada. (2013). *Employability skills 2000+.* Ottawa, ON: Author.

Critcher, C. (2008). Moral panic analysis: Past, present and future. *Sociology Compass, 2*(4), 1127–1144.

Darling-Hammond, L., Hammerness, K., Grossman, P., Rust, F., & Shulman, L. (2005). The design of teacher education programs. In L. Darling-Hammond & J. Bransford (Eds.), *Preparing teachers for a changing world: What teachers should learn and be able to do* (pp. 390–441). San Francisco, CA: Jossey-Bass.

Davies, S., & Guppy, N. (1998). Race and Canadian education. In V. Satzewich (Ed.), *Racism and social inequality on Canada: Concept, controversies and strategies of resistance.* Toronto: Thompson.

Davies, S., & Guppy, N. (2010). *The schooled society* (2nd ed.). Toronto: Oxford University Press.

Davis, M. (2003). What's wrong with character education? *American Journal of Education, 110*(1), 32–57.

DeFaveri, I. (1995). Multiculturalism and education. In L. Roberts & R. Clifton (Eds.), *Crosscurrents: Contemporary Canadian educational issues* (pp. 271–284). Toronto: Nelson Canada.

Demers, S., & Bennett, C. (2007). *Single-sex classrooms* Retrieved April 24, 2013, from www.edu.gov.on.ca/eng/literacynumeracy/inspire/research/demers.pdf.

Dewey, J. (1971). Why study philosophy? In J. A. Boydston (Ed.), *John Dewey: The early works 4: 1893–4.* Carbondale: Southern Illinois University Press.

Douvanis, G., & Hunsley, D. (2002). The least restrictive environment mandate: How has it been defined by the courts? *EC Digest, 629.*

Downs, A. (1972). Up and down with ecology: The "Issue-Attention Cycle." *The Public Interest, 28,* 38–50.

Dweck, C.S. (1975). The role of expectations and attributions in the alleviation of learned helplessness. *Journal of Personality and Social Psychology, 31,* 674–685.

Earl, L. (1999). Assessment and accountability in education: Improvement or surveillance? *Education Canada, 39*(3), 4–6, 47.

Edwards, A., Gilroy, P., & Hartley, D. (2002). *Rethinking teacher education: Collaborative responses to uncertainty.* London: Routledge Falmer.

Eiserman, J. (2009). They can still act Chinese and be Canadian at the same time: Reflections on multiculturalism and the Alberta art curriculum. *Canadian Review of Art Education, 36*(7), 67–82.

Elder, L., & Paul, R. (2007). *A critical thinker's guide to educational fads*. Dillon Beach, CA: Foundation for Critical Thinking Press.

Farmer, S. (2010). Criminality of Black youth in inner-city schools: "Moral panic," moral imagination, and moral formation. *Race Ethnicity and Education, 13*(3), 367–381.

Fendler, L. (2003). Teacher reflection in a hall of mirrors: Historical influences and political reverberations. *Educational Researcher, 32*(3), 16–25.

Floden, R.E., & Buchmann, M. (1993). Between routines and anarchy: Preparing teachers for uncertainty. *Oxford Review of Education, 19*(3), 373–382.

Floden, R.E., & Clark, C.M. (1988). Preparing teachers for uncertainty. *Teachers College Record, 89*(4), 505–524.

Freire, P. (1970). *Pedagogy of the oppressed*. New York: Herder & Herder.

Fryer, R., Jr. (2010). *Financial incentives and student achievement: Evidence from randomized trials* (NBER Working Paper No. 15898). Cambridge, MA: NBER.

Fullan, M. (2001). *Leading in a culture of change*. San Francisco: Jossey-Bass.

Fung, A. (2004). *Empowered participation: Reinventing urban democracy*. Princeton, NJ: Princeton University Press.

Furedi, F. (2011). The objectification of fear and the grammar of morality. In S. Hier (Ed.), *Moral panic and the politics of anxiety* (pp. 90–103). Abingdon, UK: Routledge.

Gaines, D. (1994). Border crossing in the U.S.A. In A. Ross & T. Rose (Eds.), *Microphone fiends: Youth music and youth culture* (pp. 227–234). New York: Routledge.

Garan, E.M., & DeVoogd, G. (2008). The benefits of sustained silent reading: Scientific research and common sense converge. *The Reading Teacher, 62*(4), 336–344.

Gardiner, S. (2001). Ten minutes a day for silent reading. *Educational Leadership, 59*(2), 32–35.

Ghosh, R. (2008). Racism: A hidden curriculum. *Education Canada, 48*(4), 26–29.

Giroux, H. (2000). Postmodern education and disposable youth. In P.P. Trifonas (Ed.), *Revolutionary pedagogies, cultural politics, instituting education, and the discourse of theory* (pp. 174–195). New York: Routledge.

Giroux, H. (2005). *Schooling and the struggle for public life* (2nd ed.). Boulder, CO: Paradigm.

Glegg, A. (2005). Anatomy of a tragedy: The assisted schools of British Columbia and the death of Mabel Jones. *Historical Studies in Education, 17*(1), 145–164.

Goffman, E. (1959). *The presentation of self in everyday life*. New York: Doubleday.

Goode, E., & Ben-Yehuda, N. (1994). Moral Panics: Culture, politics, and social construction. *Annual Review of Sociology, 20*(1), 149–171.

Goode, E., & Ben-Yehuda, N. (2009). *Moral panics: The social construction of deviance* (2nd ed.). Malden, MA: Wiley-Blackwell.

Gorski, P. (2008). The myth of the "Culture of Poverty." *Educational Leadership, 65*(7), 32–36.

Gosse, D. (2012). Men, masculinities, and sexualities in education and society: A call for evolution! *Education Canada, 52*(5), 16–19.

Greene, J.P. (2005). Education myths: Without reliable information, it is difficult to make good policy decisions. *Society for Quality Education Forum, 14*(4).

Greene, M. (1973). The professional significance of history of education. In M. Gillett & J.A. Laska (Eds.), *Foundation studies in education: Justifications and new directions*. Metuchen, NJ: Scarecrow Press.

Greene, M. (1995). *Releasing the imagination: Essays on education, the arts, and social change*. San Francisco: Jossey-Bass.

Gregory, M. (2007). Real teaching and real learning vs narrative myths about education. *Arts and Humanities in Higher Education, 6*(1), 7–27.

Guernsey, L. (2009, March 3). Rewards for students under a microscope. *New York Times*, pp. 1–4.

Gurian, M., & Henley, P. (2001). *Boys and girls learn differently: A guide for teachers and parents*. San Francisco: Jossey-Bass.

Halpern, D., Eliot, L., Bailer, R., Fabes, R., Hanish, L., Hyde, J., Liben, L., & Martin, C. (2011, September 23). The pseudoscience of single-sex schooling. *Science*, 333. Retrieved March 12, 2012, from www.scienceemag.org.

Hansot, E., & Tyack, D. (1982). A usable past: Using history in educational policy. In A. Lieberman & M. McLaughlin (Eds.), *Policy making in education* (pp. 1–22). Chicago, IL: National Society for the Study of Education.

Hare, W. (1993a). *Attitudes in teaching and education*. Calgary: Detselig.

Hare, W. (1993b). *What makes a good teacher?* London, ON: Althouse Press.

Helsing, D. (2007). Regarding uncertainty in teachers and teaching. *Teaching and Teacher Education, 23*, 1317–1333.

Helsper, E., & Eynon, R. (2010). Digital natives: Where is the evidence? *British Educational Research Journal, 36*(3), 503–520.

Helwig, C., Turiel, E., & Nucci, L. (1997). *Character education after the bandwagon has gone*. Paper presented at the American Educational Research Association, Chicago.

Henig, J.R., Hula, R.C., Orr, M., & Pedescleaux, D.S. (1999). *The color of school reform: Race, politics, and the challenge of urban education*. Princeton, NJ: Princeton University Press.

Herdt, G. (2009). Introduction: Moral panics, sexual rights, and cultural anger. In G. Herdt (Ed.), *Moral panics, sex panics: Fear and the fight over sexual rights* (pp. 1–46). New York: New York University Press.

Heubert, P., & Hauser, R.M. (1999). *High stakes: Testing for tracking, promotion and graduation*. Washington, DC: National Academy of Sciences.

Holt, J. (1982). *How children fail* (Revised ed.). New York: Seymour Lawrence.

Hornby, G. (2011). Inclusive education for children with special education needs: A critique. *International Journal of Disability, Development and Education, 58*(3), 321–329.

Horne, M. (2004). Breaking down the school walls. *Forum, 46*(2), 6.

Hubbs, D.L., & Brand., C.F. (2005). The paper mirror: Understanding reflective journaling. *The Journal of Experiential Education, 28*(1), 60–71.

Hunt, L.C. (1970). Effect of self-selection, interest, and motivation upon independent, instructional, and frustrational levels. *Reading Teacher, 24*(2), 146–151.

Hyslop-Margison, E.J., & Strobel, J. (2007). Constructivism and education: Misunderstandings and pedagogical implications. *The Teacher Educator, 43*(1), 72–86.

Irwin, W., Conrad, M.T., & Skoble, A.J. (Eds.). (2001). *The Simpsons and philosophy: The d'oh of Homer*. New York: Open Court.

Ivinson, G., & Murphy, P. (2007). *Rethinking single-sex teaching*. Open University Press.

Jackson, C. (2002). "Laddishness" as a self-worth protection strategy. *Gender and Education, 14*(1), 37–51.

Janis, I.L. (1982). *Groupthink: Psychological studies of policy decisions and fiascoes*. Boston: Houghton Mifflin.

Kahneman, D. (2011). *Thinking, fast and slow*. New York: Farrar, Straus & Giroux.

Karsenti, T., & Collin, S. (2013). Why are new teachers leaving the profession? Results of a Canada-wide survey. *Education and Urban Society, 3*(3), 141–149.

Katz, L. (1995). *Talks with teachers of young children: A collection*. Norwood, NJ: Ablex.

Kearns, L. (2011). High-stakes standardized testing and marginalized youth: An examination of the impact on those who fail. *Canadian Journal of Education, 34*(2), 112–130.

Kerr, D., Mandzuk, D., & Raptis, H. (2011). The role of the social foundations of education in programs of teacher preparation in Canada. *Canadian Journal of Education, 34*(1), 118–134.

Kindler, A., Badali, S., & Willock, R. (1999). *Between theory and practice: Case studies for learning to teach*. Scarborough, ON: Prentice Hall, Allyn & Bacon Canada.

Kochhar, C.A., West, L.L., & Taymans, J.M. (2000). *Successful inclusion: Practical strategies for a shared responsibility*. Upper Saddle River, NJ: Prentice-Hall.

Kohn, A. (1996). *Beyond discipline: From compliance to community*. Alexandria, VA: Association for Supervision and Curriculum Development.

Kohn, A. (2010). How to create nonreaders: Reflections on motivation, learning, and sharing power. *English Journal, 100*(1), 16–22.

Kostogriz, A. (2006, November 27–30). *On strangers, "moral panics" and the neoliberalization of teacher education*. Paper presented at the Annual Conference of the Australian Association for Research in Education, Adelaide, Australia.

Krashen, S. (2001). Is in-school free reading good for children? Why the National Reading Panel Report is (still) wrong. *Phi Delta Kappan, 86*(6), 444–447.

Krinsky, C. (2008). *Moral panics over contemporary children and youth*. Farnham, UK: Ashgate.

Lawson, B. (2001). *The language of space.* Oxford, UK: Architectural Press.

Leinweber, K., Donlevy, J.K., Gereluk, D., Patterson, P., & Brar, J. (2012). Moral education polices in five Canadian provinces: Seeking clarity, consistency and coherency. *Interchange, 43*(1), 25–42.

Leithwood, K., Fullan, M., & Watson, N. (2003). What should be the boundaries of the schools we need? *Education Canada, 43*(1), 12–15.

Levin, B. (2010, October 27–28). *Improvement, not innovation, is the key to greater equity.* Paper presented at the Canada–United States Colloquium on Achieving Equity through Innovation, Toronto.

Linn, R. (1998). *Assessments and accountability.* Los Angeles, CA: Centre for the Study of Evaluation.

Lipman, M. (1991). *Thinking in education.* Philadelphia: Temple University Press.

Liston, D., Witcomb, J., & Borko, H. (2009). The end of education in teacher education: Thoughts on reclaiming the role of social foundations in teacher education. *Journal of Teacher Education, 60*(2), 107–111.

Lortie, D. (1975). *Schoolteacher: A sociological study.* Chicago: University of Chicago Press.

Losh, E., & Jenkins, H. (2012). Can public education coexist with participatory culture? *Knowledge Quest, 41*(1), 16–21.

Lukianoff, G. (2013). Emily Bazelon and the danger of bringing "anti-bullying" laws to campus [Electronic Version]. *Huffington Post.* Retrieved August 20, 2013, from www.huffingtonpost.com/greg-lukianoff/emily-bazelon-and-the_b_3006539.html?utm_source=Alert-blogger&utm_medium=email&utm_campaign=Email%2BNotifications.

Lynch, K., & Feely, M. (2009). *Gender and education (and employment): Gendered imperatives and their implications for women and men. Lessons from research for policy makers.* Brussels, Belgium: European Commission.

Lynn, R. (2010, October 2). *Constructing parenthood in moral panics of youth, digital media, and "sexting."* Paper presented at the American Sociological Association.

Mader, C.E. (2009). "I will never teach the old way again": Classroom management and external incentives. *Theory into Practice, 48*(2), 147–155.

Maher, F.A., & Tetreault, M.K. (1994). *The feminist classroom.* New York: Basic Books.

Mallea, P. (1999). *Getting tough on kids: Young offenders and the "law and order agenda."* Winnipeg, MB: Canadian Centre for Policy Alternatives.

Mandzuk, D., & Hasinoff, S. (2010). *Slices of life: Managing dilemmas in middle grades teaching: Case studies for professional development.* Westerville, OH: National Middle School Association.

Marinak, B.A., & Gambrell, L. (2008). Intrinsic motivation and rewards: What sustains young children's engagement with text? *Literacy Research and Instruction, 47*(1), 9–26.

Marwick, A.E. (2008). To catch a predator? The MySpace moral panic [Electronic Version]. *First Monday,* 13. Retrieved August 29, 2013, from http://journals.uic.edu/ojs/index.php/fm/article/view/2152/1966.

McCracken, R.A. (1971). Initiating sustained silent reading. *Journal of Reading, 14*(8) 521–524, 582–583.

McCreary, T. (2009). The myth of the multicultural patchwork: Anti-racist education and the problem with multiculturalism. *Briarpatch* (September/October), 6–7.

McEwin, C.K., Dickinson, T.S., & Jenkins, D.M. (2003). *America's middle schools in the new century: Status and progress.* Westerville, OH: National Middle School Association.

McGregor, J. (2004). Space, power and the classroom. *Forum, 46*(1), 13–18.

McRobbie, A., & Thornton, S.L. (1995). Rethinking "moral panic" for multi-mediated social worlds. *British Journal of Sociology, 46,* 559–574.

Meier, D. (2002). Standards versus standardization. *Phi Delta Kappan, 84*(3), 190–198.

Mendelson, E. (1976). *W.H. Auden: Collected poems.* Toronto: Random House.

Mercer, A. (2012). Beware of bandwagons. *Education Forum, 38*(2), 16–19.

Michaels, S., O'Connor, M.C., Williams Hall, M., & Resnick, L.B. (2010). *Accountable Talk® sourcebook: For classroom conversation that works.* Retrieved May 7, 2013, from ifl.lrdc.pitt.edu/ifl/index.php/download/index/ats/.

Moffatt, K. (2006). Grading as the coding of student desire in the context of lacking. *Radical Pedagogy, 8*(2).

Moss, G., Francis, B., & Skelton, C. (2009). *Addressing gender and achievement: Myths and realities.* London, UK: Department for Children, School and Families.

Murphey, K. (2011). A matter of class. *History of Education Quarterly, 51*(2), 254–263.

Murphy, E. (1997). Constructivism: From philosophy to practice [Electronic Version]. Retrieved December 21, 2012, from www.ucs.mun.ca/~emurphy/stemnet/cle.html.

Murphy, K., & Sideman, L. (2006). Fadification of emotional intelligence. In K. Murphy (Ed.), *Critique of emotional Intelligence: What are the problems and how can they be fixed* (pp. 283–300). Mahwah, NJ: Lawrence Erlbaum.

Nansel, T.R., Overpeck, M., Pillar, R.S., Ruan, W.J., Simons-Morton, B., & Scheidt, P. (2001). Bullying behaviors among U.S. youth: Prevalence and association with psychosocial adjustment. *The Journal of the American Medical Association, 285*(16), 2094–2100.

National Institute of Child Health and Human Development. (2000). *Report of the National Reading Panel. Teaching children to read: An evidence-based assessment of the scientific research literature on reading and its implications for reading instruction: Reports of the subgroups.* (NIH Publication No. 00-4754). Washington, DC: US Government Printing Office.

Nieftagodien, N. (2011). Youth in history, youth making history: Challenging dominant historical narratives for alternate futures [Electronic Version]. *Yesterday and Today, 6*, 1–10. Retrieved November 24, 2012, from www.scielo.org.za/scielo.php?script=sci_arttext&pid=S2223-03862011000100005&lng=en&nrm=iso.

Nikiforuk, A. (1994). *If learning is so natural, why am I going to school?* Toronto, ON: Penguin.

Noguera, P.A. (2004, October 17). Transforming urban schools through investments in the social capital of parents. *In Motion Magazine.* Retrieved September 4, 2013, from www.inmotionmagazine.com/er/pn_parents.html.

Nussbaum, M.C. (1997). *Cultivating humanity: A classical defense of reform in liberal education.* Cambridge, MA: Harvard University Press.

Nuthall, G. (2005). Cultural myths and realities of classroom teaching and learning: A personal journey. *Teachers College Record 107*(5), 895–934.

O'Connell, T., & Dyment, J. (2011). The case of reflective journals: Is the jury still out? *Reflective Practice: International and Multidisciplinary Perspectives, 12*(1), 47–59.

OECD. (2013). *Trends shaping education 2013.* OECD Publishing.

Olweus, D. (1993). *Bullying at school: What we know and what we can do.* Malden, MA: Blackwell.

Ontario Confederation of University Faculty Associations. (2013). *Worldviews Conference pledges to "commit sociology."* Retrieved May 31, 2013, from http://ocufa.on.ca/2013/worldviews-conference-pledges-to-commit-sociology/.

Osborne, K. (2001). Review of the books "Knowing, teaching and learning history" and "L'histoire à l'école: Matière à penser." *The Canadian Historical Review, 82*(3), 548–555.

Pellegrini, A.D., & Long, J. (2002). A longitudinal study of bullying, dominance, and victimization during the transition from primary school through secondary school. *British Journal of Developmental Psychology, 20*, 259–280.

Pennington, M. (2009). Educational fads: What goes around comes around. Retrieved January 15, 2013, from http://penningtonpublishing.com/blog/reading/educational-fads-what-goes-around-comes-around/.

Pennington, M. (2011). Why sustained silent reading (SSR) doesn't work [Electronic Version]. *Pennington Publishing Blog.* Retrieved May 5, 2013, from http://penningtonpublishing.com/blog/reading/why-sustained-silent-reading-ssr-doesn%E2%80%99t-work/.

People for Education. (2012). *Annual Report on Ontario's Publicly Funded Schools 2012.* Retrieved May 5, 2013, from www.peopleforeducation.ca/wp-content/uploads/2012/05/Annual-Report-2012-web.pdf.

Phillips, D.C. (1995). The good, the bad, and the ugly: The many faces of constructivism. *Educational Researcher, 24*(7), 5–12.

Pierce, W.D., Cameron, J., Banko, K.M., & So, S. (2003). Positive effects of rewards and performance standards on intrinsic motivation. *The Psychological Record, 53*(4), 561–579.

Pilgreen, J. (2000). *The SSR handbook: How to organize and manage a sustained silent reading program.* Portsmouth, NH: Boynton-Cook.

Pink, D.H. (2009). *Drive: The surprising truth about what motivates us.* New York: Riverhead Books.

Polites, N. (1975). Two books speculate on how

environment affects learning. *The Phi Delta Kappan, 56*(5), 369–370.

Popham, W.J. (2000). *Modern educational measurement: Practical guidelines for educational leaders.* Boston: Allyn & Bacon.

Porter, S.E. (2013). *Bully nation: Why America's approach to childhood aggression is bad for everyone.* St Paul, MN: Paragon House.

Posner, G.J. (Ed.). (2000). *Field experience: A guide to reflective teaching* (5th ed.). New York: Addison Wesley Longman.

Prensky, M. (2001). Digital natives, digital immigrants: Part 1. *On the Horizon, 9*(5), 1–6.

Proshansky, H.M. (1978). The city and self-identity. *Environment and Behavior, 10*(2), 147–169.

Purpel, D. (1999). *Moral outrage in education.* New York: Peter Lang.

Putnam, R. (2000). *Bowling alone: The collapse and revival of American community.* New York: Simon and Schuster.

Putnam, R. (2004). *Education, diversity, social cohesion and "social capital."* Dublin, Ireland: OECD Education Ministers.

Ravitch, D. (2003, April 15). *Does education really need more innovation in the age of scientifically based research?* Paper presented at the Office of Innovation and Improvement Innovations in Education Conference, Harvard University, Cambridge, MA.

Ravitch, D. (2011, September 29). School "reform": A failing grade. *New York Review of Books.*

Robertson, H. (1998). *No more teachers, no more books: The commercialization of Canada's schools.* Toronto, ON: McClelland & Stewart.

Rosenthal, R., & Jacobson, L. (1968). Pygmalion in the classroom. *Urban Review, 3*(1), 16–20.

Rubin, D.I., & Kazanjian, C.J. (2011). "Just another brick in the wall": Standardization and the devaluing of education. *Journal of Curriculum and Instruction, 5*(2), 94–108.

Ruitenberg, C.W. (2011). The trouble with dispositions: a critical examination of personal beliefs, professional commitments and actual conduct in teacher education. *Ethics and Education, 6*(1), 41–52.

Russell, B. (1973). *The problems of philosophy.* London: Oxford University Press.

Ryan, K. (2002). Moral education [Electronic Version]. *Gale Encyclopedia of Education.* Retrieved September 34, 2013, from www.answers.com/topic/moral-education.

Ryan, R.M., & Deci, E.L. (2000). Intrinsic and extrinsic motivations: Classic definitions and new directions. *Contemporary Educational Psychology, 25,* 54–67.

Saha, L. (2010). Sociology of education. In T. Good (Ed.), *21st century education: A reference handbook* (pp. 229–307). Thousand Oaks, CA: Sage.

Salomone, R. (2006). Single-sex programs: Resolving the research conundrum. *Teachers College Record, 108,* 778–802.

Sanders, M.G. (2001). The role of "community" in comprehensive school, family, and community partnership programs. *Elementary School Journal, 102*(1), 19–34.

Sandwell, R. (2011). History is a verb: Teaching historical practice to teacher education students. In P. Clark (Ed.), *New possibilities for the past: Shaping history education in Canada.* Vancouver: UBC Press.

Sarason, S.B. (1996). *Revisiting "The culture of the school and the problem of change."* New York: Teachers College Press.

Scheffler, I. (1973). *Reason and teaching.* Indianapolis, IN: Bobbs-Merrill.

Schissel, B. (2008). Justice undone: Public panic and the condemnation of children and youth. In C. Krinsky (Ed.), *Moral panics over contemporary children and youth* (pp. 15–30). Farnham, UK: Ashgate.

Schuck, S., & Buchanan, J. (2012). Dead certainty? The case for doubt in teacher education. *Australian Journal of Teacher Education, 37*(8), 1–11.

Schwab, J.J. (1973). The practical 3: Translation into curriculum. *The School Review, 81*(4), 501–522.

Schwab, J.J. (1977). Structure of the disciplines: Meanings and significances. In A.A. Bellack & H.M. Kliebard (Eds.), *Curriculum and evaluation* (pp. 189–207). Berkeley, CA: McCutchan.

Schwartz, B. (2009). Incentives, choice, education and well-being. *Oxford Review of Education, 35*(3), 391–403.

Segal, R. (2011). What is mythic reality? *Zygon: Journal of Religion and Science, 46*(3), 588–592.

Seixas, P., & Peck, C. (2004). Teaching historical thinking. In A. Sears & I. Wright (Eds.), *Challenges and prospects for Canadian social studies* (pp. 109–117). Vancouver: Pacific Educational Press.

Shirley, D. (1997). *Community organizing for*

urban school reform. Austin, TX: University of Texas Press.

Shor, I. (1997). *When students have power.* Chicago: University of Chicago.

Shulman, L. (1990). Reconnecting foundations to the substance of teacher education. *Teachers College Record, 91*(3), 300–310.

Shulman, L. (1996). "Just in case . . .": Reflections on learning from experience. In J.A. Colbert, P. Desberg, & K. Trimble (Eds.), *The case for education: Contemporary approaches for using case methods.* Boston: Allyn & Bacon.

Shulman, L. (2005). Pedagogies of uncertainty. *Liberal Education* (Spring), 18–25.

Siegel, H. (1988). *Educating reason: Rationality, critical thinking, and education.* New York: Routledge.

Simpson, J.S., James, C.E., & Mack, J. (2011). Multiculturalism, colonialism, and racialization: Conceptual starting points. *Review of Education, Pedagogy, and Cultural Studies, 33*(4), 285–305.

Smith, P.K. (2004). Bullying: Recent developments. *Child and Adolescent Mental Health, 9*(3), 98–103.

Sojourner, R.J. (2012). The rebirth and retooling of character education in America [Electronic Version], 1–19. Retrieved September 17, 2013, from www.mcgraw-hillresearch foundation.org.

Sommer, R. (1977). Classroom layout. *Theory into Practice, 16*(3), 174–175.

Sommers, C.H. (2000). *The war against boys: How misguided feminism is harming our young men.* New York: Simon & Schuster.

Sommers, S. (2011). *Situations matter: Understanding how context transforms your world.* New York: Penguin.

Spalding, E., & Wilson, A. (2002). Demystifying reflection: A study of pedagogical strategies that encourage reflective journal writing. *Teachers College Record, 104,* 1393–1421.

St Denis, V. (2011). Silencing Aboriginal curricular content and perspectives through multiculturalism: "There are other children here." *The Review of Education, Pedagogy, and Cultural Studies, 33*(4), 306–317.

Stroot, S., Keil, V., Stedman, P., Lohr, L., Faust, R., Schincariol-Randall, L., et al. (1998). *Peer assistance and review guidebook: Developmental stages of teachers.* Columbus, OH: Ohio Department of Education.

Sullivan, A., Joshi, H., & Leonard, D. (2010). Single-sex schooling and academic attainment at school and through the lifecourse. *American Educational Research Journal, 47*(1), 6–36.

Sullivan, F.R. (2012). Deconstructing digital natives: Young people, technology, and the new literacies. *Teachers College Record.*

Surrey School District Research and Evaluation Department. (2010). Silence is not always golden: Examining research into silent reading. *Research Currents, 1*(2), 1–2.

Sykes, G.G., & Bird, T. (1992). Chapter 10: Teacher education and the case idea. *Review of Research in Education, 18,* 457–551.

Tarr, P. (2001). Aesthetic codes in early childhood classrooms: What art educators can learn from Reggio Emilia. *Art Education, 54*(3), *33-39.*

Tauber, R. (1998). *Good or bad, what teachers expect from students they generally get!* Washington, DC: ERIC Clearinghouse on Teaching and Teacher Education.

Teitel, E. (2011). Bullying 2.0 is more like a drama class [Electronic Version]. *Maclean's.* Retrieved August 30, 2013, from http://www2.macleans.ca/2011/10/11/bullying-2-0-is-more-like-a-drama-class/.

Tennent, L., Taylor, C., Farrell, A., & Patterson, C. (2005, 27 November–1 December). *Social capital and sense of community: What do they mean for young children's success at school?* Paper presented at the International Education Research Conference, Sydney, Australia.

Tepperman, L. (2010). *The sense of sociability: How people overcome the forces pulling them apart.* Don Mills, ON: Oxford University Press.

Thiessen, V. (2009). *The pursuit of post secondary education: A comparison of First Nation, African, Asian and European Canadian youth.* Vancouver: Canadian Labour Market and Skills Researcher Network.

Thompson, K. (1998). *Moral panics.* London: Routledge.

Thompson, T., & Ungerleider, C. (2004). *Single sex schooling: Final report.* Vancouver: Canadian Centre for Knowledge Mobilisation.

Thorpe, K. (2004). Reflective learning journals: From concept to practice. *Reflective Practice, 5*(3), 327–343.

Thurlow, C. (2007). Fabricating youth: New-media discourse and the technologization of young people. In S. Johnson & A. Ensslin (Eds.), *Language in the media: Representations, identities, and ideologies*. London: Continuum.

Trelease, J. (2001). *The read-aloud handbook* (5th ed.): Penguin Books.

Tyack, D., & Tobin, W. (1994). The "grammar" of schooling: Why has it been so hard to change? *American Education Research Journal, 31*(3), 453–479.

Ullucci, K. (2007). The myths that blind: The role of beliefs in school change [Electronic Version]. *Journal of Education Controversy, 2*. Retrieved February 10, 2011, from www.wce.wwu.edu/resources/cep/ejournal/v002n001/a006.shtml.

Ungerleider, C.S., & Burns, T. (2002, April 30–May 2). *Information and communication technologies in elementary and secondary education: State of the art review.* Paper presented at the Pan-Canadian Education Research Agenda Symposium: Information Technology and Learning, Montreal.

Vacalopoulos, A.E. (1976). *The Greek nation, 1453–1669: The cultural and economic background of modern Greek society* (I. Moles & P. Moles, Trans.). New Brunswick, NJ: Rutgers University Press.

Valentine, J.W., Clark, D.C., Hackmann, D.G., & Petzko, V.N. (2002). *A national study of leadership in middle schools:* Volume 1, *A national study of middle level leaders and school programs.* Reston, VA: National Association of Secondary School Principals.

van Huizen, P., van Oers, B., & Wubbels, T. (2005). A Vygotskian perspective on teacher education. *Journal of Curriculum Studies, 37*(3), 267–290.

Violas, P.C. (1990). The role of history in the education of teachers. In S. Tozer, T.H. Anderson, & B.B. Armbruster (Eds.), *Foundational studies in teacher education: A reexamination.* New York: Teachers College Press.

Warnock, M. (2005). Special educational needs: A new look. London: Philosophy of Education Society of Great Britain.

Warren, M.R. (2001). *Dry bones rattling: Community building to revitalize American democracy.* Princeton, NJ: Princeton University Press.

Warrington, M., & Younger, M. (2001). Single-sex classes and equal opportunities for girls and boys: Perspectives through time from a mixed comprehensive school in England. *Oxford Review of Education, 27*(3), 339–356.

Wartella, E., & Jennings, N. (2000). Children and computers: New technology—old concerns. *The Future of Children, 10*(2), 31–43.

Watts, A. (1995). *The Tao of philosophy.* North Clarendon, VT: Tuttle.

Weaver-Hightower, M. (2003). The "Boy Turn" in research on gender and education. *Review of Educational Research, 73*(4), 471–498.

Weick, K. (1976). Educational organizations as loosely coupled systems. *Administrative Science Quarterly, 21*, 1–19.

Willis, P. (1977). *Learning to labour: How working class kids get working class jobs.* Westmead, UK: Saxon House.

Wineburg, S., Martin, D., & Monte-Santo, C. (2011). *Reading like a historian: Teaching literacy in middle and high school history classrooms.* New York: Teachers College Press.

Woolcock, M. (2001). The place of social capital in understanding social and economic outcomes. *Canadian Journal of Policy Research, 2*(1), 11–17.

Wotherspoon, T. (2009). *The sociology of education in Canada* (3rd ed.). Don Mills, ON: Oxford University Press.

Yu, T. (2004). *In the name of morality: Character education and political control.* New York: Peter Lang.

INDEX